*A beautiful scene in Twyford cutting
showing the 10.45 HST Paddington to
Cardiff at 125 mph* (Brian Morrison).

# TWO MILES A MINUTE

## O.S.Nock

BSc, C Eng, FICE, FI Mech E

The story behind the conception and
operation of Britain's High Speed
and Advanced Passenger Trains

### Foreword by Sir Peter Parker, MVO
Chairman, British Railways Board

 **Patrick Stephens, Cambridge**

First published in 1980

**British Library Cataloguing in Publication Data**

Nock, Oswald Stevens
   Two miles a minute.
   1. Railroads—Great Britain—History
   —20th century
   I. Title
   385'.0941        HE3018

   ISBN 0 85059 412 X

Text photoset in 10 on 11 pt English Times
by Manuset Limited, Baldock, Herts.
Printed in Great Britain on 100 gsm
Pedigree coated cartridge and bound by
The Garden City Press, Letchworth
for the publishers Patrick Stephens Limited,
Bar Hill, Cambridge, CB3 8EL, England.

# Contents

2097657

# Foreword by
# Sir Peter Parker, MVO

## Chairman, British Railways Board

It seems like a numbers game to congratulate 'Ossie' Nock on his tremendous achievement of writing 100 books on railways as his 'century' comes in the 150th anniversary year of the world's first 'Inter-City' line, the Liverpool and Manchester Railway, and the subject is British Rail's achievement of 125 mph in regular daily service. But there is more to it than mere numbers can convey, for the last 150 years of main line railways represent a catalogue of technological progress which this latest book from Britain's most prolific railway author brings right up to date with his examination of British Rail's high speed operations.

There is probably nobody better qualified to make an objective examination than Mr Nock, who has travelled on trains all over the world for more than seven decades—virtually half the period of railway history. His writings, in the *Railway Magazine* as well as in so many books, have helped sustain and encourage interest and more faith in railways. Many railwaymen and students of this most romantic form of transport who began their interest as schoolboys noting engine numbers have been weaned on to a more adult form of enthusiasm by Mr Nock's writings.

He embodies the reality of enthusiasm: the amateur can take a deep and worthwhile interest in the performance of different types of railway traction in service. The presence of stopwatches in the pockets of a fair proportion of regular train passengers is an indication of this form of study which extends far beyond recording speeds to assessments of horsepower achieved, involving calculations of such matters as the rolling resistance of different coach types and the impact of side winds.

Not that this book will appeal only to the technically-minded. Although written by an engineer on a subject steeped in engineering, the development of BR's 125 mph trains is told in an interesting, readily understood fashion which brings to life an achievement now almost taken for granted.

In the 1960s when the last of the steam locomotives were being withdrawn from regular service, there were those who believed that the railway enthusiast fraternity would dwindle and nobody would want to read about the new diesels and electrics, far less take an enthusiastic interest in watching them and travelling by them. Yet books on railway subjects covering the modern scene

**Left** *Further into the future: a prototype APT demonstrates its unique tilting action through a high speed curve* (British Railways).

have never had higher sales and I am very encouraged to see the renaissance of railways so positively promoted in *Two Miles a Minute*.

When Ossie wrote *Rail, Steam and Speed* some ten years ago, he described the 'terrific' sensation of speed when, as a young man, he watched a London and North Western Railway express at Lancaster doing no more than 70 mph. I am sure that young enthusiast of almost 60 years ago never dreamed that the day would come when he could write about a 125 mph train as providing an almost 'non-existent' impression of speed. But thanks to continuously-welded rails, modern suspension, new types of wheel based on years of research and other technical innovation, the day has arrived.

One wonders what the future holds. Ossie is sure it lies on the rails; whatever it is, I am certain he is right.

*Sir Peter Parker,* MVO
*January 1980*

# Author's introduction

In writing the story of the inception, development, and daily work of British Railways' High Speed Trains, the fastest diesel trains in the world, one is dealing with a unique activity. Over the years many famous trains have been established as the world's fastest on the basis of their start-to-stop average speeds; but, like 'The Cheltenham Flyer', 'The Flying Hamburger', the Rock Island 'Rockets', 'The Coronation' and others, they were isolated spurts amid a general level of considerably slower trains. In more recent times the Japanese introduced a new conception of high speed train travel on their Shinkansen line—a line nevertheless used exclusively by a regular interval, very fast service. The British Railways HST is something quite different. It exemplifies the injection of a very fast and frequent service on to lines already carrying a busy and notably 'mixed' traffic. It has been a project involving the most careful and experienced timetable planning, and the most rigorous and exhaustive maintenance of the new trains to ensure the very high standard of reliability needed to keep the schedules advertised with train-sets that are averaging between 800 and 1,000 miles (1,280 and 1,600 km) a day.

It has been a fascinating and privileged task to write this book, and I am deeply indebted to Mr Ian Campbell, Chief Executive of the British Railways Board, for his help and encouragement and for authorising the granting to me of countless privileges for seeing the trains under construction and in course of maintenance, for travelling widely, and of riding in the driving cabs on many occasions and on a variety of routes. I have enjoyed immensely my various visits to Derby, Crewe, York and Bristol on many fact finding trips while, ever since their introduction on the Western Region, the HSTs have become an indispensable aid to my ordinary business travelling between Bath and London. I have come to rely implicitly on their punctuality. I always take detailed records of the running, but the uniformity of performance is such that I have long since ceased to note the numbers of the individual train sets. They are all so completely alike in the results they give.

And then there is the APT, which to a far greater extent than the splendid HSTs, is surely the train of the future. At the time of completing this book the prototype train is still on trial between Carlisle and Glasgow, and I have seen it flashing along several times during my journeys in the north country. The APT is the train that will make substantial acceleration of service possible on routes where the curvature is such that the full potentialities of the HST cannot be realised. I hardly need add that although the prototype APT is electric, there is no problem in building a diesel-powered version. In these days the press, radio and TV are making us very conscious of what is called the energy crisis. In view of this it is all the more important to emphasise the astonishing economy in fuel consumption of the HST in comparison with other forms of transport, and not only in respect to other trains. The appendix, which contains a number of vital statistics, is a section of this book to which particular attention can be directed.

My warmest thanks are due to the many senior officers of British Railways who have given up their time to put across the various aspects of this great enveloping project for which they are responsible, and especially to Mr David S. Binnie, General Manager of the London Midland Region, as the first user of the APT, for his views on its potentialities and the problems of its commercial introduction. Mr D.J. Joiner, Press Officer of the British Railways Board, has provided the necessary liaison with all the various activities that I wished to study, and I was particularly grateful to my old friends of the Western Region for their invitation to join, and act as official recorder of, the record making run of the 09.20 from Paddington to Chippenham on April 10 1979. The Japanese National Railways may hold—for the time being—the record for the fastest scheduled start-to-stop run in the world, but BR on that memorable day broke the world's record for an actual start-to-stop run, at an average of 111.6 mph (178.5 km/h).

In conclusion my special thanks are due to Mrs Linda Glyde. In days gone by, as a typist in my office at Westinghouse, she typed humdrum memos about design and production matters. Now she has typed, at a speed that almost matches that of the HST, the manuscript of this book—and this, in spite of the fact that my handwriting has not improved with the years!

*O.S. Nock*
*Batheaston, Bath, May 1980*

**Chapter 1**

# Historical introduction

Fifty years ago the hallmark of a top class express passenger train was a start-to-stop average speed of 60 mph (96 km/h). Then, in the summer of 1929, the Great Western Railway began to draw ahead with one train, the 3.45 pm from Swindon to Paddington, which was accelerated to make the run of 77.3 miles (124 km) in 70 minutes, an average of 66.2 mph (106 km/h). It was an isolated move, with a relatively unimportant train that originated at Cheltenham. It so happened that the run up from Swindon over an ideally straight and slightly favourable road was well suited to making a fast start-to-stop average quite easily, having regard to the relatively light loading of the train—usually not more than 250 tons. So easily was the accelerated schedule maintained that in 1931 it was cut still further to 67 minutes and, in 1932, as if to emphasise the margin they still had in hand, the Great Western staged an exhibition run on Monday June 5. With the engine *Tregenna Castle* and a load of only 195 tons, the run from Swindon to Paddington was made in 56 minutes 47 seconds, an overall average speed of 81.7 mph (131 km/h). The booked time was subsequently cut to 65 minutes, a start-to-stop average of 71.3 mph (114 km/h), and this remained in force until the outbreak of war in September 1939.

The 'Cheltenham Flyer', as it became known, remained a completely isolated service. No other train from that area had a timing that was anything like so fast. There was, in fact, no real justification for such a fast run, save for the prestige value of having by far the fastest train in Great Britain. When the London and North Eastern Railway introduced the 'Silver Jubilee' streamlined train in the autumn of 1935 the circumstances were not quite analogous. This provided a fast service from Tyneside to London in the morning and a correspondingly fast return service at night. The journey time between Newcastle and Kings Cross was four hours in each direction, involving an overall average speed of 65.8 mph (105 km/h) and $3\frac{1}{2}$ hours in London. While this was an attractive proposition for businessmen, there was no corresponding service northbound in the morning and returning in the early evening. The ordinary express trains took roughly one hour longer in each direction. Concurrently with the introduction of the 'Silver Jubilee' service to Darlington and Newcastle, the Great Western put on a new fast train to Bristol, covering the distance of 118 miles (189 km) in 105 minutes; but like the 'Silver Jubilee', the 'Bristolian' was a single 'out and home' service; down from London in the morning at 10 am and returning at 4.30 pm. There was no corresponding service in the reverse direction.

These trains brought a spectacular and sorely needed lustre to the image of

*The first British high speed streamlined train: 'The Silver Jubilee' of the LNER, here seen on the southbound run between Potters Bar and Hadley Wood, hauled by the pioneer streamlined 'A4' Pacific No 2509 Silver Link (Real Photographs Co Ltd).*

British railway passenger train working, and the runs of the 'Cheltenham Flyer' on June 5 1932 and of the 'Silver Jubilee' on September 27 1935 brought world speed records to Great Britain; but although the impact of these two runs in particular was sensational, their contribution to the overall pattern of train service offered to the public was very slight. I well remember a conversation in the bar-lounge of a hotel in the West Highlands of Scotland. A close friend with whom I had travelled north by the 'Silver Jubilee', as the first stage of a fortnight's tour of the north, was so enthusiastic about the experience that he dilated at some length upon the glories of that train. A fellow guest, whose ideas of a holiday in the Highlands ran entirely upon the fishing rather than of the trains that helped to get one there, cut into this panegyric with the down-to-earth question: 'where does this train run, does it come to Glasgow or Edinburgh?'; and my own reply left him entirely unmoved. A train, however fast, that stopped short at Newcastle, was beneath the notice of a Scottish businessman! Similarly of course, the 'Cheltenham Flyer', and the 'Bristolian', however brilliantly they might run, were of no interest to a senior executive visiting the Westinghouse works at Chippenham!

However much the publicists paraded their achievements, and however much devotees of the stop-watch travelled for the sole purpose of logging fast runs, the plain fact was that the British railway network was not yet ready for general acceleration on so sweeping a scale. In fact, the safe running of these much faster trains was a distinct embarrassment to the other railway engineering disciplines. The brake equipment then in standard use was not adequate to stop them in the distances then existing between the home and distant signals when they were travelling at their maximum permissible speeds of 90 mph (144 km/h), and special regulations had to be devised to permit their safe running. On the

*The 'Bristolian' of the GWR shortly after its introduction in 1935, near the top of Filton bank and hauled by engine No 6027* King Richard I (G.H. Soole).

Great Western Railway very elaborate measures were introduced. The routes over which they ran were divided into sections covering a number of ordinary block sections, each approximately ten miles long. Within such a section there would be four or five intermediate signal boxes, each with its distant signals spaced at the existing standard distance from the corresponding home signal. For purposes of explanation the signal box at the beginning of such a ten-mile section will be referred to as 'A', the intervening ones as 'B', 'C', 'D', 'E' and 'F', and that at the end of the section and the beginning of the next as 'G'.

The procedure for an ordinary express train was for it to be signalled stage by stage from one signal box to the next, from A to B, B to C and so on. It only needed the line to be clear from A to B for the starting signal to be lowered and the train allowed to go forward; but with a high speed train, either the 'Cheltenham Flyer', or the 'Bristolian', the entire ten-mile (16 km) section had to be clear from A to G. There was no positive interlocking to ensure that this was so; it was entirely a case of the individual signalmen working to the rules laid down for progressing these extra fast trains. When the 'Silver Jubilee' was first put on the London and North Eastern Railway, the sections between Kings Cross and York and between Northallerton and Newcastle were equipped entirely with mechanically worked semaphore signals, on the ordinary block system, and to compensate for inadequate brake power on the new train the working regulations required that *two* sections ahead, instead of one, should be clear before the train was allowed to proceed. This was a process known as 'double blocking'. The 30-mile (48 km) section between York and Northallerton, however, had not long previously been equipped with colour light signalling, with many of the intermediate units working automatically. The distances from signal to signal were as inadequate as elsewhere in providing safe

**Above** *The up 'Coronation', the streamliner of 1937 Edinburgh to Kings Cross near Lamesley and hauled by 'A4' Pacific No 4498* Sir Nigel Gresley *(the late W.B. Greenfield).*

**Below** *126 mph in 1938!* Mallard *standing at Barkston, before starting south on the record-breaking test run, with the dynamometer car next to the engine.* (H.M. Hoather).

braking allowance, but because of the automatic working the palliative of 'double-blocking' could not be used; and one had in consequence the anachronism of the train being limited to a maximum speed of 70 mph (112 km/h) over the one stretch fitted with the most modern system of signalling.

As on the Great Western, the acceleration of an isolated train had been pushed forward without any regard to the various co-related aspects of traffic working. It seems extraordinary in retrospect that trains of such exceptional maximum speed capacity as the 'Silver Jubilee' should have been introduced when they were incapable of being stopped within the existing parameters of signalling and brake power. The Great Western was in a slightly better position as regards braking, because it used not only a higher degree of vacuum—25 in (63.5 cm), as against 21 in (53.3 cm) on other British railways—but a more rapid application of the brake was obtained by use of direct-admission valves on each coach. This latter device, which enabled the reduction of vacuum at a brake application to be made locally, instead of relying on propagation down the length of the brake pipe from the engine, was less important on short trains like the 'Cheltenham Flyer' and the 'Bristolian' than it would have been on the 14-coach 'Cornish Riviera Express'; but it was, nevertheless, an extra worth having. 'The Silver Jubilee', however, went into service with nothing except the standard vacuum brake. It was typical of the parochialism of the railways, even in the grouping era, that the LNER did not take up the direct admission valve, which Stanier took to the LMS when he moved there in 1932. After the introduction of the second high speed service in 1937, the 'Coronation', LNER began experiments with the Westinghouse QSA (Quick Service Application) valve, which gave a considerably improved performance over the standard vacuum brake.

The 'Coronation' and its LMS counterpart, the 'Coronation Scot', both introduced additional train mileage, but it is doubtful if they proved really worthwhile investments, other than in terms of publicity. The 'Coronation', running at the same standard of speed as that of the 'Silver Jubilee' south of Newcastle, provided an entirely new late afternoon service between London and Edinburgh, completing the 392.7 miles (628 km) in a level six hours. The 'Coronation Scot', on the other hand, replaced the 'Midday Scot' between Euston and Glasgow, leaving the latter name to be carried by a second train conveying the Edinburgh and Aberdeen sections, plus a small portion for Glasgow to cater for traffic from intermediate sections that were bypassed, and to collect at Crewe the through carriages from Plymouth. The 'Coronation Scot', although the fastest train in the world (making a non-stop run of all but 300 miles—Euston-Carlisle—299.2 miles (479 km) in 283 minutes) did not involve payment of any supplementary fare, whereas the high speed streamlined trains of the LNER did require a small extra.

How this slight movement towards higher speeds would have developed, but for the onset of war in 1939, is debatable; but an important paper read before the Institute of Transport in December 1938 by Mr S.H. Fisher, Assistant Chief Operating Manager of the LMS, and the subsequent discussion, gave some interesting indications of the way certain leading personalities in the railway world were then thinking. The consensus was in favour of the general speeding up of train services, rather than undue concentration on a relatively few ultra-high speed trains. It was particularly interesting to hear a very high officer of the

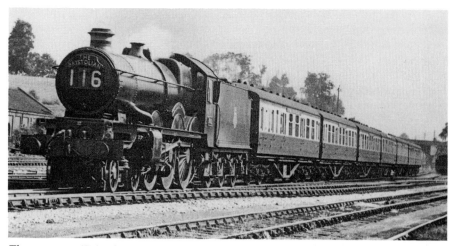

*The post-war 'Bristolian' passing Chippenham at high speed hauled by 4-6-0 No 7032
Denbigh Castle (K.H. Leech).*

LNER stressing the difficulty of providing the timetable paths for the very high
speed trains, when others were running late, and the margins ahead were
reduced. Signalmen were inclined to sidetrack late running ordinary trains
unduly early to give the streamliners a clear run, with the result that the initial
lateness became much greater. It was generally agreed that one common level of
speed, as far as was practicable, gave better prospects for punctuality than an
increase in the number of high speed trains. In this respect it was significant that
the speed of the 'Coronation Scot' between Euston and Crewe was much the
same as that of the fastest 'ordinary' expresses on the London-Liverpool and
London-Manchester services of that period.

The interruption, and indeed disruption of any ordered policy of evolution in
passenger transport facilities by rail caused by the war is evidenced by the long
interval which elapsed before any fully coordinated plans for reconstruction
afterwards began to take shape. The nationalisation of British Railways, and
the subsequent rush to replace steam by other forms of traction, continued the
period of upheaval and uncertainty, and all the time traffic receipts were
dwindling. The suggestion not infrequently voiced in high quarters, 'We shall be
all right once we get rid of steam', was one of the greatest fallacies of all. So also
was the view held by some senior officers of the immediate post-nationalisation
period, that there was no need to shorten journey times. The mere change in the
form of traction would restore prosperity! Fortunately wiser councils prevailed,
and much notable improvement of train services took place from 1960 onwards.
With most of the traction changed from steam to diesel in the ten-year period
from 1955 to 1965, and a small amount of main line electrification commissioned, the maximum speed of running was raised gradually to 100 mph
(160 km/h). Average journey speed was improved, and a welcome increase in
passenger travel resulted. Having replaced *all* traction within a decade however,
consideration had to be given to its renewal in the late 1970s and early 1980s, and it
is the policy formulated by British Railways, and its implementation, with which
the remaining chapters of this book are concerned.

# Chapter 2

# A new philosophy of operation

With the commissioning of the full electric service beween Euston, Liverpool and Manchester in April 1966 a new philosophy of operation on British Railways took its first practical form. Until then passenger train timetables had followed a traditional pattern that had not varied a great deal from the time when railways were undisputedly the pre-eminent, and indeed the only acceptable means of long distance travel in Great Britain. The market had contracted to an alarming extent between the two world wars, and the first really determined attempt by the four main line railway companies to gain public support for changes in legislation, in the winter of 1938-9, had barely got under way when war came once again. But the introduction of the new electric service from Euston in April 1966, with frequent regular-interval departures and entirely new standards of speed, brought outstandingly successful results. In the four years following completion there was an increase in passenger journeys of

*The first moves away from steam for main line work: the diesel electric No 10000 of the LMS, on the up Midland line express near Radlett* (E.D. Bruton).

**Above** *When the Midland still ran through to Manchester: the diesel-electric No 10000 on the 7.15 am up to St Pancras near St Albans* (E.D. Bruton).

**Below** *The diesels get larger: one of the 2,300 hp; 'Peak' class, originally numbered D2, and named* Helvellyn *on the up Midland line express from Manchester to St Pancras near Mill Hill* (British Railways).

*one hundred per cent.* This public reaction to a high quality, high speed service provided a base of experience of the utmost value when consideration had to be given by British Railways to the manner in which replacement of the traction and rolling stock forecast for the late 1970s and early 1980s would most advantageously be made.

The electrification of the Euston route, even though not yet extended north of Liverpool and Manchester, had involved very heavy capital expenditure, and, as things eventuated, had brought rich returns; but any investment in the passenger business is essentially a long term operation. Those with memories of steam days in Great Britain may remind me that it did not take Sir Nigel Gresley and his staff long to design and build the 'Silver Jubilee' train in 1935; that no more than six months elapsed between the successful trial runs to and from Newcastle, with a standard 'Pacific' engine and standard coaching stock, and the sensational Press run of the new streamlined train three days before it went into revenue-earning service. That, however, as I emphasised in the previous chapter, was very much a unilateral project of one department of the railway. To launch a major change of product, taking account of all the various disciplines, engineering and commercial, and integrating them into an acceptable all-round pattern, can take up to ten years, and therefore the decision to embark upon any such investment requires a considerable amount of foresight. Fortunately, after the introduction of the fast electric service from Euston, a passenger survey had been carried out to find out why members of the public had returned to railway travel in such numbers. Between 40 and 50 per cent of those who responded to the survey had been attracted by the speed and the fact that the journeys were less tiring than by other means of travel. Another ten to 20 per cent appreciated a quiet, smooth journey on which they were able to read, work, write or sleep. Other considerations, including that of price, accounted for less than ten per cent of those who filled in the questionnaire.

An assessment of the competitive market indicated that railways were favourably placed up to a total journey time of about three hours. With the electric service from Euston providing hourly departures through the day to Liverpool and Manchester, and journey times of 2 hours 35 minutes in each case, their success was amply explained, but when the journey times considered in this market research extended beyond three hours there was a progressive decrease, and loss of business to air. Proportionate accelerations to those on the Euston route if applied to London-West Riding, London-South Wales routes seemed to promise profitable returns, although service to the Tees-side and Tyneside areas from London would require acceleration considerably beyond the standards of the Euston route in order to bring the overall times below the three-hour norm. When considering the possible introduction of still higher speeds, having particular regard to what had been achieved on the entirely new high speed line in Japan, supplementing an established 3 ft 6 in gauge (106.6 cm) network, it must be emphasised that very little of the British railway system was designed with such high speeds in mind, and much of the route mileage, even on trunk lines, has a high percentage of curves that limit maximum speeds. Nevertheless detailed consideration was given to the possibilities of major speeding-up on four principal main lines: East Coast: London to Edinburgh; West Coast: London to Glasgow; Western Region: London to Bristol, Cardiff and the West of England; and South-West to North-East—Bristol and South Wales to the West Riding, York and Tyneside.

*British Railways principal Inter-City trunk lines.*

*One of the most powerful of British diesels, a 'Deltic' No 55006* The Fife and Forfar Yeomanry *on the up Anglo-Scottish express just south of Tweedmouth* (D. Haviland).

The inclusion of the West Coast main line was significant because, although with electrification a substantial acceleration of the London-Glasgow time to the level five hours had been made, this potentially profitable traffic still lay well outside the three-hour norm. To apply this to the London-Glasgow 'axis' would involve an end-to-end average speed of 135 mph (217 km/h) and, because certain railway administrations in other parts of the world were investing in entirely new routes to achieve high uniform speeds, a study was conducted within British Railways to find out if a comparable investment would be justified here. It was concluded that no case could be made for the construction of a new high speed route in a country that is compact, highly developed and intensively populated, and a decision was taken to direct the whole of technical research towards the better use of the existing network.

As early as 1966 the first results from this research were able to present to the British Railways management two ways of moving into the highly desirable era of higher speed passenger trains. The first was the more conventional. It involved the use of well established traction and rolling stock technology to produce a train capable of continuous running at 125 mph (200 km/h) and having braking equipment that would permit stopping distances under service conditions no greater than those of existing trains travelling at speeds up to 100 mph (160 km/h). Thus reconstruction of the signalling would be unnecessary. There remained, however, the question of the speed of the train around curves. With the exception of two among the various routes considered for service acceleration, the majority have a high percentage of curves; and since many of these could not be improved economically, the restraint thus imposed would make the improvement in overall journey time less than ideal, even though maximum speeds up to 125 mph might be attained on favourable lengths of line. On the other hand, on routes where improvements in alignment *could* be carried out economically, substantial accelerations could be made, with all the advantages of re-equipping with stock based on established technology.

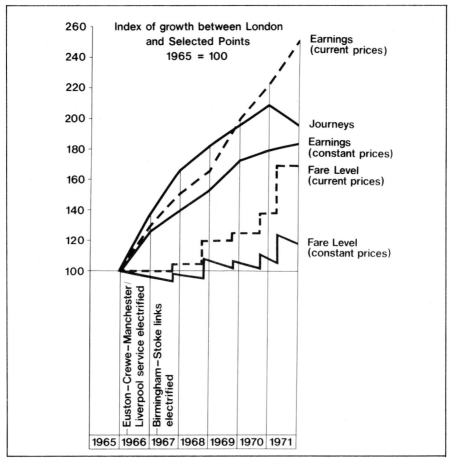

*Growth in Inter-City business: Euston-Manchester/Liverpool electrification.*

This, of course, would be no more than treating the tip of the iceberg, giving no more than marginal improvement on certain major trunk routes, and leaving completely beyond the pale arteries of business travel such as Liverpool-Manchester-West Riding and Manchester-Sheffield, where regular passenger travel has sunk to dismally low proportions despite the hazards and frustrations of private car transport across the Pennines as an all-weather proposition. Fundamental research had, however, shown that there was a second possibility, of a new train capable not only of much higher speeds but incorporating a tilting mechanism that would enable existing curves to be negotiated safely at a considerably higher speed. With such a train it was felt that a London-Glasgow time close to four hours, although beyond the three-four norm established from the experience of the London-Liverpool-Manchester electrification, would be very attractive to travellers, providing a journey in a time, from city centre to city centre, of little more than would be involved with air travel. This idea, of the tilting mechanism, first mooted within British Railways in 1966, would allow higher average speeds on a severely curved route, and bring into an acceptable speed level routes that would otherwise lie well outside, and remain dead areas so far as competitive passenger traffic was concerned. In 1970, however, the timescale within which technological success could be achieved with the novel features of this second form of high speed train was the unknown factor, and this uncertainty heavily influenced the development of an investment policy for the re-equipment of the Inter-City services of British Railways.

These two alternatives presented management with a difficult decision, whether to plump for a modernised High Speed Train that would give substantial service improvement on a few routes, but no more than marginal improvements elsewhere, or to take a chance on a new technology that offered greater potential advantages but also greater risks of failure in achievement. The British temperament has, however, a genius for compromise, and the decision eventually taken was to invest in both, taking advantage of the High Speed Train for a limited number of routes on which its benefits could be exploited most readily, and to press ahead with the development of the Advanced Passenger Train, with its feature of tilting on curves to allow much higher speeds in such locations than would be permissible with conventional rolling stock. In taking these decisions it was a case of replacing the entire stock on certain selected routes with the new trains and this introduced a philosophy that was largely new in many areas.

One of the great difficulties that has beset British railway operation in the past has been the very wide diversity in train speeds on almost every main line— greater perhaps than on any other railway in the world. It arose fundamentally from our retention of the loose-coupled, unbraked freight train, which ambled between block posts at a maximum speed of little more than 40 mph (64 km/h), and which, if of any length, required a portentously long time to stow in a siding to clear the line for a faster train. But it was not only the freights that were

*90 mph up Shap: one of the Class '87' electrics No 87006, with the morning Bristol-Glasgow express, demonstrating the approaching new era in railway passenger travel (Derek Cross).*

extravagant in line occupation. On the former Great Western Railway, on the tracks of which the new High Speed Trains first went into revenue-earning service, there had been a great deal of difference between trains like the 'Cheltenham Flyer' and 'Bristolian', and those at the lowest end of the speed scale to carry express train headlamps. The Great Western was essentially a line serving the rural shires through which its crack express trains ran, and in its operating philosophy it provided for them as thoughtfully as it took holiday makers to the Cornish Riviera or hauled Welsh coal in 1,000-ton loads to London. On the same tracks as those used by the 'Cheltenham Flyer' and 'Bristolian' there ran express trains that did not need to exceed a maximum speed of 60 mph (100 km/h) to keep their schedules. They were timed thus so that horseboxes or other four-wheeled stock could be attached to them, or detached, at intermediate stations, and the station times were generous to allow the necessary marshalling—sometimes, as at Swindon and Bath, by a horse!

Although such homely picturesque procedures were suitable for the country branch line and the slow pick-up goods, in the modern drive to make optimum use of the existing railway network, maximum utilisation and revenue earning can best be attained, with better punctuality, by running as many trains as possible at similar speeds. The electric service introduced on the line from Euston in April 1966 incorporated the principle of running *all* the express passenger trains at standard point-to-point times, and one had, for the first time in Great Britain, the spectacle of 'flights' of four or five trains following each

*The prototype HST, No 252001, showing the distinctive driving cab, on a test run passing Swindon in June 1976, with Test Car No 6 marshalled next to the leading power car (Brian Morrison).*

other down the line at five-minute intervals and all running at 90 to 100 mph (150 to 160 km/h). There were no specially favoured schedules; they áll ran equally fast. It was so successful and brought so much more business that when the time came for the vital decision of how the first-line traction and rolling stock should be replaced, the investment consisted of enough diesel-propelled High Speed Trains to take over, firstly, the entire passenger service between Paddington, Bristol and South Wales, and later that of the East Coast main line, except for Kings Cross-Humberside expresses, Kings Cross-York semi-fasts and overnight trains which remain locomotive hauled. Both groups of lines included considerable mileages of straight track, and many sections that, while not immediately suitable for running at 125 mph, could be upgraded at a relatively moderate cost.

It was not to be merely a case of replacing existing trains with new ones running to faster timings. The whole service was to be re-cast to provide many more trains running at regular intervals, and with somewhat smaller coach formations than previously. By having power units at each end of trains of seven or eight coaches, permanently coupled, light engine movements at the terminals would be eliminated. It was considered that the provision of trains of this kind in the late 1970s would represent an attractive proposition, highly competitive in their own particular sphere, and give a much accelerated service in the interim period before the Advanced Passenger Train was fully developed and proved. It is hoped that the latter, because of its ability to round curves at much higher speeds, will prove the eventual answer to *general* acceleration throughout the network of British Railways. It would, however, be wrong to suggest that the Advanced Passenger Train is the ultimate solution. It is hard to imagine a state of affairs in the future in which there would be no further development, but it seems that each major technological advance that involves most, if not all of the different engineering disciplines, is likely to take about ten years from conception to its becoming a revenue-earning proposition.

Before coming to a detailed account of how the new trains have already been absorbed into the Western Region Bristol and South Wales services, and into those of the East Coast main line, the extent of the investment so far may be noted. On the Western Region lines a total of 27 trains has been in operation since May 1977, and the first injection of eight trains on to the East Coast main line was made in May 1978. This was followed by progressive addition of more trains until the total allocation of 32 was reached in May 1979. The East Coast train sets differed from those of the Western Region in having eight coaches instead of seven, although having the same traction—two 2,250 hp power units one at each end of the train.

Since then additional HST sets have been put into service on the London-Plymouth and Penzance route of the Western Region, and are being introduced on the cross-country route from the West Country via Bristol, Birmingham and Sheffield to the North East. On these routes the opportunities for maximum speed running at 125 mph are more limited, but the high tractive capacity of the trains—providing power for rapid acceleration from speed restrictions and an ability to climb intermediate gradients at considerably higher speed than the present trains of conventional stock—will produce some shortening of end-to-end times and provide a welcome interim improvement before a major impact can be made by general introduction of the Advanced Passenger Train, although no decision has yet been taken on possible use of the APT on such routes.

# Chapter 3

# Planning the timetables

It would, perhaps, be an over-simplification to say that, out of the great diversity of problems associated with the introduction of a new high speed train service, the production of a train that would run at 125 mph—purely as a piece of traction engineering—was the simplest. After all, British steam trains had attained speeds of well over 100 mph, admittedly in favourable conditions but, in the 40 years that have elapsed since those stirring feats of the 1930s, technology has greatly advanced, and much more could be expected. The mere task of making a train run fast is one of the least of the many considerations to be taken into account in planting new high speed train services on to the crowded tracks of British Railways. Keeping in mind the prime desideratum of running trains of all classifications with the minimum likelihood of delay to each other, and each at its maximum economic speed, the difficulty of solving this fascinating jig-saw puzzle becomes amply apparent. A piece of simple arithmetic applied to the London Midland main line out of Euston puts no more than one side of it.

One of the present locomotive-hauled electric trains running at an average speed of 100 mph would cover a stretch of 75 miles (120 km) in 45 minutes, and in normal timetabling arrangements one has four or five of such trains following each other at five-minute intervals; but an HST or an Advanced Passenger Train at 125 mph would cover the same distance in 36 minutes, and on the timetable chart would occupy the space of *four* 100 mph trains! So at first sight it would seem as though the introduction of these very fast trains would be something of an embarrassment to a timetable planner anxious to make the best possible use of his track capacity. Financial considerations preclude any ideas of changing *all* passenger trains on the line into 125 mph units and, even though the locomotive-hauled trains may be capable of sustaining 90 to 100 mph, their rate of acceleration to that speed is considerably less than that of the 125 mph sets. Naturally the aim would be to put the new units on to the busiest and most popular routes, and these inevitably carry the greatest diversity of train speeds and traffic requirements.

The skill with which four HST services in every hour have been worked into the intense programme of departures from Paddington between the very busy hours of 16.30 and 18.30 can be appreciated from the accompanying graph, which shows the occupation of the down main line between Paddington and Reading. Beyond the latter station there is some relief because of certain trains passing on to the Berks and Hants line, while from Didcot the traffic thins out still further, by the divergence of certain trains for Oxford, Banbury and

Worcester. But as the diagram shows there are 26 main line departures in two hours. The ordinary express trains running in 'flights' of five have a headway of no more than three minutes, and the standard average speed over the 21.9 miles (35 km) from Southall to Twyford is 87.5 mph (140 km/h), whereas the HST sets on the Bristol and South Wales services are timed at exactly 125 mph between the same two stations. On starting from Paddington the minimum headway between an ordinary express train and an HST is nine minutes, and it will be seen from the diagram how quickly the faster trains 'catch up', requiring diversion of the last of the ordinary express flight to the relief line no further out of Paddington than Maidenhead, 24.2 miles (38.7 km).

This diagram provides an almost classic study in line utilisation at really high speed; but while it could be said that the Western Region is fortunate in having four tracks available from Paddington to Didcot, there are no less than 22 relief line departures from Paddington in the same two hours, and the rapid and punctual working of these well-loaded commuter services is essential in order to provide clear paths for the express trains to cross from main to relief lines punctually at their scheduled points, at Slough, Maidenhead or Twyford. The clear, undelayed running of HST services such as the 17.20 and 18.20 departures from Paddington (by which I travel frequently, and which often pass Reading nearly one minute early) is an indication that not only one train but a whole complex network is moving with precision and complete punctuality.

Busy and intense as the utilisation of this section of line is in the early evening peak period, the Western Region is fortunate in having no interruption in its four-track system for 53 miles (85 km) out of London. On the second route to

*Timetable: main line departures from Paddington 16.30 to 18.30 hours.*

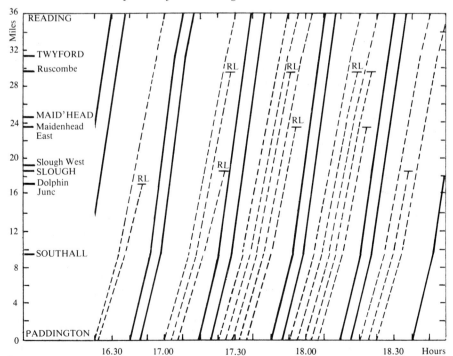

**Above** *The prototype HST running trials at Swindon, showing Test Car 6 attached to the leading power car* (Brian Morrison).

**Below** *The prototype HST in revenue earning service in April 1976 working the 15.15 Bristol (Temple Meads) to Paddington* (Brian Morrison).

*The prototype HST on trials in the Eastern Region, at speed near Hatfield* (British Railways).

which HST sets were allocated, the East Coast main line from Kings Cross, the commuter services are electrically operated as far out as Hitchin, 31.9 miles (51 km); and although these are thus assured of regularity in working, and very rapid acceleration from station stops, there is a serious double-line bottleneck extending from a mile north of Welwyn Garden City across the Welwyn viaduct and through the Welwyn South and North tunnels to Woolmer Green, a total distance of 2½ miles (4 km). Some very careful timetabling was necessary to introduce HST paths through this area without undue disruption of a busy and well-patronised local service. In other respects, however, the East Coast main line was similar to the Western Region routes from London to Bristol and South Wales in favouring the introduction of HSTs. Both had lengthy stretches that could be made suitable for running at 125 mph without undue expense.

It is in the introduction of the diesel-powered HSTs on to routes where the track geometry is not so favourable that many additional problems have arisen. The first of these applications, on to the West of England main line of the Western Region, is in some ways an extension of the Paddington-Bristol-South Wales scheme, and will have certain services integrated with it. In 1980 (summer Saturdays excepted) there are eight HST runs from Paddington through to Penzance, using the Berks and Hants line from Reading, while three of the present Bristol services will be extended to provide an HST working to Paignton. It will be appreciated that some considerable modification of service would be needed for Saturdays during the summer when the accommodation on the fixed formation of HST sets would not be suitable without the provision of a substantial number of relief and additional trains. It is not, however, the

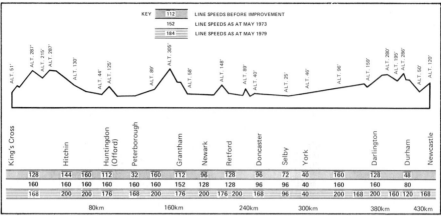

*East coast main line London, Kings Cross to Newcastle showing distance, gradients and line speeds.*

matter of peak period traffic that poses the greatest difficulty towards the introduction of HST sets on this route. It is what has been aptly called the track geometry.

Unlike Brunel's magnificent 'Great Way Round' to the West Country, via Bristol, much of the direct route from Reading to Cogload Junction was never intended to be a fast express route. It is true that at one time Brunel himself had an idea for an 'Exeter Great Western', which would have continued from the then-extremity of the Berks and Hants single-line branch to pass through Yeovil and Honiton, to block the westward aspirations of the London and South Western. If built it would no doubt have been in the most grandiose Brunellian style; but as matters eventuated, long after the days of Brunel, the shortened GWR route to the West of England was a chain of bits and pieces. Some sections, like the Sturt and Westbury cut-off and the Castle Cary-Langport stretch, were built as express routes; but a number of awkward curves and junctions remained, which the Westbury and Frome bypass lines of the 1930s went no more than part of the way to removing. In the steam locomotive interchange trials of 1925 and 1948 the visiting enginemen were severely handicapped by the constant succession of curves over lengthy stretches of this line.

Since then much has been done to upgrade the route, and between the Reading junctions and the approach to Exeter the line maximum speed is now 90 mph (144 km/h) throughout. But there are eight locations, where over short distances a restriction to 80 mph (128 km/h) is in force; two others, at Midgham, and near Bruton where the limit is 70 mph (122 km/h), and three, at Hungerford, the Grafton curves near Savernake and at Cowley Bridge Junction, where the limit is 60 mph (96 km/h). In these conditions, when the HST sets were first introduced on this route it was not possible to reduce the non-stop time between Paddington and Exeter below 134 minutes for 173.5 miles (277 km), an average of 77.7 mph (124 km/h). This, of course, included a spell of 125 mph running between Acton Yard and the approaches to Reading, but otherwise keeping within the present speed limits west of the latter junction. This represented an improvement of 15 minutes over the best time previously operating, but little enough to justify the introduction of the HSTs.

The timetables of 1979-80, however, are no more than a beginning. A programme of important civil engineering works has been authorised which, when completed, will enable the general speed limit to be raised from 90 to 100 mph, while on certain favourable stretches—favourable from the track geometry point of view—the limit will be raised to 110 mph (176 km/h). Even so, as the diagram overleaf shows, the overall situation on this line will still be restrictive, compared, for example, to the long stretches of the Bristol main line where 125 mph can be sustained continuously. Nevertheless, the accelerations of October 1979 brought Plymouth within a measurable distance of the three-hour norm considered the maximum journey time by train at which the railway can effectively compete with air travel. The extension of certain of the Bristol HST workings to Paignton naturally does not provide such a fast overall service time from Paddington to Exeter, although the fastest of these, taking 2 hours 25 minutes, involves some smart running between stations, with, at present, no increase in maximum speed limits over 90 mph on the 'Bristol and Exeter'.

Westward from Exeter I always remember the remark of a locomotive running inspector in Great Western days. He said: 'Beyond Exminster the line belongs to the engineer!' From October 1979 it is true that the 'Cornish Riviera Express' left Paddington ten minutes later and arrived at Penzance 19 minutes earlier, but only seven minutes of this acceleration took place beyond Plymouth. The fastest down train in Cornwall in that timetable was actually the

*Arrival of an HST from Bristol, at Paddington. The additional length of the trailer cars will be evident from comparison with the train of locomotive-hauled stock alongside (British Railways).*

17.40 from Paddington—the 'Golden Hind'—which, by omitting the stops at
Camborne and Hayle, covered the 79.5 miles (127 km) from Plymouth to
Penzance in 107 minutes, although the overall time from Paddington is longer
than that of 'The Limited', because of the additional stops at Taunton and
Newton Abbot. It is interesting to see how the pattern of train service in
Cornwall has changed over the years. There used to be a popular jibe against the
'Cornish Riviera Express' that it passed all the larger stations, except Truro.
When I first travelled on it, in 1924, the only intermediate stops were Truro,
Gwinear Road and St Erth. Now all trains call at Liskeard, Bodmin Road, St
Austell and Redruth in addition to Truro, and there seems a good deal of
profitable intermediate business. The HSTs certainly provide very rapid
accelerations from rest, and climb the banks practically at line maximum speed.

The fourth route on which HST sets are shortly to be introduced is a vastly
different proposition. The former Midland Railway always considered their
'West of England' main line to be one of their most important passenger routes,
although the speeds run over it were not exactly heroic. In this modern age,
however, a route that links such a chain of industrial and business centres as
Bristol, Birmingham, Derby and Sheffield, with the equally important

*West of England HST route.*

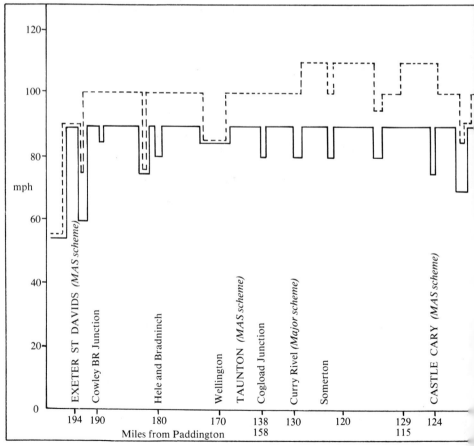

connections to Newport, Cardiff, Swansea and Plymouth in the south-west, and to Leeds and the West Riding, York, Tees-side, Durham and Newcastle, would seem a potential money-spinner. Much of the passenger business is city to city, rather than of long through journeys, and fortunately the track alignment over a considerable part of the mileage is capable of being upgraded without unduly heavy capital expenditure. On the other hand, in looking to possible important accelerations by use of HST sets, one becomes very conscious of the 'mixed' nature of the traffic, with heavy and profitable freight hauls over sections of the line where only two running lines are available. Clearly to fit in really fast Inter-City services some very intricate timetable planning will be needed.

A very important feature of train working over this route that has been developed to great advantage since the electrification of the West Coast main line has been the pattern of cross-platform connections made at Birmingham New Street, and the 'flighting' of the express trains between Birmingham and Gloucester. One could have, for example, a Cardiff-Newcastle and a Plymouth-Liverpool express following each other closely north of Gloucester, arriving within a few minutes of each other at opposite faces of the same platform at Birmingham, and providing admirable and quick cross connections. There are

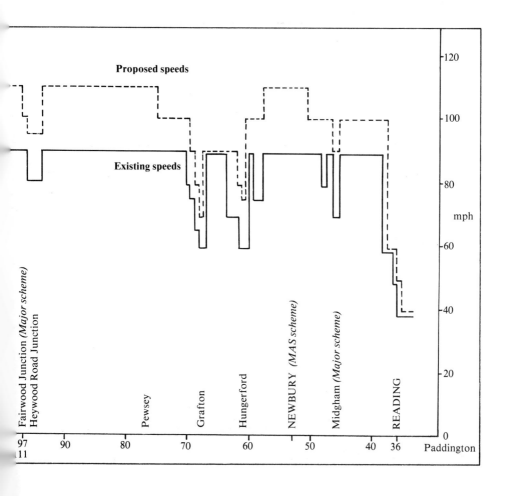

plans, still subject to Government investment approval at the time of writing, for Liverpool and Manchester to have HST services to and from the South Coast, the West of England, and South Wales, via Birmingham. Some interweaving would be practicable, allowing the faster member of a southward 'flight' from Birmingham to overtake the slower while the latter is taking the Worcester loop. The main line south of Bromsgrove would seem likely to witness 125 mph running before so very long, and as the most intensively used part of the line so far as through passenger traffic is concerned, its use will be critical. It will be interesting to see how the old Brunellian main line into South Wales may be developed in future, from Gloucester to Severn Tunnel Junction, because the alignment there is mostly very good.

The old Midland line north of Birmingham can also be upgraded into a really fast route, other than the Sheffield loop, while George Stephenson's excellent alignment of the North Midland main line should be capable of being built into an inter-City speedway for Sheffield-Leeds traffic. One is, of course, aware that the frequency of service by HST between Birmingham-Derby-Sheffield-Leeds will not at first equal that already enjoyed by the Paddington-Bath-Bristol 'axis'. It will be most interesting to see how the HST workings will be developed on what is now known as the North-East to South-West route, covering at its longest extent Newcastle to Plymouth. But it is time I was done with pleasurable speculations as to HST services of the future, and getting down to the superb engineering that has made the present situation possible.

*The first Inter-City 125 HST handed over to the Eastern Region being welcomed on arrival at York by a special fanfare of trumpets of The Royal Scots Dragoon Guards, on September 7 1977* (British Railways).

**Chapter 4**

# The foundations for high speed

At the time of writing this chapter the full HST service on the Bristol and South Wales routes of the Western Region has been in operation for two years and, as a regular traveller between Bath and Paddington, one of the most enjoyable features of the service is the way the smooth excellence of the ride has been consistently maintained. There has been no discernible deterioration. Later chapters of this book deal with the detail design of the power and trailer cars, and the methods of their routine maintenance. Such matters, of course, make a massive contribution to the quality of the ride; but below the rolling stock is the track, and no amount of skilful and ingenious vehicle design can make up for deficiencies below rail level.

Since the introduction of the intense electric service on the London Midland main line northward from Euston, with its hourly flights of six 100 mph expresses within a single half hour, repeated throughout the day, a great deal of experience has been amassed as to the behaviour of modern track in such severe conditions. Equally on the East Coast main line the frequent passage of heavy express trains hauled at 100 mph—sometimes a little more—by the powerful 'Deltic' locomotives has added to the accumulating bank of experience in building and maintenance of track carrying very fast and frequent service. On the London Midland Region in particular the effect of certain varieties of electric locomotive, nominally limited to a maximum speed of 100 mph, but frequently attaining maxima of up to ten per cent in excess, has provided an invaluable experience for the civil engineers. In approaching the era of regular and frequent running at 125 mph on diesel-operated routes, even with all the experience that had been gained, the civil engineers were taking a step into the unknown, just as much as for 100 mph running with electric locomotives when this was first introduced on the London Midland Region.

Fortunately the days of isolationism between the various engineering departments on British Railways are long past; no longer is there risk of repetition of the classic confrontations of history between civil and locomotive engineers. Theoretical research, backed by the experience with the existing high speed services had shown how necessary it was to keep the dynamic forces exerted by wheels on the rails to a minimum to avoid track deterioration and rail breakages. To do that it is necessary to keep axle loads to a minimum and, what is more important, to keep the unsprung weight on each axle to a minimum. When the prototype High Speed Train was under construction, and it was expected that the maximum axle load would not exceed 18 tons, civil engineers with experience of the 'Deltic' locomotives on the East Coast main line

**Left** *Track laying in progress. Note the bridging vehicle resting entirely on the temporary outer rails* (British Railways).

**Right** *The new track laid in, before ballasting* (British Railways).

anticipated that the effect of the HST, at 125 mph would be no worse than that of a 'Deltic' at 100 mph. Again with diesel locomotives of classes '45', '47', and the diesel-hydraulic class '52', all three of which the Western Region had ample experience, the indications were that the HSTs would be little, if at all worse. Before the prototype HST began its trial running, some tests at 125 mph had been made on the West Coast main line at Cheddington, with several types of locomotive, and these gave useful experience on continuously welded rail, with concrete sleepers, including a specially prepared dipped joint, at which the response was measured.

Every detail of the 'road', from the bottom upwards needs the most careful scrutiny and attention. The formation, that is the ground on which the railway is built, is the first consideration. In the south of England, on the fast-running main lines radiating from London, the formation varies from clay to sand, gravel or chalk, and of these only sand and gravel are safe materials on which to build a modern railway without some special treatment. If the ballasting of the track is built directly upon clay and chalk it has been found that a muddy mess, known techically as slurry, works up through the ballast and makes good maintenance impossible. On some lines built with economy in view, when traffic was slower and lighter, reasonably good service has been given for many years with ballast laid on chalk; but relaying with heavy pre-stressed concrete sleepers and continuous welded rails has proved too much for stability. On such stretches of line one of the most effective solutions has been to lay a blanket of sand between the clay or chalk formation and the ballast; this blanket must be not less than 6 in (15 cm) thick, and it is often reinforced by a sheet of polythene at mid-thickness of the sand, to form a sandwich. The process of blanketing is, of course, a major operation and requires absolute possession of the track in question.

The quality of the ballast itself is very important. In days before the grouping

2097657

of the railways of Britain, in 1923, a great variety of materials were used, mostly with a view to minimum initial cost, and cost of haulage to site. Thus one found tracks ballasted with gravel, ash, or even shingle from sea beaches. It was only on some of the more wealthy railways, like the London and North Western, that stone was used in any quantity. In more recent years, crushed limestone has been extensively used, but under very fast and heavy traffic it is subject to attrition, and bad spots consisting of stone-powder and ballast can develop into areas of slurry in wet weather. Such areas can make the maintenance of a good road difficult, if not impossible. Today the aim is to provide a hard stone ballast, preferably granite, or basalt, and to have a deep layer between the sleepers and the formation, whether of the natural ground if this be sand or gravel, or of the blanketing in other cases.

Unfortunately the geology of the country injects its own form of economics into the situation. East of a line drawn from Exeter to Humberside there is no igneous rock (the very hard granites and basalts formed in prehistoric times by the results of volcanic action; and while the resources of the famous Meldon quarries on the northern slopes of Dartmoor have been extensively developed, the supply is not nearly enough to satisfy the needs of the Southern Region, let alone the Western, the territory of which lies largely outside the area of igneous rock. To convey granite, or basalt from the north-west or Scotland would be totally uneconomic. So limestone has to be used extensively, and care taken to guard against the effects of attrition. Today a depth of ballast 15 in (380 mm) below the underside of sleepers is standard, in good conditions, for lines carrying traffic at 100 to 125 mph although this is increased in certain areas, as found necessary. Modern techniques are in use for determining the depth, and these require a careful study of the subsoil. But in any locality it goes almost without saying that good drainage is essential.

It is, however, one thing to specify and install good modern ballasting on a

*A modern tamping machine used in the job of consolidating and levelling the track, which makes use of an electronic beam device for checking the alignment and levels* (British Railways).

satisfactory natural or a prepared blanketed formation; but there is an old joke that the permanent way is so called because it is the *least* permanent part of the whole railway! Once installed it is equally important to maintain it in first class condition. Some of the old railway companies of pregrouping days were famed for the immaculately high standards of their track maintenance; but this was achieved by labour-intensive methods, at a time when traffic was neither so fast nor so frequent as now. In the economic conditions of today one has not only to design for maximum mechanisation of the work, but also to bear in mind the greatly reduced time available for maintenance, if the flow of traffic is not to be seriously disrupted. At a time when there are so many people ready to detract from the public image of British Railways, it is clear that every effort has to be made in avoiding disruption of train services, however essential engineering work on the line may be. It needs no more than a glance at the timetable diagram of the Western Region reproduced on page 25 to appreciate that there is precious little time even for examination, let alone for actual work when traffic is flowing at such densities.

While good ballasting is essential for ensuring a smooth ride, it is equally important for minimising the deterioration of the track superstructure. The vertical and horizontal forces created by the passage of trains at high speed are distributed through the rails, sleepers and fastenings to the ballast, and if the ballasting has weak spots because of slurry formation or ineffective packing, the rails themselves and the sleepers will take a disproportionate share of the loading and, by deterioration in level and alignment, will hasten failure, not to mention bad, or even dangerous riding. Machines for aligning the track, and others for tamping, or packing ballast under the sleepers, are in extensive use today, but they can only be used to maximum effect if the ballast itself is kept in first class condition. Some very interesting new techniques and machinery are now in operation on British Railways for ballast cleaning on track used by 125 mph trains. Even so there are, as yet, no convenient methods for cleaning the ballast, and separating out the contaminating elements, that do not involve digging out the ballast from underneath the track. But the latest machines in service enable the job to be done without removing the track itself.

As can well be imagined such a machine is a mighty piece of equipage, which together with its service vehicles makes a train of its own. Most types now in use are indeed capable of travelling to the site under their own power, though in actual practice they are usually moved by locomotive. The complete unit is marshalled thus: match-runner wagon, machine wagon, power wagon, followed as required by box wagons for tools, and a living van for the crew. The match-runner wagon supports the spoil conveyor, while the machine wagon comprises the excavating equipment, conveyors, screening plant and the control gear. It will be appreciated that to dig the ballast out while the track is in position means attacking it from *outside* the width of the sleepers. The extent to which the trough connected with the traverse cutter bar does extend will be seen from any picture showing the RM62 type in action. Careful pre-planning of any ballast cleaning operation is necessary, where obstructions such as station platforms, signalling equipment and such like exist on the sections of track selected for treatment.

All ballast that has supported track carrying heavy and fast traffic will have become compacted to some extent, and when it becomes broken up by the action of the cutter chain it will naturally increase in volume, and there is a tendency for it to push upward in the spaces, or 'cribs' between the sleepers. This can cause a situation that needs watching. The cutter bar passes beneath this upward bridging and, when the loosened materials below is extracted, this crust falls back and could result in some dirty ballast being left behind. The matter of obstructions is regarded differently by men in the different engineering disciplines on the railway. I always remember an occasion very many years ago when I was lecturing on modern signalling practice to a gathering of permanent way men, and I was roundly abused—in the most jocular manner!— for 'cluttering up the track, with new fangled electrical gadgets'. Recalling this, I was very amused to read in an article published a few years ago on ballast cleaning machines, of the most gigantic proportions, the following sentence: 'In practice permanent structures such as drains, signalling equipment, monument blocks and other engineering structures are encountered and it is necessary, if damage to the machine is to be avoided, to be able to assess machine clearance'. Damage to the *machine* . . .!

The civil engineers must forgive my pulling their legs. They have a difficult enough job keeping the ballast in good shape for the traffic that has now to flow, and there are other factors than mere cleanliness that must be taken into account. There is the matter of drainage. To improve this, ballast cleaning is often carried out with one end of the transverse cutter bar lower than the other so as to provide a cross fall. It is, however, not always possible to do this, because it depends upon there being a layer of material that is impervious to moisture below the ballast that is required to be removed for cleaning. But impervious layers can of themselves be a severe handicap. If there should be good ballast at the lower layers all could be well, but often one digs down to clay before an impervious layer is reached, or to another kind of formation. Clay is a horrible material to handle in a ballast cleaner, and slows down operations so much that crossfalls are not usually attempted in such localities. In general they are limited to areas where the lower levels of the ballast are sufficiently good to obviate the need for removing them.

More problems occur during the ballast cleaning operations due to the temporary sinking of the track level. The removal of a considerable depth of ballast from beneath the sleepers will result in a fairly abrupt change of level ahead of the machine wagon. This could result in the setting up of high stresses in the rails, while derailment of the machine could take place. Furthermore, if a high proportion of the stone is to be returned to the track after cleaning, much labour would be involved in raising the rails so that packing beneath the sleepers could recommence. To avoid these difficulties, arrangements have to be made for temporary support of the track, on blocks of timber or other suitable means. Usually an attempt is made to limit the inclination in the rails before and after a cut to 1 in 20.

The speedy execution of track maintenance work is becoming increasingly important at a time when timetable planning is becoming more complex, when

*Vertical profile measuring system.*

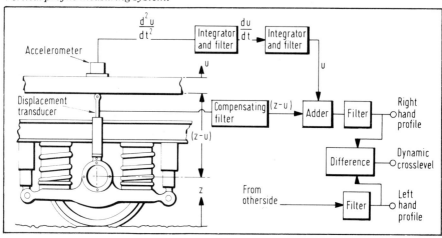

*The ultrasonic test car—rail contact equipment for detecting flaws in rails* (British Railways).

there is an increasing necessity to make more intense use of the very large investment represented by the main railway lines of this country, and to improve the public image of the railways by better all-round adherence to the published timetables. Heavy civil engineering work involving 'absolute possession' of one or more tracks must of necessity be done mainly at weekends, and it is in a feeling of resignation that those of us who have to make journeys at such times accept diversion of trains to longer and less speedy routes, long delays, and other inconveniences. But although traditional it is not good for the image, particularly at a time when the restricted train service normally available at weekends is well patronised. It may well become a question of whether investment in still more elaborate machines for quicker and more effective track maintenance would pay off.

At the same time it must be emphasised that a ballast cleaning operation usually involves something of a compromise between a number of largely unrelated factors, such as site conditions, how readily the spoil may be disposed of, the mechanical capacity of the machines available, whether new clean ballast is conveniently to hand, how long the traffic department can afford to give absolute possession of the track, and other considerations. One important feature of the design of the actual cleaning machines is giving them the facility for unloading the spoil end-wise, instead of into wagons on an adjoining track. Such a machine enables the work to be done with possession of only one running line, and could be done during temporary single line working, rather than total possession. I have written at some length on this subject of ballast cleaning, because even with previous standards of speed and line occupation dirty ballast can be the 'Achilles-heel' of track maintenance work, not to mention the effect that dirty ballast can have upon the reliable operation of the track circuits of the signalling system. The whole subject becomes of far greater importance on a line carrying many trains running at 125 mph.

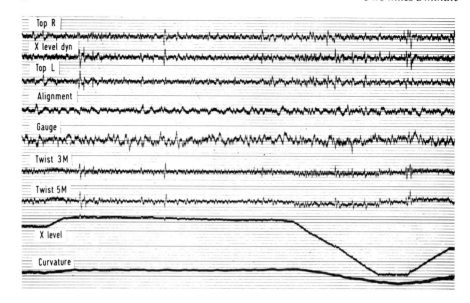

Equally important is the checking of what can be called the geometry of the track. In years gone by the permanent way inspectors brought a lifetime's experience to the job, usually invigilating upon deviations from correct 'top' and line by personal observation backing up the daily walk-throughs of the gangers. The intensification and acceleration of todays traffic demand quicker and more scientific methods. The latest practice is to measure and assess the details of the track not by human observation at rail level, but by observing the effects upon a special test vehicle capable of operation at 125 mph. For this purpose a special car has been designed and built at Derby, which is capable of measuring the following details of the track:

1. Vertical profile, or the 'top'
2. Horizontal profile, or alignment—'line'
3. Accuracy of the gauge
4. Super-elevation on curves
5. Twist
6. Horizontal curvature
7. Gradients

The recording car contains a wealth of highly scientific equipment for measuring the foregoing. In respect of the horizontal profile in particular, for which a beautiful optical system is used, one thinks instinctively of the old, delightfully simple, but rough and ready method of the whitewash bucket. This was mounted in the floor of the car in such a way that when a sideways swerve or lurch took place some of the whitewash was thrown out and slopped on to the track. It told the men on the ground there was a spot that the car did not like, but of course gave little in the way of a quantitative measurement, except that a big splash obviously indicated a bigger defect than a small one! In the new car, bogie-mounted projectors, line scanners on the coach body, and video processing units produce a continuous graphic record of the exact variation along the line.

**Left** *Ultra-violet record of track profiles.*

**Right** *View inside the ultrasonic test car—showing test equipment for locating faults in rails* (British Railways).

Through a series of electronic recording and processing features, a comprehensive chart is produced, on which all seven of the quantities previously enumerated are recorded, so that the complete picture for any section of line is presented in precise relation one with another; the accompanying diagram shows part of a typical chart. 'Top' is measured for both left-hand and right-hand rail and one can see, for example, how 'twist' can give rise to variations. It is a magnificent tool of engineering management, that will enable track maintenance operations to be selectively scheduled as a result of test runs over the high speed train routes.

The extent to which the track itself has been developed in recent years is perhaps not generally appreciated. To this the pre-stressed concrete sleeper has made a massive contribution. They are some four or five times as heavy as the former standard timber, of 10 in × 5 in cross section and, although as such need machine handling, the improvement in stability is such that they do not need any of the day-to-day fettling, by platelayers, that was a feature of track maintenance in earlier days. There used to be 24 sleepers to a 60 ft rail; now there are 28 sleepers on lines carrying speeds of 100 mph and over, and 26 everywhere else on main lines. Although the rail section now being laid in on main lines with the heaviest traffic is of the same weight, 113 lb per yard, as that used when the changeover from bull head rails was first made, in 1948, the present section is actually the fourth that has been used on British Railways. The first was actually a British standard, that had been supplied to overseas railways; but after some experience a change was made to a new section, 109 lb per yard. Then, in 1960, the UIC 54 section was adopted: 54 kilogrammes per metre, which became known as the British '110A' rail. Then, in November 1967, there came the terrible accident on the Southern, at Hither Green, due to a broken rail, and a new section was developed, the '113A', which was generally the same so far as overall dimensions were concerned but had a thicker web 0.79 in (20 mm) parallel against a tapering section with a minimum thickness of 0.62 in (15.9 mm). The metallurgical content of the rails has remained virtually unchanged, being what is known as a 'medium manganese steel', having a manganese content of 0.95 to 1.25 per cent.

In connection with continuous welded rails, which have made such an outstanding contribution to the stability of modern track and to the smoothness of ride, the question is often asked as to how the expansion and contraction of the material, due to atmospheric temperature changes, is provided for. Modern practice is to pre-stress them so that they are stress free between the range of 21 to 27 degrees C, that is from 70 to 81 degrees F. Above 81 degrees compressive stresses would be set up, and below 70 degrees there would be some tension. In practice this has worked very well, and perhaps, as might be expected, the relatively very few incidents of failure are mostly due to tensional cracks in very cold weather. The number of outright fractures, and consequent delay to traffic, has been greatly reduced by the introduction of rail flaw detection apparatus, by which defects are pin-pointed before they become serious enough to cause a fracture.

The rail flaw detection car works over a line under observation at 20 mph and because of this has necessarily to operate at night. Originally, by ultrasonic methods, it produced a film strip that indicated, by a 'jerk' in the trace, the location of a flaw. The examination of these traces, after a run, was a somewhat laborious—and, it may be added, sleep inducing—task, and the records are now analysed by computer. The work of the rail flaw detection car is now supplemented by a pedestrian ultrasonic detector. The application of these two methods of rail stress analysis has resulted in the location of no less than three times as many flaws—and thus potential causes of rail failure—as the cases that actually lead to broken rails. This is a remarkable forestalling of probable causes of outright failure.

*This photograph of a southbound HST, approaching Oakleigh Park at high speed, shows the close packing and great depth of ballast installed on the main lines used by these trains* (Brian Morrison).

# Chapter 5

# Signalling, brake power and sighting

In many schemes of multiple aspect signalling commissioned as part of the great modernisation plan of 1954 on British Railways, the layouts were designed to provide for 100 mph running with air braked trains. In the busier areas, where a liberal admixture of slower traffic gave ample evidence of the 'mixed' nature of the operation, four-aspect signals were installed to enable trains running to schedules needing maximum speeds greatly less than 100 mph to work at close headways by using the double-yellow indication of the four-aspect signals as their all-clear. In certain other areas, with considerably less density of traffic, three-aspect signals were adequate, so spaced as to provide full braking distance from one signal to the next for air-braked trains travelling at 100 mph.

Multiple aspect signalling, though a vital necessity in any modern railway operation, is nevertheless expensive, and in any considerations towards high running speeds attention had to be given to brake power, to enable the faster trains to stop from their maximum speed in the same distance as that taken by the existing air-braked trains, locomotive hauled, and running up to 100 mph. Unless this could be done, new trains with a maximum speed of 125 mph could not be run without extensive, and very expensive alterations to signalling over many hundreds of miles of main line. The standard stopping distance curve for passenger trains permits a distance of 2,200 yards (2,030 m), from 100 mph and a curve showing the minimum braking requirement, for existing signalling, was used as a guideline in designing brakes for the new trains. To provide for varying rail conditions, which in certain circumstances can have some effect upon braking distances, just as they can on the highway, the new braking equipment was designed to have a rate of deceleration equal to nine per cent of that caused by gravity, in other words a rate of retardation of 2.9 ft (88 cm) per second. The diagram overleaf shows the stopping distances provided by this design parameter in comparison with those required by the existing multiple aspect signalling. From this it will be seen that, whereas the existing air-braked trains take 2,200 yards in which to stop from 100 mph, the designers of the high speed train set out with the objective of stopping from 125 mph in 1,979 yards (1,810 m), and from 100 mph in no more than 1,200 yards (1,100 m). How it was done is referred to in some detail in a later chapter; but at this stage all that need be said is that the design parameter has been more than fulfilled.

So far as plain line was concerned the requirements had been met, and the new High Speed Trains could be run at 125 mph in safety on lines equipped with multiple aspect signalling. Also, after much consultation between all the various parties, it was agreed that with the equipment of all lines concerned with the

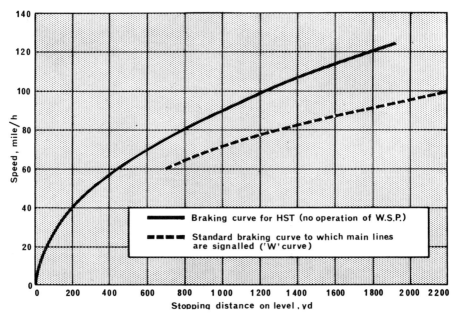

**Above** *Designed braking performance of the HST at 125 mph is well within the limits set for 100 mph locomotive-hauled trains.*

**Below** *Swansea-bound HST leaving the tunnels between Gaer Junction and Newport, showing colour light signals and direction indicators* (J. Brennan).

automatic warning system (AWS) throughout, the increase in maximum speed from 100 to 125 mph was still within acceptable limits for observation of signals by the drivers. No additional aids were considered necessary. The question of signal observation is very important on a system such as British Railways, carrying a remarkably 'mixed' traffic. On the Japanese Shinkansen lines, operating at maximum speeds of 131 mph (210 km/h) sustained over very long stretches of line, there are no wayside signals at all. The drivers work entirely on cab indications showing the speed at which they should run, and any change in this requirement is advised not only by visual indication on his control console but also by audible warning. Such a system is, of course, applicable only to a single-purpose railway. On a mixed railway it is generally considered that there must be wayside signals; but modern technology may cause some modification of this view in time to come.

It is, however, not only other classes of traffic, but also the High Speed Trains that need to be diverted from the maximum speed line. On the Western Region, for example, the South Wales HSTs diverge at Wootton Bassett Junction, and those bound for Penzance diverge at Reading West. Other instances will arise as the service of High Speed Trains is increased. In addition to major diverging junctions at which HST sets are following their regular scheduled routes, the introduction of transitioned crossover roads, over which speeds of 70 mph (112 km/h) are permitted along the diverging route, has enabled temporary crossover movements to be made, on four-track systems

*A scene in the approach to Paddington showing colour light signals, and direction indicators on gantry controlling approach to the terminus* (Brian Morrison).

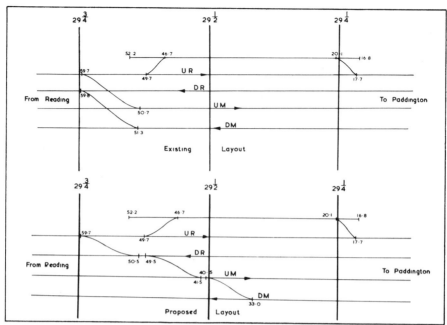

**Above** *Western Region: Ruscombe Crossover (29½ miles from Paddington) showing the original layout (top) and the present layout with high speed crossover roads (bottom).*

**Below** *One of the HSTs supplied to the Western Region on commissioning trials on the East Coast main line south of Thirsk, passing colour light signals signifying approach to crossovers between main and relief lines (British Railways).*

with much less delay than previously. Referring to the timetable diagram on page 25 in Chapter 3, the crossover movements of the 17.03, 17.29, 17.56 and 18.03 departures from Paddington are made at Ruscombe, over the track layout shown in the accompanying diagram. While none of these trains are HSTs they are sharply timed, lower down the speed scale, and their drivers require adequate preliminary warning of the divergence from the straight track, even though it may be a regularly scheduled movement. When HSTs need to be diverted, as a temporary measure, the operation becomes one for special consideration.

It is important to review the standard practice of British Railways for junction signalling that existed until the coming of the High Speed Trains. The methods can be divided into two categories, the first in which speed over the diverging route must not exceed about 40 mph (65 km/h), as in the case of trains taking the Berks and Hants line at Reading West Main; the second category covers a junction like Wootton Bassett, before the days of HSTs, and high speed crossovers on quadruple track, like Ruscombe, referred to previously. The first category was previously dealt with by approach control of the junction signal. This was held at red, with the associated restrictive aspects leading up to it, until the train had occupied the berth track circuit for a time calculated to ensure that the driver had reduced speed to the stipulated figure for the junction ahead. Then the signal cleared to display an aspect appropriate to the state of the line ahead and the white lights of the junction indicator would be illuminated. The complexity of this necessary arrangement may well be contrasted with the simplicity of signalling in GWR days, when all that was thought necessary was to provide a splitting distant semaphore arm on the station home signal, from which it was inferred that the driver's knowledge of the road would ensure that a suitable reduction of speed over the actual junction would be made. That no doubt was adequate when the speed of approach to the area was around 70-75 mph (112-120 km/h), and no one would mind very much if the junction points were taken at nearer 50 than 40 mph (80 than 65 km/h).

At what would now be regarded as medium speed locations, where the diverging route could be taken at 50-70 mph (80-112 km/h), pre-HST practice was to hold the signal *beyond* the junction at red, so that the lead up to the turn out would find the actual junction signal, with its directional indicator at single yellow, and the indicator illuminated. With the braking equipment fitted to the HST sets, a train could, however, be approaching a 'single yellow' aspect at nearly 100 mph and still be able to make a comfortable stop at the red. This was clearly a case where the existing signalling was not adequate for dealing with the HSTs, because in such an instance the junction points could be taken at considerably more than 70 mph. The line beyond the 'red' on the diverging route might be completely clear, but a time release control was imposed on that signal, and when it cleared, of course, the junction signal would clear from single yellow to a less restrictive aspect. But it was the approach to the junction that could be misleading, particularly to the driver of an HST who was being diverted through a crossover system like Ruscombe, but who thought he was being warned of the run-up to a red aspect along the straight line.

The problem having arisen, the question naturally came up as to how to provide selectively for the High Speed Trains. But after due consideration the British Railways Board, in consultation with the railway inspectorate of the Ministry of Transport, concluded that it was not exclusively a problem where

**Left** *The northbound 'Flying Scotsman', after the introduction of HSTs on the East Coast main line, threading the intricate track layout on the east/north side of Newcastle Central station* (G.S. Cutts).

**Above** *A northbound HST in Selby station. Note the overhanging structure (top right) to provide clear sighting for the colour light signals* (G.S. Cutts).

High Speed Trains were concerned. Injecting a personal sentiment at this point, I have always been a little sensitive about junction signalling arrangements since my own involvement, fortunately without injury but not without memories, in the alarming high speed derailment at Didcot on September 27 1967, when the train in which I was travelling took a system of crossovers like that in the diagram on page 46, though limited to 25 mph (40 km/h) at about 70 mph. To meet the modern requirements of traffic working, British Railways are now introducing the first departure—or rather the first elaboration—from the standard code of colour light signalling aspects set up as a result of the deliberations of the Three Position Signalling Committee of the Institution of Railway Signal Engineers, whose report was published in December 1924. From some time now there has been talk of introducing a fifth aspect, with some combination of yellow and green lights; but with the present disposition of lights in a standard four-aspect colour light signal, there would not have been sufficient colour separation between the green and the yellow, and an additional unit would have been necessary above the existing signal head.

Rather than go to this elaboration for certain junction layouts, and to make provision for a sixth, as well as a fifth aspect, British Railways have introduced flashing single yellow and flashing double yellow aspects, and a number of junction layouts have been selected for this application. The philosophy involved is designed with a two-fold purpose: to ensure, as far as possible, the accurate observance of a speed restriction over a diverging junction where the limit is less than line maximum speed, and to give additional warning of the approach to such a junction. In the run-up the train will first encounter a flashing double yellow; next, a flashing single yellow, and then a steady single yellow with the junction indicator above it appropriately lighted. Whatever the state of the line beyond the junction there will be three successive audible warnings in the driver's cab from the AWS system, at the flashing double yellow, at the flashing single yellow and on passing over the AWS magnet before the junction signal. At such locations the approach control on the junction signal previously used is now removed, and instead the signal clears to a less restrictive aspect, if conditions on the line ahead are suitable, only when the locomotive passes over the AWS magnet, 200 yards (185 m) before the signal itself.

While this book is primarily concerned with the High Speed and Advanced Passenger Trains, the use of flashing aspects is not to be confined to lines where the maximum speed is 100 mph and over. The following guidelines have been laid down, as a general principle:

| Straight route Speed mph/km/h | Minimum turnout speed mph/km/h |
|---|---|
| 100/160 or over | 50/80 |
| 96/153 or less | 40/65 |
| 75/120 or less | 24/38.5 |

The first junction to be equipped was on the Western Region, at Didcot East Junction, for crossover movements from down main to down relief line, used by express trains from London to the Oxford and Worcester line.

Taking a look now into what one hopes is the not-too-distant future, there is the running of the Advanced Passenger Train to be considered. In Chapter 9 of this book the mechanism by which the APT is able to run through curves at

*The up 'Flying Scotsman' approaching Newcastle, showing colour light signals and the electric-pneumatic point operating gears* (Brian Morrison).

*A high level view of the approach to Paddington, looking west, with an HST from Swansea approaching. The positioning of signals can be seen* (Brian Morrison).

considerably higher speed than other trains is described. When these trains are introduced into revenue-earning service on the West Coast main line they will be driven by men in the regular links, whose normal duties include the 100 mph electric expresses, liner trains and so on, and they will need some positive means of discriminating between existing speed restrictions, and the considerably higher values applicable only to the Advanced Passenger Trains. Although these trains have a maximum speed potential higher even than that of the HST, up to 155 mph (250 km/h) in fact, it is not the immediate intention to schedule speeds above 125 mph and for this the existing signalling will provide adequate braking distances. But the question of how best to indicate to drivers of the APT the higher speeds at which many of the curves could be negotiated, had to be considered from several angles. There was the relatively cheap possibility of erecting additional signs at the track side, applying only to the APT; but this was soon discarded, not only on the grounds of proliferation, but from the undoubted risk of misinterpretation, both by APT drivers and by drivers of ordinary trains. Instead it was decided that the permissible APT speeds throughout the route should be given to the driver in the form of a cab display presented continuously throughout the journey.

It is important to appreciate how this differs in basic principles from the aids to running given to drivers on certain other high speed services elsewhere in the world. On the Japanese Skinkansen lines there are no wayside signals and the driver has a continuous visual indication of the speed at which he should run. On the Deutsches Bundesbahn in Germany the driver has a series of charts in the form of a book, the pages of which he turns over as the journey proceeds, showing the maximum speed limit of the line, and the speed at which he should run to maintain the schedule of his train. On the British APT the cab indications are no substitute, nor even an adjunct to the indications of the wayside signals and the audible signals received in the cab via the AWS apparatus. The train has to be driven in accordance with the indications of the ordinary signals, and the cab display is a continuous reminder of the permanent speed restrictions applying to the APT. In addition to the visual indication, three types of audible indication are given. First, the approach to a section of more restricted speed. This is made at such a time previously that would give braking distance, plus a short time for driver reaction. As with AWS indications, if a warning of restricted speed ahead is not acknowledged by the driver the brakes are automatically applied. Secondly comes a notification of the point at which a restriction begins, and thirdly an indication of change to a higher speed.

The activating source of the continuous display of permissible speed limits in the cab of an APT is a series of passive electrical devices known as transponders, mounted in the track. On plain line there is a transponder at every kilometre. It is a passive electrical device with no external cabling or power supply, and having a tuned aerial, and together with electric circuitry corresponds to a particular speed, such as 100 or 125 mph. The train-borne equipment consists of an aerial tuning unit fed from a high-frequency supply, and as this aerial passes over each transponder a high frequency signal from the train triggers off a response corresponding to the speed for which the transponder is adjusted. This response is then amplified, de-coded as it were, checked and translated into the visible display before the driver of the train. There are times, of course, when temporary speed restrictions have to be enforced, because of track repairs and such like. Then the Advanced Passenger Trains would be subject to the same restrictions as all other trains throughout the affected area. At such times transponders will be put out of action throughout the lengths concerned, by fitting a padlocked screening device over them. In consequence there will be no cab display from the time of approaching the warning boards at the lineside. It becomes operative again on passing the first transponder beyond the speed restriction T sign.

I mentioned earlier that the APT is designed for a maximum speed of 155 mph (250 km/h). At the moment this is a prospect only for the future because it is generally considered that regular running at more than 125 mph is beyond the limit at which the existing signalling can be satisfactorily observed; special additions to the signalling are at present under consideration to provide for safe operation in such conditions. Any decision to raise the train speed above 125 mph (200 km/h), and the measures required to assure continental safe operation, will depend upon the experience now being gained from operating at speeds up to 125 mph (200 km/h).

*Typical arrangement of transponders on plain line; in junction areas the regular interval is reduced from 1,000 to 500 metres.*

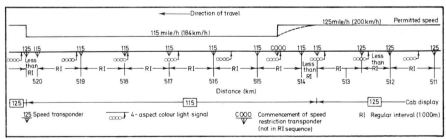

**Chapter 6**

# Power to pull

With the target of performance set at a sustained service speed of 125 mph on level track there are cynics who have said that such a speed was not that wonderful. After all, they remind us, *Mallard* did 126 mph as long ago as 1938, and even today I see occasionally those hoary old chestnuts of American locomotive history brought out that claimed a speed of 112.5 mph (180 km/h) for a New York Central 4-4-0 as long ago as 1893, and for a Pennsylvania 'Atlantic' the still more startling maximum speed of 127 mph (203 km/h). These old claims have long been discredited in the eyes of all connoisseurs of locomotive performance, and of course *Mallard's* epic run, although genuine enough so far as the maximum speed claimed, was very much a once-only feat! In setting out deliberately to produce trains that will have the capacity to run regularly at such speeds, with sufficient traction power to overcome the resistance of adverse weather conditions, and provide a reliable all-year-round public service, it was a very different situation from that of taking a picked individual unit, with a driver and fireman of exceptional tenacity, and then thrashing the engine almost beyond its limit on a very favourable stretch of line.

In the case of the High Speed Trains intended for the Western Region, the East Coast main line, and later for the North East-South West route, the commercial departments asked for rakes of seven or eight coaches of the Mark III type 75 ft long (23 m), and providing seats for 96 first class and 288 second class passengers, apart from the accommodation in buffet and kitchen cars. The tare weight of an eight-car train was estimated at about 280 tonnes, or a little short of 300 tonnes, fully loaded with passengers and luggage. Since the nationalisation of British Railways a great deal of experimental work has been carried out to establish accurate records of the rolling resistance of coaching stock over the entire range of speeds that were required in passenger service, until the project of regular running at 125 mph was launched. The experimental work was very comprehensive, and the results gave not only the estimated coach resistance when running in still air, but also in two conditions of adverse wind. The graphs showed that at 90 mph the resistance in still air would be 14.5 lb per ton (6.6 kg/tonne), but 17 lb per ton (7.7 kg/tonne) against a 10 mph head wind blowing at an angle of 45 degrees to the track. Train resistance, however, is not proportional to the speed. It follows a parabolic type of curve, and increases rapidly with increase of speed. At 100 mph that earlier BR evaluation showed a resistance of 17.5 lb per ton, in still air. From this one could guess it might be around 25 lb per ton (11.3 kg/tonne) at 125 mph, or 30 lb per ton (13.6 kg/tonne) *plus* in bad weather. Although resistance is still quoted, as of old, in lb per ton,

**Above** *Power to pull! Youthful enthusiasts discuss the merits of an HST at Newcastle* (Brian Morrison).

**Below** *In Newcastle Central station: the up 'Flying Scotsman' (HST) beside one of the '45' Class diesel electric locomotives, No 45 039* (Brian Morrison).

with HST and APT coaching stock the resistance is very little relevant to the actual deadweight, but far more so to the aero-dynamic features of the stock, which has been the subject of intense development.

A provision of at least 3,000 hp would have to be made for haulage of the coaches alone. But on both the Eastern and the Western Regions there are long gradients on which it was desirable to maintain speed fairly near to the maximum for the line, to enable high start-to-stop averages to be reliably scheduled, and the decision was eventually taken to provide an engine horsepower of 4,500, with a power car at each end of the train. This provision, which was very convenient from the operating point of view, in that no light engine movements would be required at terminal stations, was also interesting from the viewpoint of train resistance. When the LNER introduced the 'Coronation' streamlined train in 1937 the rearmost vehicle was an observation car with a streamlined 'beaver tail', as it was termed. It was a striking and attractive car; but although it was in some quarters regarded as a publicity 'gimmick' it virtually eliminated the tail end eddies that are inseparable from the rear end of a locomotive-hauled train of conventional stock. One had only to watch the manner in which the exhaust steam from the locomotive trailed smoothly over it. Of course the reduction in train resistance created by this rear-end streamlining on the 'Coronation' was far more outweighed by the job of hauling the car itself, which provided no additional revenue-earning seating space. During the winter months when most of the journey between Kings Cross and Edinburgh was in darkness, the observation car was not run. On the HST sets, with an air-smoothed power car at each end, one has the advantage of some tail-end streamlining.

The resistance of the HST sets at 125 mph is 22 lb per ton (10 kg/tonne) which, as one might expect, is considerably less than that of conventional British Railways coaching stock. Related particularly to the long 1 in 200 gradients of the East Coast main line, which observation has shown are climbed at a sustained speed of about 110 mph (180 km/h), the total resistance would be 9,700 lb rolling and aero-dynamic and 5,000 lb gravity, total 6,500 kg, and the power required around 4,000. On the Western Region the steepest gradient of any length to be mounted at or near maximum line speed is 1 in 300, on the Badminton line. With the seven-car trains standard on the London-South Wales HST service the horsepower required at 125 mph would be around 3,800. This is just about up to the maximum capacity of the power cars. From my own numerous observations on both the Eastern and Western Region HST services the use of eight-car trains on the former has brought the requirements for power much nearer to the maximum capacity of the engines than the seven-car trains of the Western Region. As discussed in Chapter 3 of this book, it was necessary to have low axle loading in the power cars, to reduce peak wheel loads on the rails, and from this it was evident that the power requirements could be met only by a gas turbine, or by *high speed* diesel engines. The gas turbine alternative was very thoroughly investigated, but no turbine was available that could compete with the diesel in all matters of cost, whether in initial price, maintenance or fuel charges.

I have emphasised that the alternative to the gas turbine was a high speed diesel. British Railways already had experience with the Paxman-built 'Ventura' engine. Initially two 12-cylinder 'Venturas' rated at 1,135 hp (at 1,530 rpm) were fitted to one class 42 Swindon-built Bo-Bo diesel hydraulic locomotive.

Subsequently the same size of engine, but rated at 1,350 hp (1,500 rpm) was fitted during re-engining of the North British Bo-Bo diesel electric locomotives of the Scottish region, which were then designated class '29'. In addition 6-cylinder 'Venturas' (650 hp at 1,500 rpm) were incorporated in the 56 diesel hydraulic 0-6-0 locomotives when built for the Western Region. This, in contrast to the marine-type diesels fitted to the main line class '40', '45', '46' and '47' locomotives, is a quick-running engine, working at 1,500 rpm against 850. The engine chosen for the HST power cars is the Paxman 'Valenta', which is a more powerful version of the 'Ventura', having 12 instead of six cylinders. The same cylinder diameter and stroke are used, but while a straight doubling up of the 'Ventura' would have provided only 1,300 hp the HST engine needed to be 2,250. The increased power was obtained by a new design of turbo-charger with increased pressure ratio, and by a new design of fuel injection equipment to give high injection rates and pressures. The cylinders are arranged in 'V' form, with their centre lines inclined at 60 degrees to each other.

To accommodate the increase in power, various features of the 'Valenta' engine had to be strengthened, although maintaining the general design features of what had proved a very satisfactory engine in service, and one having the attractive reduced weight characteristics of a quick-running engine, as distinct from the basically heavier slow-running marine types in the express passenger main line diesel locomotives but still having electric transmission. The principal changes in design, as between the 'Valenta' and 'Ventura' engines were: crankcase, cylinder heads, connecting rods, pistons and bearings redesigned to suit higher firing pressures; crankshaft stiffened by increasing the pin and journal sizes; improved cylinder head and piston cooling arrangements to withstand higher pressures; redesigned gear train, to be suitable for higher loadings; and various other detailed improvements.

*HSTs at the south end of York station. This photograph was taken during commissioning trials, and the power car in the foreground is one destined for the Western Region (British Railways).*

*Two of the Eastern Region HSTs used on the West Riding services at Bradford Exchange station* (British Railways).

It will be appreciated that the whole 'Valenta' design was very carefully worked over, in all its detail, because it was emphasised at the outset that to be economically justifiable the utilisation of the new HST trains would be very high. Additionally, the marketing of speeds so much higher than anything previously scheduled would inevitably draw a high degree of publicity. Any failures, or even mild interruption of service, would in the context of the present age be magnified out of all proportion, on the principle that only troubles and accidents make 'news'! Thus the designers had not only to prepare for exceptionally high utilisation, but to achieve it with a microscopically small incidence of failures.

The authority to design, develop and build a prototype High Speed Train was given in August 1970, and it was completed in June 1972. Unhappily, as a result of the kind of reactionary and obstructive attitude that today goes by the non-committal term of 'industrial action', the running trials of the prototype train were delayed for many months; but when it was eventually possible to run at high speed, in June 1973, the results were generally very successful. Although a number of detail modifications were called for when it came to building the production trains, it was evident that in all its basic essentials the prototype HST was proved equal to the service specifications originally laid down. Although the object of the trials in 1973 was not primarily directed towards record breaking, I may add that in running between Darlington and York a maximum speed of 143 mph (230 km/h) was attained. On a demonstration run that I was privileged to accompany I logged a maximum speed of 137 mph (221 km/h) between Northallerton and Thirsk southbound. Here I actually clocked one half-mile in exactly 13 seconds, that is 138.4 mph (223 km/h), but I prefer to regard the maximum on that occasion as 137 mph. The 'power to pull' was certainly there for the HST.

In Chapter 2 of this book the philosophy behind the development of two entirely new and dissimilar types of passenger train by British Railways was described, and it is interesting to recall that authority to build an experimental version of the second alternative, the Advanced Passenger Train, with the special tilting feature, was actually given some two years before authority to build the prototype HST was received. While the novel aspect of the APT was, of course, the tilting feature, the provision of 'power to pull' was a most important consideration seeing that a target maximum speed of 155 mph (250 km/h), had been set. As in the case of the HST, gas turbine propulsion was considered. In 1969 this alternative had more than just a research engineering interest. In the previous year British Leyland had begun developing a gas turbine with regenerative heat exchangers, for possible commercial application to traction generally in the 1980s, and British Railways were glad enough to incorporate in the experimental APT a form of engine that could well have proved attractive, when fully developed by its manufacturers. In fact, it was a multiple installation with five engines in the power car and electric transmission. The gas turbine has the advantage of lightness and compactness, and as compared with the diesel enables twice as much power to be installed within a given space.

One of the route rationalisation schemes undertaken by British Railways following the epoch-marking Beeching plan involved the closing of the former Midland main line between Nottingham and Melton Mowbray, and running Nottingham-London services via Trent and Leicester. This closed line included a high proportion of curved track, and because of its relative proximity to the Railway Research Centre at Derby provided an ideal test route for running with the experimental APT. In the testing of the gas turbine-powered train on the Nottingham-Melton line, tractive power was not the principal consideration; it was the novel principle of the tilting mechanism that had to be examined in all its many ramifications. As it eventuated, however, the idea of using gas turbines for propelling the APT on non-electrified routes was killed by the world oil crises of 1974, which led to the suspension of the Leyland turbine development programme. Any introduction of the APT on non-electrified routes would have to rely upon diesel traction. It was evident also that gas turbine propulsion was not going to yield the economies originally expected. The control gear of the heat exchangers proved troublesome, and the manufacturers had no confidence in the heat exchangers themselves. Even if they had eventually been successful, the fuel consumption of the gas turbines would have been slightly greater than for a diesel; but in actual running the control gear of the heat exchangers was more trouble than it was worth, and the exchangers were removed.

It was business strategy, however, and not anything connected with power plant problems, that led to the prototype APT sets being designed for direct electric traction. Their first application was to be on the West Coast main line, between Euston and Glasgow, and any future non-electric introductions are likely to be diesel-powered. Nevertheless, before passing on to the power requirements of the West Coast main line, the potentialities of the APT for train service improvements on routes over which the track alignment admits of no more than minimal degrees of acceleration by the use of the HST, was dramatically demonstrated by a test run from St Pancras to Leicester—an important main route, which has much restrictively curvy mileage in its length of 99 miles (159 km). So far as track geometry is concerned it may be compared very unfavourably to the 94 miles (152 km) of the Western Region main line between Paddington and Chippenham, engineered by I.K.Brunel, where today the only restrictions below 125 mph are through the busy junction stations of Reading and Swindon.

Today, running up to maximum recovery standard, that is deducting the recovery time included in the schedules, the fastest time between St Pancras and Leicester is 80 minutes, representing a start-to-stop average of 74.2 mph (119.6 km/h), whereas between Paddington and Chippenham, with HST sets, the fastest 'net' time is only 53 minutes, an average of 106.2 mph (171.2 km/h). Despite their capacity for speed, HST sets could not greatly improve upon the London-Leicester time, because of the continuous incidence of curves. But on this special run with the experimental APT, the journey was completed in 58½ minutes, at an average speed of 101 mph (163 km/h) start to stop. Allowing for an appropriate amount of recovery time, this is equivalent to a service schedule of 62 minutes, against the present best of 84 minutes. This saving of 26 per cent in journey time gives an excellent impression of the service improvement that would be possible after introduction of the APT on lines that include too much curvature to enable the HST to make an effective contribution. This test run is referred to in detail in Chapter 10.

In view of the earlier reference in this chapter to the rapidly increasing values of train resistance with increasing speed it might be questioned whether the fuel cost of the higher speeds practicable and actually run by these high speed trains are not inordinately high. In this connection it is interesting to study the accompanying graph which shows the tractive energy consumption per second class seat for the HST and APT, in comparison with that for a conventional

*Comparison of tractive energy consumptions per equivalent second class seat. (All passenger and catering accommodation assumed to be second class seating.)*

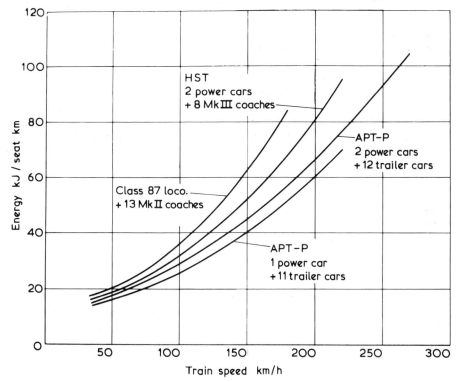

**Above left** *In the centre of York station, before HSTs went into revenue earning service. The train at platform 8a is on trial, while the down 'Flying Scotsman', still Deltic-hauled, comes slowly through from the south* (Brian Morrison).

**Left** *An impressive aspect of '254 018' leaving Kings Cross with the down 'Talisman'* (Brian Morrison).

**Above** *HST from Bristol passing under the huge viaducts that span the track outside Paddington* (Brian Morrison).

train of Mark II coaches hauled by an electric locomotive of class '87'. The HST curve relates to one of the East Coast main line sets, with eight Mark III coaches, while the APT curves show two projected variations. In the latter the power cars are placed in the centre of the train, and the maximum number of trailers that can be hauled by one power car, at a maximum service speed of 125 mph, is 11. For the designed maximum speed of 155 mph (250 km/h), when it is possible to operate this, two power cars will be needed, and a maximum of 12 trailer cars may then be taken.

From this group of curves it will be seen that at 100 mph the respective energy consumptions are 69, 56 and 43 KJ* per seat km for the locomotive-hauled Mark II coaches, the HST, and the APT with one power car and 11 trailers, and that the latter again with 11 trailers at 125 mph actually consumes less energy than a class '87' locomotive hauling 13 Mark II coaches at 100 mph. This is a most interesting and significant achievement, testifying to the efficacy and skill of the research work that has been put into these notable developments in railway traction. It is important also to emphasise that the above figures represent useful energy consumption at the rail, and do not take into account losses in the prime mover (whether at the power station or in the HST power car) and in the transmission. The overall energy consumptions lie between three and four times the above figures.

* KJ = Kilojoules, or 1,000 joules. The joule is the metric unit of work representing that necessary to move a weight of 10 kilograms a distance of one metre. In Imperial measure a joule is equal to 0.737 ft lb.

**Chapter 7**

# The relationship of track and train

As a regular traveller by train since 1921 and a rider on locomotives since 1934, I have naturally recollections of many kinds of ride. Until the last twenty years or so my experiences as a passenger at speeds of much over 80 mph (130 km/h) were relatively few, compared to my aggregate railway mileage, and in that speed range memories of rough and uncomfortable rides are few—except on the express multiple-unit electric trains of the Southern Line. I can recall, however, many rough trips on locomotives (non-steam included!) and when the prospect opened up of regular running at 125 mph (200 km/h) it was no more than natural that one had some slight feelings of apprehension. This was the more understandable on the Paddington-Bristol route of the Western Region, where memories of the execrable riding of the 'Blue Pullmans'—a scant recompense for higher than standard fares!—was still a live issue, not to mention the riding of the 'Warship' class diesel-hydraulic locomotives, which could be frightening. There were also recent experiences on the class '86' electric locomotives of the London Midland Region at speeds up to 100 mph (160 km/h), which a Longsight driver once prefaced, as we got away on a Wilmslow-Euston non-stop run, with the stirring words: 'Ride her, cowboy!' Before we had gone very far what the scientists would call the 'vertical accelerations', and their frequencies, made one think of those intrepid young men at a rodeo in the Wild West!

Since those early days of modernisation, however, an immense amount of research has been made into the complex factors that contribute to the riding qualities of both locomotives and coaching stock, and by the time the High Speed Trains went into revenue-earning service in the Western Region in 1977 the travelling public was presented with an immaculate ride, up to 125 mph (200 km/h)—and sometimes, in those first months of their introduction, considerably more. I had one instance of an exceptionally smooth run at a speed sustained at 136 mph (219 km/h) for some distance on an ordinary service train. Far more important, however, than any first impressions, or the recollections of individual instances of very fast running, is the way in which the quality of the ride has been subsequently maintained. I travel regularly between Bath and Paddington, on an average about once a fortnight throughout the year, and today, after about two years in which the fleet of HST sets in the Western Region is averaging a quarter of a million miles (400,000 km) per annum by each train, the quality of the ride remains as excellent as when the trains were first put into service. Some of the factors that have contributed to this highly commendable situation may now be discussed.

In a notable paper presented in Frankfurt-am-Main in October 1977 Mr E.S. Burdon, HST Project Engineer, said: 'One of the single most critical areas of the Power Car design is undoubtedly the derivation of the suspension parameters to give a good quality of ride, both vertical and lateral, as well as providing an adequate margin of stability beyond the maximum service speed. The type of bogie suspension chosen was based on experience with high speed bogies previously and successfully developed for use with electric locomotives . . . .' This development arose out of the need to cure the rodeo-like riding of the class '86' electric locomotives on the West Coast main line, and resulted in the application of a different form of suspension on the class '87' and '86/2' locomotives. The new arrangement consisted of coil-spring primary and secondary units, with the wheelsets located by four resilient links of the Alsthom type, incorporating lateral restraint rubbers. There was, however, not enough space on the HST bogie to adopt this design in its entirety, and the first proposal was to make the Alsthom links narrower than those on the class '87' electric locomotives.

It was realised that such a deviation, from what had been a very successful arrangement, would be something of a compromise and it was not embodied in the final design without further study. In so doing use was made of modern computer techniques in the Research Department of British Railways. A study was made, by analogue computer of bogie critical speeds, feeding into the computer all the design features of the bogie, and it was shown that in the worst conditions that would be acceptable for wheel type wear, and so on, the critical speed was around 90 mph (150 km/h). This, of course, would have been useless on trains planned to run at 125 mph (200 km/h) and, still on the theoretical

*High Speed track: a southbound East Coast HST, doing 125 mph passes the London-Edinburgh half-way sign, near Tollerton, Yorkshire; it was here that steam locomotive crews used to change, through the corridor tender, in the days of the London-Edinburgh run of the 'Flying Scotsman'—later 'The Elizabethan' (British Railways).*

basis, dampers were introduced to check and limit the yawing action. This had the desired effect, but the theoretical analysis of the design was not yet completed. On a different computer, studies were made of the vehicle reaction to track, both vertically and laterally, with related actions such as body pitching, bogie pitching, body bounce and body sway. Such is the capability of modern computer science that the numerous effects could be laid bare before a single piece of actual manufacturing had begun. One looks back a little wistfully to episodes in the history of railway mechanical engineering and ponders upon how the course of development might have been changed had the great men of the past had such aids to design analysis as now exist.

Even so, the prototype HST was not absolutely right from the outset; nor, really, could one expect such a revolutionary development to be so. On the first run, when speed was worked up to 125 mph (200 km/h) the riding was completely stable, but on attempting to make repeat runs up to that speed severe hunting of the bogies developed at speeds above 112 mph (180 km/h). To quantify the extent and effect of the lateral oscillation, reference must be made to the term 'ride index', which is a factor by which both the vertical and lateral oscillations are judged. The significance of the various values of ride index may be seen from the following table:

| Ride Index | Effect |
| --- | --- |
| 1 | Very good |
| 1.5 | Almost very good |
| 2 | Good |
| 2.5 | Almost good |
| 3 | Satisfactory |
| 3.5 | Just satisfactory |
| 4 | Tolerable |
| 4.5 | Not tolerable |
| 5 | Dangerous in service |

The descriptive classifications of ride indices, need not be taken too literally, particularly if aspects other than those of passenger comfort are being considered. But they will be referred to later in connection with the general performance of the trains.

As first put on trial, the prototype HST train had a lateral ride index of 3.4, but when the severe hunting commenced it went up to the range of 4.2 to 4.8. When running in stable conditions the vertical ride index was 3.2, at the full 125 mph (200 km/h). The action had clearly to be analysed very thoroughly. The predominant mode of oscillation was swaying. Being mounted on resilient pads the traction motor tended to roll about its centre of gravity, in stable running; but when bogie hunting began some of the oscillating frequencies synchronised, and made things much worse. The points along the track where instability had occurred were examined, and it was found that all of them were locations where the rails had recently been transposed. This is a normal practice where the rail heads have been slightly worn to a coned profile, and it is a condition to which rolling stock must accept, as it were.

The first steps made to improve the riding and stability involved increase of the damper rates on the lateral and yaw dampers—in other words increasing the stiffness of the springs. Also to prevent the rolling and swaying tendencies by the traction motors, the mountings on the bogie cross members were made solid instead of resting on resilient pads. This cured the hunting action of the bogies, and test runs up to a maximum speed of 142 mph (228 km/h) were made without any sign of the previous trouble. But while the hunting was cured the lateral body accelerations increased, bringing the ride index up to 4.0 at 142 mph (228 km/h). Bogie pitching was still pronounced, and an attempt to eliminate this by uprating the primary damper had the opposite effect! And so the process of experimenting and observation, a combination of theory with practical trials, went on, until eventually the prototype train had covered some 248,000 miles (400,000 km). It was a continuous saga of careful and painstaking mechanical engineering persistence, not ceasing until the ride index, in both the vertical and lateral planes, was reduced to around 3.0. This, it should be emphasised, was on the power cars and not on the passenger carrying vehicles.

The salient features arising out of this long period of trial running, which met the demand for a vehicle that would still ride well when the type profiles were worn were: *a)* the intervals between reprofiling were well in excess of 112,000 miles (180,000 km), which is roughly equivalent to about six months regular service: *b)* the total aggregated depth of tread wear was approximately 0.16 in (4 mm) in 248,000 miles (400,000 km) of running and *c)* a complete absence of flange root problems, indicating a very satisfactory level of performance on curves. The results eventually obtained with the prototype train have been fully borne out in the very intensive use made of the production sets. After 12 months service—that is about a quarter of a million miles of running—the ride index at 125 mph (200 km/h) is 2.9 vertical and 3.2 lateral. These are very good results.

As finalised the HST power car bogie is an elaborate piece of modern machinery, as can be appreciated from the accompanying perspective drawing. Its most noticeable feature, as can be seen from outside, is that the axleboxes are not contained in fixed horn guides on the frame, but carried in what is termed a radius link. This is connected to the frame by the primary suspension springs, while the primary dampers referred to earlier are also prominent outside. The bogie frame itself is a beautiful piece of work. It is entirely of welded

*The first of the Western Region HST sets, No 253 001 on high speed commissioning trials between Darlington and York* (British Railways).

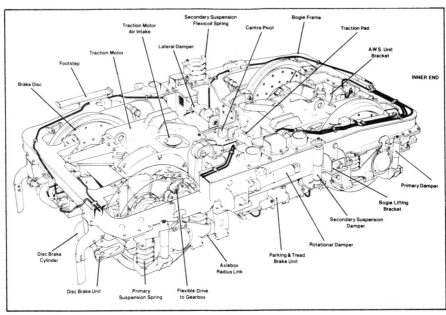

**Above** *HST power car bogie.*

**Below** *Just topping the 'Two Miles a Minute' level: the 11.45 Paddington to Weston-super-Mare passing Hayes, 11 miles out of London* (Brian Morrison).

construction, and modern computer techniques were used in design to ensure that the distribution of metal in the longitudinals and cross-sections was such as to provide the exact strength needed to resist the stresses set up in high speed running, equally in acceleration, in counteracting the sudden effects of slight irregularities in the track, and when braking. Having established the design theoretically, a prototype frame was built up and this was subjected, in a testing laboratory, to loadings arranged to simulate conditions of high speed service. Strain gauges were attached at all the critical points and the stresses measured. As a result of this practical back-up to the basic theoretical design certain modifications were made to the frame. I once heard a certain steam locomotive described as one into which more brains had been packed than any other. The more one studies the power car bogie of the HST the more one finds to admire, in the skill with which the results of so much advanced engineering practice has been packed on to that light weight bogie frame. It is indeed a powerpack of brains.

I have concentrated so far on the bogies of power cars, and by this time some readers may be thinking—yes, but what about the passengers? It is, of course, essential to have a well-nigh perfect riding power car in a train set that is close-coupled into a single unit. A bad riding power-car would not only be uncomfortable and potentially dangerous as a vehicle, but at the speed commercially required it could cause much disturbance to the track, leading to

*An eastbound HST on trial near Swindon (the first of the Western Region HST sets). Near to the church in the left background is the site of the house where the great G.J. Churchward, Chief Mechanical Engineer of the Great Western Railway, lived for more than 30 years* (Brian Morrison).

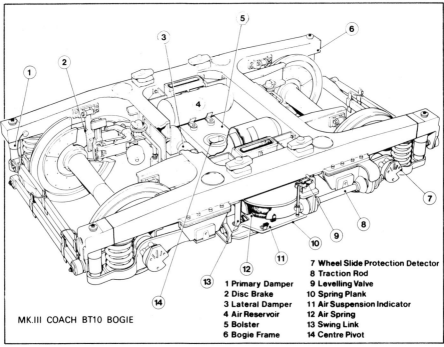

MK.III COACH BT10 BOGIE

| 1 Primary Damper | 7 Wheel Slide Protection Detector |
|---|---|
| 2 Disc Brake | 8 Traction Rod |
| 3 Lateral Damper | 9 Levelling Valve |
| 4 Air Reservoir | 10 Spring Plank |
| 5 Bolster | 11 Air Suspension Indicator |
| 6 Bogie Frame | 12 Air Spring |
| | 13 Swing Link |
| | 14 Centre Pivot |

*HST coach bogie.*

high maintenance costs. Over the years, the experience with the 100 mph electric locomotives on the West Coast main line, in very severe and continuous high speed usage has been very important, from the viewpoint of track and locomotives alike. The unusually large amount of civil engineering work on the Euston-Glasgow line at the time this chapter is actually being written is the result of the cumulative effect of very heavy utilisation, and of many electric locomotives with relatively poor ride indices. It has been assumed that much of this work on the line has been undertaken to prepare the way for the Advanced Passenger Train; but this is not so.

The trailing car bogies are those of the standard BR Mark III design, but adapted to carry the longer vehicles in the HST sets. The primary suspension is by a trailing arm, pivoted at the end nearest to the centre of the bogie, and having one coil spring per wheel, at the outer end. Lateral control of the wheel sets is by means of rubber bushed links between the trailing arms and the bogie frame, and the axlebox itself is designed to provide the anchorage points for the vertical, lateral and longitudinal springs. This design ensures accurate alignment of the wheel sets through the principle of a swinging arm. Whereas the secondary suspension of the power car bogies is through four helical springs, two on each side of the frame, the passenger cars have a secondary suspension consisting of an air cushion, at the midpoint on each side of the frame. There are levelling valves to maintain constant height of the car body, while to control body roll there are long pendulum links, with a torsion bar. The bogie pivots on a central pin, which has rubber bushed guides which transmit traction and braking forces to the bolster. This, in turn, is connected to the bogie frame by the traction rods. The weight of the car body is carried on the bolster by two side bearers of low-friction material, and these in turn control rotation of the bogie. The general arrangement of this very successful design can be studied from the drawing reproduced opposite.

The relationship between train and track has been prominently in mind during all the design stages of the High Speed Train. The necessity of providing a smooth ride for the passengers is only one side of the problem. At the outset a design pattern was established so that with any new rolling stock running at its maximum service speed the vertical impact forces imparted to the track should not exceed those of a 'Deltic' locomotive (BR Class 55) running at 100 mph (160 mk/h). The HST sets are intended for non-electrified routes, and on these the 'Deltics' constituted the most severe effect on the track. These had been the subject of an intensive study, and have been divided, so far as peak effects are concerned, into two categories. The first, designated P1, occurs at a maximum less than $\frac{1}{2}$ millisecond after passing over a rail joint. The reaction to it is taken up by rail and sleeper inertia, and in consequence of this it is the force causing rail deformation. The second peak force P2 occurs several milliseconds later, and is transmitted to the ballast. It is this force that causes degradation of the ballast, and deterioration in track 'top'—the perfection of the horizontal line of the rails. It has been established that P1, for a given standard of track, is independent of all other factors other than the speed of running, whereas P2 is dependent on the unsprung weight in a locomotive, or power car, as well as the speed.

With the design speed of the HST 25 per cent greater than that of the 'Deltic' some concern was felt as to the possible effect on the P1 peak force, and calculations gave the following results:

| Locomotive | Unsprung weight kg | Speed km/h | P1 force (N.10⁴) | P2 force (N.10⁴) |
|---|---|---|---|---|
| Deltic | 3,650 | 160 | 51.2 | 34.2 |
| HST Power car | 2,200 | 200 | 60.8 | 31.4 |

These calculations indicated that the P1 effect of the HST was more severe than could be tolerated, and instrumented track trials were carried out in two separate locations. Even with sophisticated modern equipment precise measurement of the

*125 mph track through a busy junction: the 09.35 Kings Cross to Newcastle passing Hitchin at maximum speed (Brian Morrison).*

actual forces was difficult; but the relative values, as between different types of vehicles, could be established. Tests were carried out at Didcot, Western Region, and Dinwoodie, on the West Coast main line between Lockerbie and Beattock. As might be expected from experimental work of this kind there was considerable variation in the recorded values, variation as between repeat runs at one or other of the sites on the same day, or on successive days, and between the results obtained at Didcot and at Dinwoodie. Nevertheless there was a sufficient trend visible in the measured values for certain conclusions to be made, and in respect of the 'P2' force the results were disturbing. While the calculated values as previously quoted suggested that the HST values at 125 mph (200 km/h) would be somewhat less than those of the 'Deltics', at 100 mph (160 km/h), the measured values at Didcot and Dinwoodie showed them to be worse. Although the discrepancy between these calculated and measured values was not large it was enough to instigate further research.

In the case of the 'P1' forces the measured values were consistent in showing the same increase of HST over 'Deltic' values as had been indicated by the preliminary calculations. As previously mentioned however the 'P1' force is entirely dependent upon speed, and it is affected by unsprung weight only if that weight can be reduced to a very low value. To try and effect some improvement in this respect an investigation on a considerable scale was made towards the use of resilient wheels. A preliminary theoretical study of a proprietary type of resilient wheel suggested that the P1 force might be reduced to less than $50 \text{ N}.10^4$—that is better than the 'Deltic'—and as a result a batch of these resilient wheels was obtained for testing in service conditions. The wheel in question has a steel or light alloy centre, with a large coarse-pitched screw thread turned on its outer diameter, and a steel tyre, with a similar screw thread turned on its inside diameter. The assembly of the two materials is made with a clearance of about 0.18 in (4.5 mm) between the threads and this volume is filled with silicone rubber, the rubber being cured *in-situ* to bond the two components together. It was an ingenious design, but the severity of railway operating conditions, particularly at the designed speeds of the HST, made very careful examination necessary.

The use of rubber as an intermediate material posed a number of questions. It would obviously be advantageous in lessening the effect on the track when passing over a rail joint; but wheels are themselves subjected to several other effects. There are, in particular those connected with braking, because when a brake application is made there would be a torsional effect between the centre and the tyre portion of the wheel, which would be transmitted through the resilient material, and there would also be considerable heating of the wheel centre due to the frictional action of the brake. An extensive series of laboratory tests was made in conditions infinitely more severe than anything likely to be experienced in service, and some damage to the rubber was noted, but normal service braking appeared highly unlikely to damage it. Nevertheless the whole philosophy of safe railway operation, evolved with the experience of the 150 years that have elapsed since the opening of the first main line railway, demands that the exceptional and the unexpected must be provided against, and it was realised that the malfunctioning of the brake on any vehicle, or individual wheel, leading to dragging tread brakes, could very quickly destroy the bonding of the rubber.

At the same time the parallel research into the effect of the wheels on the track when running freely, at maximum speed, was giving such promising results that the general investigation was persisted with. Indeed the use of a resiliently sprung

*Flashback to 1937! 'I can remember when this train was so horribly slow that you could eat your meal in comfort.'*

wheel appeared to be a feasible engineering solution to the problem of reducing the P1 track forces. But there remained the possibility in extreme conditions of emergency, or malfunction braking, of the rubber bond between the wheel rim and the wheel centre being destroyed. In view of the large clearance between the internal and external screw threads at the point of interface it was essential to provide some means of locking to prevent the two portions of the wheel separating in the event of the rubber bond being destroyed. Unfortunately, with the space limitations of the HST bogie and of the brake gear, this did not prove possible. As it stood the resilient wheel design did not, unfortunately, measure up to the vital criterion of being safe in the event of a failure that could definitely be foreseen, in extreme circumstances, and thus its use could no longer be considered. Although this interesting investigation thus had negative results I have referred to it in some detail, to indicate the care and thoroughness with which every engineering aspect of the HST design has been treated.

It is perhaps significant of the fundamental importance of good riding, both in the interaction between train and track, and its ultimate effect upon the vehicle bodies, that my first detailed reference to the make-up of the HSTs has been entirely concerned with the bogies. I shall always remember a *Punch* cartoon of 1937 by the inimitable Fougasse, captioned: 'I can remember when this train was so horribly slow that you could eat your meal in comfort'. There was more truth than jest in that cartoon where some of our faster trains were then concerned; but as a 'Then and Now' tailpiece to this chapter I may add that when travelling by the HSTs I have frequently checked book proofs laid on the tables, with no strain at all to my ageing eyes, even at 125 mph (200 km/h).

# Chapter 8

# Details of the High Speed Train and its handling

The traction and suspension of the HST sets has been discussed in Chapters 6 and 7, and I now come to the trains themselves; and to those who study the history of railway carriage design in Great Britain the first point to attract attention is the length of the trailer cars, 75 ft (23 m). When Churchward began his notable programme of passenger stock modernisation on the Great Western Railway, some 75 years ago, he set out to produce coaches that would carry the maximum number of passengers, in an acceptable degree of comfort, for a minimum of tare weight, and the famous 70 ft (21 m) stock was evolved. But there were certain route restrictions. They could not be used on the West to North service via the Severn Tunnel, operated jointly with the LNWR, nor on the Wolverhampton-Bristol route, via Stratford-on-Avon. Another very noticeable restriction was on the Ilfracombe branch of the LSWR which meant that the Cornish Riviera Express of the 1920-30 period had to include one 60 ft (18 m) coach, among its many 70 ft (21 m) through carriages. On any line that had originally been broad gauge there was, of course, ample side clearance on curves.

The trailer cars of the HSTs were required to have a high route availability, in view of their ultimate use anywhere between Aberdeen and Penzance, and on the North-East to South-West route. The restrictions imposed by the traditional high platforms on British Railways, and the siting of some of the principal stations on considerable curves, such as those at York, Newcastle and Birmingham New Street, all set up hampering parameters. British coach designers are sometimes apt to look a little wistfully to Continental and North American conditions, where platforms are low, and contrariwise, climbing on board can be something of a mountaineering feat for passengers! But so far as the HST trailer cars are concerned improved design techniques and some civil engineering work made it possible to accept a length of 75 ft (23 m) as standard. The seating, for 72 second class passengers, is a great deal more spacious than for the 80 accommodated in Churchward's 70 footers, of the so-called 'concertina' type. There are some, I know, who would have liked to have seen one car in the train arranged in compartments rather than open saloon style; but the modern trend is towards the saloon, and in stock so smooth riding as the HST, the provision of tables opposite all except a very few seats is a great convenience, whether for a business man to do

**Top right** *A Western Region HST, Swansea to Paddington, approaching Westbourne Park* (Brian Morrison). **Centre right** *HST second class restaurant buffet car.* **Right** *HST open second class car.*

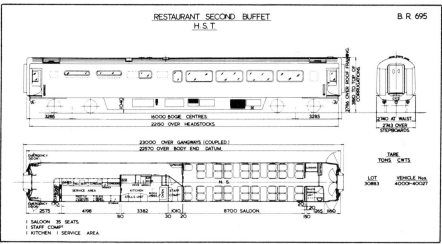

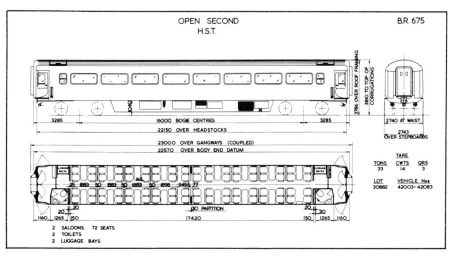

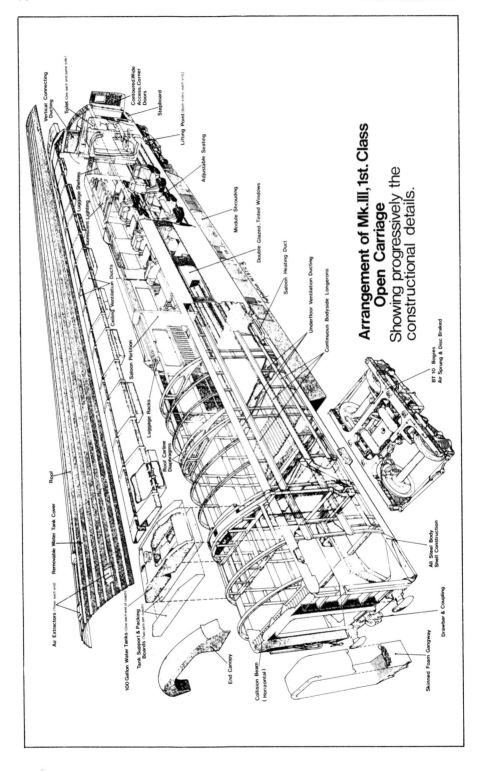

Air Extractors (Three each end)

Roof

Removable Water Tank Cover

100 Gallon Water Tanks (One each end of coach)

Tank Support & Packing Boards (Two sets per coach)

Vertical Connecting Ducting

Toilet (One each end same side)

Contoured,Wide Access,Corner Doors

Stepboard

Lifting Point (Both sides, each end)

Adjustable Seating

Module Shrouding

Luggage Shelves

Fluorescent Lighting

Ceiling Ventilation Ducts

Double Glazed,Tinted Windows

Saloon Heating Duct

Underfloor Ventilation Ducting

Continuous Bodyside Longerons

Saloon Partition

Luggage Racks

Roof Carline Diaphragms

End Canopy

Collision Beam ( Horizontal )

Drawbar & Coupling

Skinned Foam Gangway

All Steel Body Shell Construction

BT 10 Bogies Air Sprung & Disc Braked

**Arrangement of Mk.III, 1st. Class Open Carriage**
Showing progressively the constructional details.

his work, picnic parties, or for 'Auntie' to pile up the results of a shopping spree. The luggage space between the backs of abutting seats is also very welcome, avoiding the need for humping heavy suitcases on to the overhead racks.

The decor, in both first and second class saloons is very simple, but quite satisfying. Gone for ever, it seems, are the days when carriage walls were adorned with pictures of alluring tourist resorts on the line. Those on the Great Western, in colour photochrome, were some of the most attractive of this kind, so much so that patrons bought copies of the pictures for their own house decoration. It was a time when the beauties of our own country were less known than they are today when, holiday-wise, we are a much more widely travelled people. The coach bodies, which are all of uniform external dimensions, can be arranged to suit first or second class seating or, if necessary, catering cars. The window apertures are the same in all, and are spaced to coincide with seating and tables in the first class. In the second class, where the seating is not so spacious lengthwise, the tables get progressively out of phase with the windows as one proceeds towards the centre of the car; but as the windows themselves are of the large 'picture' type this 'phase displacement', if one may call it so, is not displeasing. It enables an additional four seats to be provided in both the smoking and the non-smoking sections. These 'extras' back on to the opposite sides of the central transverse bulkhead, and passengers in them have airline standard of space between them and those in the next seat ahead. There are no tables associated with these seats.

Technically, the body structure is of the stressed skin type, in mild steel, all welded. To give maximum strength and stiffness, with light weight, and minimum first cost, computer-based analysis techniques were used. The details of construction may be studied from the perspective sectional drawing opposite. Special features to be noted are the double-glazed, sealed, tinted windows, and the self-opening doors, automatically operated by treadmats on the approach floor areas. The access doors from the station platforms are an important feature. The days of lengthy, socially pleasant station stops once so typical of the Great Western Railway, have gone for ever, and with the HST services two minutes or less is all that is allowed, even where there is a considerable interchange of passengers. The wide doors and roomy entrance vestibules provide for easy circulation of passengers. In contrast to many crack services on the continent of Europe and elsewhere, there is very little seat reservation. The only exceptions are the breakfast-time business trains, such as the 07.25 Kings Cross to Leeds, and 08.00 Kings Cross to Edinburgh.

A very pleasing and successful feature of the High Speed Trains is the air-conditioning system which—one adds with bated breath!—has solved at last the vexed question of how much, or how little air circulation there is to be in a compartment, or a saloon. In the old days of individually opening windows no two passengers would ever agree as to the amount of air that should be allowed to enter. Altercations grim and great were frequent, and when the first air-conditioned coaches were introduced some people felt that with sealed windows British Railways had taken a high-handed course, shutting us all in, and providing a temperature that one could approve, or lump it; there was no alternative. The cynics said that air conditioning is all right as long as it works; and I can sympathise with their fears, having had some unspeakable journeys in the USA, when the air conditioning failed, and the temperature outside was 100 degrees F (38 degrees C)! On the HSTs the apparatus is set to provide an interior temperature of 70 degrees F (21 degrees C) when the temperature

outside is in the range from 21 degrees F or 11 degrees below freezing
(–6 degrees C) up to 82 degrees F (28 degrees C). Above 82, which after all is not
very common in England, it gets a little warmer inside, but nothing remotely to
compare with the grilling I, and many other passengers, had to endure for
several hours on the Santa Fe.

I wish I could write more enthusiastically about the catering. It seems a great
pity when such a superb standard of engineering and operational reliability has
been built into these trains that the provision of refreshments should be so
apparently haphazard. So far as my own travelling experiences are concerned it
is not so much a question of the quality of the food, but whether there is any
service on the trains at all. All too often it is a case of 'British Railways
regret . . . .' When the HST service was first put on, a trolley service of drinks
was provided down the train, but these seem nowadays to have disappeared

*Cab of the production HSTs, showing (centre) the seat for the driver and (right) that for
the co-driver* (British Railways).

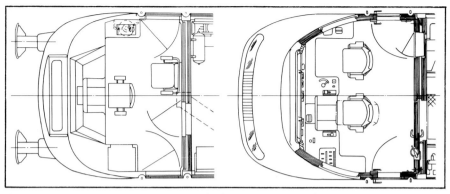

**Above left** *HST prototype power car cab showing position of seat for co-driver.* **Above right** *HST production power car cab with seat for co-driver alongside and to right.*
**Below** *Building the reinforced plastic moulded cabs for the HSTs at Crewe works* (British Railways Board).

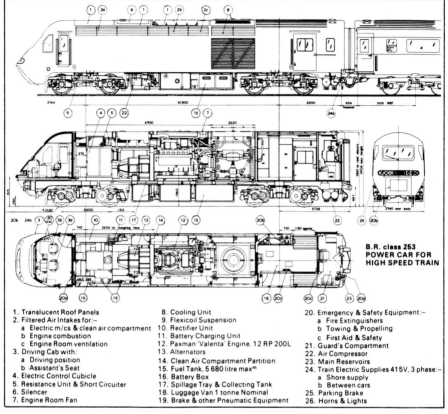

1. Translucent Roof Panels
2. Filtered Air Intakes for:-
   a Electric m/cs & clean air compartment
   b Engine combustion
   c Engine Room ventilation
3. Driving Cab with:
   a Driving position
   b Assistant's Seat
4. Electric Control Cubicle
5. Resistance Unit & Short Circuiter
6. Silencer
7. Engine Room Fan

8. Cooling Unit
9. Flexicoil Suspension
10. Rectifier Unit
11. Battery Charging Unit
12. Paxman 'Valenta' Engine, 12 RP 200L
13. Alternators
14. Clean Air Compartment Partition
15. Fuel Tank, 5 680 litre maxᵐ
16. Battery Box
17. Spillage Tray & Collecting Tank
18. Luggage Van 1 tonne Nominal
19. Brake & other Pneumatic Equipment

20. Emergency & Safety Equipment:-
    a Fire Extinguishers
    b Towing & Propelling
    c First Aid & Safety
21. Guard's Compartment
22. Air Compressor
23. Main Reservoirs
24. Train Electric Supplies 415V, 3 phase:-
    a Shore supply
    b Between cars
25. Parking Brake
26. Horns & Lights

**Above** *BR Class '253' power car for HST.*

**Below left** *HST prototype power car cab* **Below right** *HST production power car cab with air conditioning equipment in the nose.*

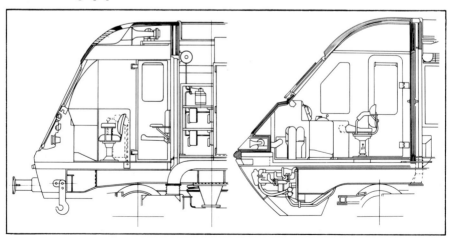

completely. Of course, with the shortening of journey times the need for snacks and light meals is very much less, and with reduced demand the costs of staffing buffet cars become disproportionately high. One can understand the need to economise wherever possible, but some crews have a way of using the public address system to announce they are closing down long before journey's end is reached. On the longer journeys of the Eastern Region there is a better opportunity for good meal service, and the situation is decidedly better. I hope I may be forgiven this little grouse, mainly directed towards the HSTs I use most frequently; but against such a superb engineering background it is a pity there has been a deterioration in a direction that must inevitably somewhat tarnish the image of the HSTs in public esteem.

Reverting to engineering features, the construction of the power car body is extremely interesting. The superstructure and underframe, examples of which I saw under construction at Crewe, form a completely integrated welded assembly, except for the driving cab. As in the case of the trailer cars it was necessary to provide maximum strength and stiffness with minimum weight, and the stressed-skin technique was applied, aided by stress analysis by computer. The design has in general been developed with the utmost ease of maintenance in mind. Reference to Chapter 13 of this book will show how little time is available for maintenance work during the night hours, and there must be no awkward procedures if units have to be taken out for attention and replaced by others. Two main cross-stretchers carry the bogie centre pivots, and three secondary cross-stretchers support the main engine/alternator set.

The cab, which is a separate unit, is an extremely interesting piece of modern construction in plastic materials. On the prototype train, as will be seen from some of the photographs reproduced, there was a centrally placed windscreen, and no side windows; but the basic form of construction in the production trains is unchanged. For a train designed to run at such high speed a streamlined nose was essential, and this could be formed most economically using plastics, rather than light weight steel, formed to the desired shape. Mass production techniques such as those used in the forming of automobile bodies to streamlined shapes were not economically justifiable, having regard to the relatively small number of cabs required. Furthermore, in view of the high running speeds the most careful consideration had to be given to protecting the crews from flying ballast and vandalism.

The thickness of the cab is 2 in (50 mm) made up of a sandwich. The outer and inner skins are of glass-reinforced polyester, between which is a foam core of polyurethane. This not only gives a high degree of strength in relation to the weight, but provides a strong resistance against impact from stones, or missiles. During impact tests of the material, a sharp object travelling very fast might penetrate the outer skin, but would have its effect absorbed finally by the polyurethane sandwich between the outer and the inner skins. There is a considerable difference between the shape and the internal layout of the prototype and production cab. Originally, as shown in the top drawing on page 77 the driver actually manipulating the controls was seated centrally, while the second man was positioned in the rear and slightly to the right of his colleague. The cab had a single side window in front, but no windows at the side. As a result of experience with the prototype train, the drivers' trade unions expressed a preference to have the two-man crew seated side by side, and a redesign had to be undertaken. With this was coupled a request for side windows as well.

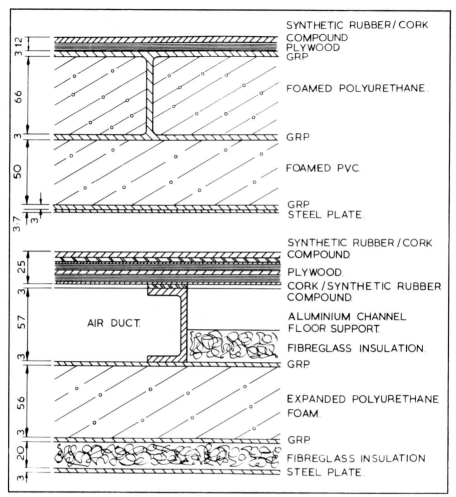

*Cab floor section.* **Top** *Prototype version.* **Above** *Production version.*

The redesign involved was a good deal more extensive than might have been imagined. Certainly it was a relatively simple matter to move the driver over to the left of the centre line of the car, and provide space to seat his co-driver alongside him, and to the right; but to preserve his line of sight to lineside signals and other objects the front windscreen had to be made considerably wider. This, together with the side windows, would have so increased the total window area that on sunny days the cab would have become undesirably hot. At the intended speed of running there could be no question of opening windows to cool the atmosphere inside, so the cabs had to be air conditioned. As originally designed, with the driver seated centrally and no side windows in the cab, there were cupboards housing certain equipment on each side of the driving console. Space had to be found for this elsewhere and this, together with the air-conditioning machine, was accommodated in an extension of the front nose of the car. The resulting difference in the transverse profile of the cab is shown in the two cross-sectional drawings on page 78.

The cabs of the production HSTs are very pleasant places in which to ride. On the various occasions when I have been privileged to enter and travel in this 'holy of holies' I have usually made my observations and notes standing in a position between the two driver's seats. I have found the riding perfectly steady and comfortable and I have been able to write with ease. From a great variety of experiences at the 'head end' of trains in many part of the world the HSTs are second to none in their smoothness in the power car, and very quiet. So far as the crew is concerned this is not only an amenity—it is a definite requirement. It was considered essential to conform to the rules of the International Union of Railways that govern the layout of driving cabs, which lay down a maximum sound level. On the prototype train, measurements made over the entire speed range showed that what has been termed the 'cab noise environment' was better than that of existing diesel electric locomotives up to about 100 mph, but it became definitely worse above that speed. This examination was yet another manifestation of the value of having an experimental prototype to run, before the new trains went into regular service.

To meet the UIC criteria of sound level in the cab the design was modified in four ways:

**1** An improved form of resilient mounting between the cab itself and the steel frame of the car.

**2** A re-design of the floor structure to include four acoustically and structurally de-coupled layers, and the inclusion of a number of layers of acoustically absorbent material. The extensive change to the floor design can be well appreciated from the drawings opposite, relating to 'before and after'.

**3** An acoustically absorbent trim was added to the inner skin above the windscreen level.

**4** Finally, in an attempt to reduce noise at its source, greater precision was introduced in the manufacture of the gears, to provide quieter running.

These measures proved successful, with the pleasant result apparent to anyone experienced in 'footplate' travel who rides in the cabs of the production trains at maximum speed.

The look-out ahead is exceptionally good, and as one makes observations and notes, even in the worst of weather, my own thoughts always go straying back to the many thousands of miles I have ridden on large 'Pacific' steam engines, peering ahead past the narrow viewpoint of a long and large diameter boiler, with a very limited view of the line ahead. I rode one of the HSTs on a day when we had pouring rain unceasingly from Kings Cross to Darlington, and never once was the visibility impaired. The controls are all very conveniently placed for the driver, but although the power car, and its twin at the rear end of the train, could be dismissed as just another diesel-electric locomotive there are important considerations that make a period of driver training necessary before one of these trains can be taken out in passenger service. There are many enginemen today on British Railways who have ample experience of driving diesel-electric locomotives at 100 mph. Some, when there is time to be made up, are tempted—with the confidence born of long experience—to go a bit more; but a jump from 100-125 mph is another matter.

Of course not all enginemen who are now handling HSTs are required to run at maximum speed, even on parts of their routes. The extension of some of the East Coast workings northward from Edinburgh to Aberdeen is a case in point. It will be the same between Plymouth and Penzance. In the Eastern Region

*The 16.00 Kings Cross to Newcastle passing Hadley Wood* (Brian Morrison).

training is centred on a number of depots, and extends over three weeks, with 12 men in a class. The first week covers theoretical class-room instruction, after which they go on to the trains. The instruction covers not only the actual driving, but sufficient in the way of general knowledge of the equipment to enable drivers to cope with minor, or isolated failures. So far as actual driving is concerned, in coming to handle a train-set that is capable of doing 125 mph, it is necessary to give drivers confidence in their brakes, and one of the first essays in handling, before they are invited to run at anything approaching 125 mph, is for them to try the brakes, and get the 'feel' of them. Nothing generates confidence more quickly than to be assured you can stop!

On one of my journeys, in the cab, between Newcastle and Edinburgh, I was privileged to witness a very impressive example of driver training. It brought vividly back to mind a very interesting parallel example that I saw in France, because the similarity was most striking. In the latter case I was riding on *L'Etendard,* one of the 125 mph *rapides* between Paris and Bordeaux. As on British Railways we had two fully experienced drivers, who had changed over duties at about the half way point of the journey, and then, on arrival at Angoulême an instructor and two trainee drivers joined us in the cab, and one of the latter was put immediately into the driving seat. I gathered that he, and his fellow trainee were in the final stages of their instruction, because first one and then the other handled the great 7,500 hp locomotive with confidence and skill on the run between Angoulême and Bordeaux. On my first trip with 'The Flying

Scotsman', after the introduction of the HST sets a similar party entered the cab at Newcastle, of all the greater interest and pleasure to me in that the instructor was a man with whom I had ridden steam more than 30 years previously, on the 'A2' Pacific engine *Wolf of Badenoch,* when it had recently been converted from a 2-8-2, and not to its puissance or general advantage! So, on the HST 'Flying Scotsman' north of Newcastle we had the regular driver, and the inspector who was my own guide and philosopher, and Bobby Johnston, and his two protégés. These two latter were actually from Ferryhill shed, Aberdeen. They were not learning the road south of Edinburgh, but were learning the HST power car.

As in the French instance previously mentioned the two trainees shared the driving between Newcastle and Edinburgh. At that time there was no stretch on that route where the train was required to run at more than 100 mph and thus only one regular driver was needed. Apart from the awkward start out of Newcastle, over the crossings and round the sharp curve at Manors station the road is a fairly straightforward one, with plenty of opportunity for getting the feel of the HST at speeds up to 100 mph. It was extremely interesting to note the excellent way in which the train was handled. Scheduled time for the distance of just 124.4 miles (200 km) was $107\frac{1}{2}$ minutes, requiring an average speed of 69.7 mph (111.8 km/h); but we had four slacks for engineering work, costing $4\frac{1}{2}$ minutes between them and a signal stop at Acklington, and we actually took $110\frac{1}{4}$ minutes. But deducting the time lost by the delays the net time was only 102 minutes. The second trainee driver had the better chance to do some speeding, and he was able to average 97 mph (156 km/h) over the 27 miles (43.5 km) from Cockburnspath to Prestonpans. Both men had acquired skill and finesse in handling the brake, and with the vigilance of the instructor at their elbow they gave us a smooth and well balanced ride. One would imagine that very few, if any, among the passengers on that well patronised train would have imagined that it was being run by 'learner' drivers.

Since the first introduction of the HSTs on the East Coast route the disastrous collapse of the roof of Penmanshiel Tunnel has led to an unexpected extension of driver training. The division of three HST workings, in each direction via Carlisle, with non-stop running over the Caledonian line between Carlisle and Edinburgh has necessitated the making up of an extra 'link'. With a time of 90 minutes over the 101 miles (162 km) it has been possible to schedule an overall time of 6 hours 10 minutes from Kings Cross to Waverley, by the 15.00 departures from London, an average speed of 69.4 mph (112 km/h) over this circuitous route, more than 30 miles (48 km) longer than the route via Berwick. No route learning, or driving training was necessary in the case of the cross-country section from Newcastle to Carlisle. This route has, by tradition, always been included in the route knowledge and regular working of the top link enginemen at Gateshead shed. In North Eastern Railway days, the appearance of large Atlantic locomotives at Carlisle was sometimes thought to have been a little flag-waving, to uphold the prestige of the North Eastern at a station where such a galaxy of locomotive eminence was always on display; but actually it was a case of the top-link Gateshead engines and men working across to Carlisle to boost up their weekly mileages. As will be told in more detail in a later chapter of this book the line from Newcastle to Carlisle, with its overall maximum speed limit of 60 mph (97 km/h), has proved one of the most constrained of all HST routes.

# Chapter 9

# Evolution of the APT principle

The main obstacle in the way of substantial acceleration of journey times on a majority of British main lines is the existence of so many curves. The historic background to this situation lies in the very large investment in railways in the Victorian era, when many lines were constructed to provide communication between one centre of population and another without any particular regard for the speed potential of the resulting alignment. Routes were established in some cases to suit the convenience of individual landowners, or to avoid the hostility of others, and the result in many instances assumed the look of the proverbial 'dog's hind leg'. This was of no consequence at a time when railways were the pre-eminent, and often the only means of public transport; but it became a serious handicap when private cars, and road transport over new, finely engineered modern highways began to provide faster and more convenient transit times than the railways. Perhaps the most extraordinary instance was that of the cities of Edinburgh and Perth, no more than 30 miles (48 km) distant from each other as the crow flies, but between which the passenger service, by express train making few, brief intermediate stops was around 85 minutes, and is very little better today.

The situation was aggravated because the substantially built double track railways were very much under-utilised; they were likely to become still more so, unless means were found of providing a vastly improved passenger service. Although the case quoted, of Edinburgh and Perth, is one of extremes, in overall terms the situation in respect of track alignment is nation wide. Statistics show that roughly 50 per cent of the total main line mileage of Great Britain is on curves, and of these about half are quite sharp, at between $\frac{1}{3}$ mile and $1\frac{1}{4}$ mile (0.5 and 2 km) radius. It is indeed a remarkable, but little appreciated fact that on most routes, worked by conventional, locomotive hauled trains the average speed tends to be governed not by locomotive power, gradients, or the loads to be hauled but by the frequent incidence of speed restrictions on curves. On many of these routes it was not until the increase in locomotive power, and the demands of the commercial departments for average speeds in the 70-80 mph (113-130 km/h) range, instead of the previously accepted standard of 55-60 mph (90-100 km/h) that the restrictions potentially inherent in the track alignment became apparent; and because major re-alignment schemes, or the building of brand new lines were far too costly, some means had to be found of negotiating the existing curves at very much higher speeds. Only by such methods could the average speeds be raised to a level of competing successfully with other forms of transport.

In general, speed restrictions on curves are, at present, imposed not for reasons of safety but for the well being of the passengers. When rounding a curve the constraint imposed upon the train and everything within it sets up a centrifugal force, which is a tendency to fly out tangentially. The pressure of the outer rail on the wheel flanges and also the tread forces checks this tendency in the case of the vehicles, but passengers feel the sensation of outward thrust, and loose articles like items of luggage, and crockery in the restaurant cars, can be thrown sideways. To counteract this effect the track is superelevated, or canted; but such adjustment is necessarily a compromise. The cant is proportional to the square of the speed, and inversely proportional to the radius of the curves, so that it is only at one speed that it can precisely counteract the effect of the centrifugal force. Above and below that speed the effect of the curve will be felt, one way or the other. The first diagram below shows how the cant neutralises the centrifugal force effect, but two numerical examples will show the factors that have to be taken into account, when deciding on the amount of cant to be provided on any length of railway. The cant necessary on a curve of 1.24 miles radius (2 km) for a speed of 60 mph (97 km/h) is 2.2 in (56 mm), but for 80 mph (129 km/h) it is 3.95 in (100 mm).

If the cant provided is exactly that required to compensate for a speed of 60 mph (97 km/h) a considerable force would be exerted on the outer rail if a train took the curve at 80 mph (129 km/h), and to use a colloquialism, the

**Below left** *Cant angle exactly compensating for centrifugal force C. Resultant (R) of C and W (weight of vehicle), exactly at right angles to slope of track.* **Below right** *Higher speed—higher centrifugal force, producing cant deficiency.*

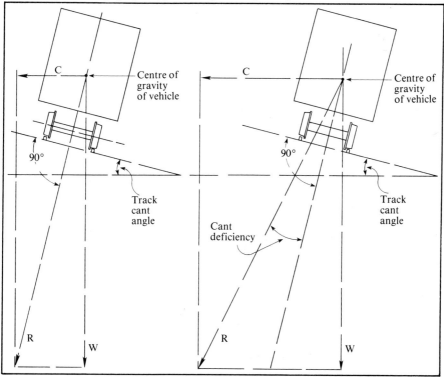

passengers would know all about it. This case introduces the quantity known as cant deficiency. The second diagram helps to amplify this point. When a vehicle is travelling round a curve there are two forces acting upon it: its weight, and the centrifugal force, as indicated by the arrows W and C. The combined effect of these two is the resultant R. If the centrifugal force, due to the speed in rounding the curve is large enough to deflect the resultant outside the centre line of the track, as shown in the diagram the angle between is termed the cant deficiency, and it is measured as an angle. The concensus of opinion, after a great deal of study from every point of view, is that a maximum deficiency in the cant angle of about 4 degrees can be accepted without causing discomfort to the passengers. When travelling round in a curve in such conditions there is no doubt something of it would be sensed in the train, particularly if standing, or walking along the centre aisle of a carriage. But the point then arises, that not all trains on the route will be travelling at express passenger speed. Further compromises are needed.

If all trains on a route were running to the same point-to-point times the super-elevation on curves could be arranged to give smooth running at high speeds; but with an admixture of medium and fast freight services, intermediate passenger trains and other traffic, it would be undesirable to provide everywhere the large amount of super-elevation to permit express passenger trains to traverse curves at high speed, especially through stations where slower trains had to stop. So, the cant angle in general has to be less, and speed restrictions imposed so that the maximum cant deficiency does not exceed 4 degrees. But to meet commercial needs by making the greatest impact on overall journey times, on existing routes, the maximum permissible speed must be raised, and some means found of negotiating curves in conditions that set up a cant deficiency of 9 degrees. This latter is the considered maximum for safe running so far as the vehicle is concerned, on existing curves, and it would enable the maximum speeds to be raised by between 20 and 40 per cent. It would, however, be quite intolerable to passengers. It was then that the concept of tilting the coach body inwards by up to 9 degrees was formed; for by so doing the comfort of travelling would be maintained, by full compensation for cant deficiency.

However brilliant in theory, a tremendous amount of technical innovation and development was foreseen before the principle of the tilting body could be established for introduction into revenue earning service. But British Railways, in embarking upon the Advanced Passenger Train programme, set their sights ace-high with the following objectives, not only including the tilting feature and greatly improved aero-dynamic characteristics but also the following, relative to the performance of existing locomotive hauled trains:

1 Maximum speed 50 per cent higher
2 Negotiate curves at up to 40 per cent faster
3 To run on existing track with existing signalling
4 Maintain standards of passenger comfort at the higher speeds
5 To be efficient in energy consumption
6 To maintain existing levels of track maintenance

and perhaps one of the most significant items—to achieve a similar cost per passenger-seat kilometre. This meant that the facility of much higher speed, with no lessening of travelling comfort, would be offered to the public at no increase over standard fares. The programme was bounded by the two

*The laboratory built for APT development at Derby houses experimental rigs, including extensive hydraulic test equipment, a brake dynamometer (foreground), a mechanical transmission dynamometer and a six-axle roller rig. The control tower (left) houses controls and instrumentation, including a mini-computer, for conducting major experiments.*

underlying parameters of a maximum speed of 155 mph (250 km/h) and a 9 degree deficiency.

At the outset, however, it was by no means certain that the tilting principle, however attractive in theory, could be established in terms of the solid reliable 'hardware' essential for everyday railway working. There were considerable technical risks. But the promise it offered for attractive and highly competitive inter-city travel was so attractive that in 1968 a three-pointed programme of development was authorised jointly by the British Railways Board and the Ministry of Transport. First of all there was to be an experimental train, gas turbine powered, which could be run up to a maximum speed of 156 mph (250 km/h); secondly, the project was considered of sufficient importance for a special laboratory to be built at Derby. This housed a number of experimental rigs, including extensive hydraulic test equipment, a brake dynamometer, a mechanical transmission dynamometer, and a six-axle roller rig. The control tower within the building housed the controls and instrumentation, and included a mini-computer. The comprehensive nature of this test house is indicative of the massive investment made into the whole APT project. To carry out the work a team of very highly qualified engineers was built up.

Laboratory testing, however, was not considered enough. Road testing was essential and it was fortunate that a section of main line relatively near to Derby was available, and could be adapted for test purposes. The former Midland

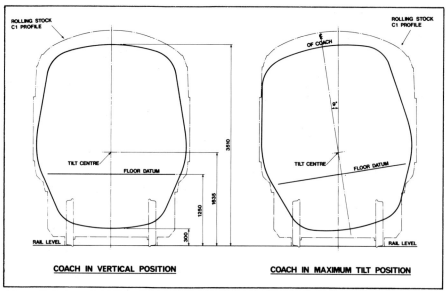

**Above** *Relation of APT body profile to C1 loading gauge.* **Below** *APT tilt suspension.*

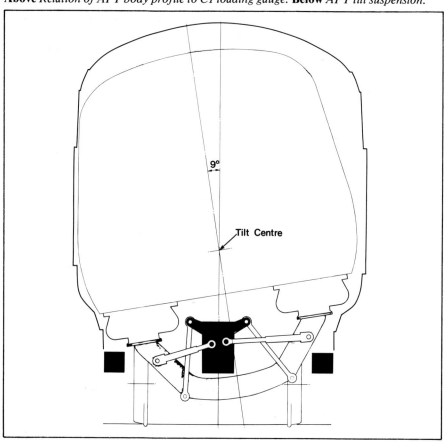

Railway had built up an elaborate system of alternative and duplicate lines north of Kettering, and one of these was the direct line from the south to Nottingham, permitting non-stop running to and from London (St Pancras). It was also extensively used for coal traffic, and virtually continued the quadruple-tracked main line northward from Kettering to the Erewash Valley, and avoided the busy area of Leicester. But in the time of general traffic recession of the 1950s and 1960s such duplication of facilities was not required, and so far as passenger trains were concerned the City of Nottingham could be served by trains travelling via Leicester. In consequence the direct line to the south was closed between Nottingham and Melton Mowbray. With its former value gone, however, it proved a veritably ideal site for APT testing. Before describing how it was adapted for this purpose reference to the APT principle itself is necessary.

A first consideration so far as any tilting of the coach bodies is concerned was, of course, to keep within the loading gauge. This will be apparent from a first study of the diagram opposite. The cross-section of the body had therefore to be somewhat smaller than that of a standard Mk III coach. The tilting mechanism is designed to operate automatically in response to the lateral accelerations experienced by the passengers. Sensing devices are installed which measure this effect, separately on each vehicle of the train, and these activate an electro-hydraulic servo mechanism. It is essential that the response should be very rapid and sensitive. At the same time the process of transition from straight track to a circular curve of constant radius has to be met. Unless severe shocks are to be experienced one cannot change from one to the other at once, and standard practice is to lay in what are termed transition curves, in which the radius is gradually reduced from infinity to that of the circular curve. On this transition curve the cant is gradually increased from nil, in proportion to the reducing radius, to the full amount necessary for the circular curve. The transition curve itself is a scientifically plotted trajectory, usually of geometrical form known as a cubic parabola. It is necessarily short, and in the case of high speed running, the time of transition from straight track to the circular curve is equally short so that it is necessary for the tilt-system to act very quickly. The parameter set is a response rate of 5 degrees of cant deficiency per second.

This diagram (above left), previously referred to in connection with clearance from the loading gauge shows also the operation of the tilting mechanism. The shaded portions show the members attached to the bogie frame, and it will be seen that the tilting bolster is suspended from the central member by two swinging links. On the centre line of this same member are pivotally attached the ends of the piston rods of two hydraulic jacks, the operation of which tilts the body. A second diagram shows (in simplified form) the control system, the initiating member of which is the accelerometer, which is instantly sensitive to any lateral acceleration of the vehicle, due to the centrifugal force set up on entering a curve. While the experimental train was powered by gas-turbines the first commercial use of the APT will be on the West Coast main line between Euston and Glasgow, and it is electrically powered. Although it is carrying the story of development some years ahead this brought problems of a different kind, because the current collection had to be by pantograph from the overhead wires. The pantograph had to be maintained in the normal position in relation to the bogie frame. It could not be subject to the tilting action of the coach body, even though it needed to be attached to it, to provide the necessary power.

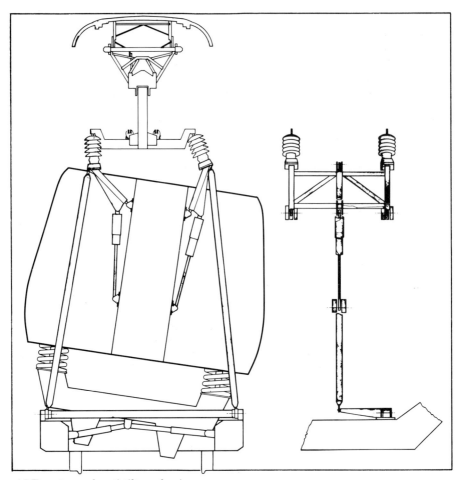

*APT pantograph anti-tilt mechanism.*

To meet this requirement the ingenious anti-tilt mechanism shown above was designed.

The broad objectives in design and development have already been stated. So far as speed through curves are concerned the improvement aimed is shown in the graph on page 91. In conformity with the current trend towards use of the metric system the values there are quoted in kilometres per hour, with the radius of curves in metres. To put them in more familiar quantities a curve of 1,000 metres is equal to 0.62 miles, or 50 chains; and it will be seen that the permissible speed with an APT round such a curve is 108 mph or 175 km/h, against 84 mph (134 km/h) with a conventional train. On a curve of 100 chains, an APT could run at 148 mph (237 km/h) against 118 mph (189 km/h). When one thinks of stretches of the West Coast main line between Carnforth and Carlisle, where maximum speeds for conventional trains of 75 to 80 mph (120-128 km/h) are enforced, the APT could, on these sections, run at 95 to 100 mph (152-160 km/h). It has been estimated that without exceeding a maximum speed of 125 mph (200 km/h) the journey time over the 401 miles (650 km) between London and Glasgow could be reduced from the present five hours to a little under four hours.

All this was originally theory. The experimental gas turbine APT was put through a series of verification tests in the special laboratory at Derby, and then activities were continued on the test track. The section between Nottingham and Melton Mowbray was originally double track maintained up to first class main line standard, but the 12 miles (20 km) length chosen for test purpose is single line, except for a short length of double track through Stanton Tunnel between the former stations of Widmerpool and Plumtree. It runs through hilly country, and while the gradients, considerable in the days of steam traction, are of no consequence with an APT, there is much curvature, which made it an ideal stretch for test observations. Furthermore there was variation in track quality. Much of it consisted of continuous welded rail on concrete sleepers, but sufficient lengths of the original jointed rails on wooden sleepers remain, fortunately including the 3 mile (5 km) straight between the Upper Broughton curve, and Stanton and round the Stanton curve. This provided experience in the worst rail conditions likely to be encountered in revenue earning service. The drawing reproduced on page 92 shows the salient features of this important test track. The track as it existed would not have provided all the variation in conditions that were required, and some money had to be spent to include these. The double track section through the tunnel was to provide conditions for aero-dynamic testing when another train was on the second track.

While the effect on passengers of the centrifugal force set up in rounding curves is eliminated by the tilting mechanism—and more important still, eliminated at all speeds by the automatic response of the sensing devices—the force itself is present, and is proportional to the square of the speed. Thus in the

*Typical APT speed improvement on curves.*

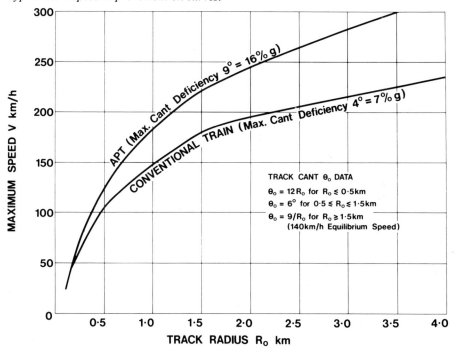

TRACK CANT $\theta_0$ DATA

$\theta_0 = 12R_0$ for $R_0 \leq 0.5$ km

$\theta_0 = 6°$ for $0.5 \leq R_0 \leq 1.5$ km

$\theta_0 = 9/R_0$ for $R_0 \geq 1.5$ km
(140 km/h Equilibrium Speed)

APT (Max. Cant Deficiency $9° = 16\%\, g$)

CONVENTIONAL TRAIN (Max. Cant Deficiency $4° = 7\%\, g$)

MAXIMUM SPEED V km/h

TRACK RADIUS $R_0$ km

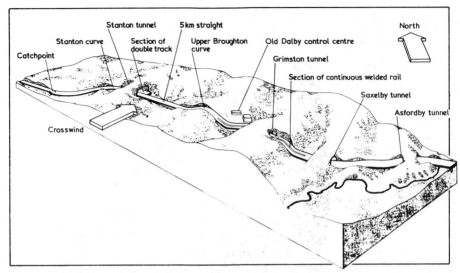

**Above** *The 20 km length of single line test track follows the alignment of the closed Nottingham to Melton Mowbray line. Much of the track is on continuously welded rails on concrete sleepers. However, sufficient stretches of the original jointed rails on wooden sleepers remain, notably the 5 km stretch and Stanton curve, to provide* worst case *conditions. The double track in Stanton tunnel allows an instrumented aerodynamics coach to stand in the tunnel whilst the APT passes.*

**Below** *The experimental Advanced Passenger Train APT-E on trials on the former Midland line between Nottingham and Melton Mowbray* (British Railways).

*The APT-E on track trials, showing the tilting action on a curve taken at high speed* (British Railways).

comparative instance quoted, of rounding a curve of 1,000 metres radius at maximum permissible speeds, namely 108 mph (173 km/h) for an APT and 84 mph (134 km/h) for a conventional train, the centrifugal force would be 65 per cent higher against a 29 per cent increase in speed. The overturning tendency had thus to be most carefully examined, even though theoretical considerations indicated that the safety margin was ample. On the APT the tendency is minimised by having a relatively low tilt centre, as shown in the diagram on page 88 and a low centre of gravity, which in normal operating conditions is maintained over the track centre line by the tilt system.

The predicted cant deficiency to cause overturning for the APT was about 25 degrees—a very substantial margin over the 9 degree maximum for which permissible maximum speeds on curves were calculated. This aspect of APT performance, however, was considered so important as to require experimental verification. Accordingly a scrap coach, modified to simulate the weight and suspension features of the APT, was tested on a relatively sharp curve of 590.5 ft (180 m) radius near Dover. The diagrams on page 85 show that the maximum safe speed for the APT on such a curve is no more than 37 mph (60 km/h), with a cant deficiency of 9 degrees. This coach was run round the curve at successively higher speeds until it overturned, at a cant deficiency of 24.3 degrees. This was a remarkably close confirmation of the theoretical prediction; but what was perhaps more reassuring in these very severe conditions was that there was no evidence of any tendency for the wheel flanges to climb the rails and cause derailment over the top, as it were.

In any apparatus designed for railway use, and particularly where passenger carrying is concerned, one must always look to the possibility of failure of different units, and ensure that any failure of which human nature can conceive will be on the side of safety. With the APT the thought that immediately comes to mind is what would happen if the tilting mechanism failed to work on one of the coaches and the train ran through the curve at a speed corresponding to the maximum cant deficiency of 9 degrees. It would not be very comfortable, but there would be no danger. So far as discomfort on curves is concerned I shall never forget journeys to Bournemouth in the late 1920s when there used to be a shocking transition (or lack of it!) in the middle of the down platform at Christchurch, and the shocks we got at any speed over about 60 mph were frightening. But nobody seemed to worry. Nowadays, of course, everyone is so conscious of any deficiency in travel comfort that a defect would instantly cause complaint. With the APT, on the Nottingham-Melton test track the engineers of BR took the question of failure to a further and altogether extreme case of having a vehicle tilted by 9 degrees in the *wrong* direction, and assumed stuck there. It was shown that, while discomforting to passengers, such a failure was not unsafe.

I mentioned earlier in this chapter the desirability of having very quick response of the tilting mechanism to the entry upon a curved section. The accompanying diagram shows the results of measurements made on the test track. The curve marked 'A' shows the lateral accelerations experienced in a conventional coach running on a curve at a speed that produced the maximum permissible cant deficiency of 4 degrees. The second curve, marked 'B' shows the corresponding effect in an APT coach at a speed to produce a 9 degree cant deficiency. There is a sudden rise to a lateral acceleration almost equal to that of the conventional coach in the first two seconds after the train enters the transition curve; but then the tilting mechanism comes into action, and for a matter of about one second, the force swings the other way, before settling down to *nil* lateral acceleration after five seconds from entering the curve.

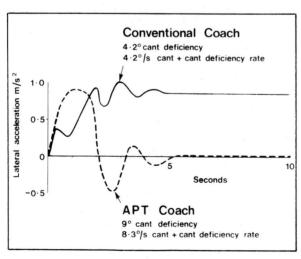

Passenger accelerations at curve entry.

# Chapter 10

# Details of the Advanced Passenger Train

While the facility for tilting the coach bodies on curves automatically, to a degree proportional to the lateral acceleration experienced by the passengers, is the underlying feature of the APT, the trains as a whole include numerous details of an interesting and novel character which would place them in a class of their own, quite apart from the unique principles embodied in the coach body suspension. It is important to emphasise, however, that the trains now coming into revenue earning service on the West Coast main line are still no more than prototypes. There may well be points of detail to be changed when the time comes to building APT sets in bulk. The prototype train can be formed in three alternative versions, as shown in the following table:

| Duty | No of power cars | No of trailer cars | Tare weight tonnes | Max speed level track km/h | Seats 1st | 2nd |
|------|------|------|------|------|------|------|
| Low power (200 km/h) | 1 | 11 | 370 | 215 | 144 | 376 |
| High power (APT-P) | 2 | 12 | 463 | 270 | 144 | 448 |
| High Power stretched | 2 | 14 | 509 | 255 | 144 | 592 |

In all these the power cars are marshalled in the centre. The trains are necessarily of the fixed formation type to avoid any light engine movements at the terminals, and in view of the high power and high speeds involved, it was considered undesirable to have two power cars at one end. When propelling, as on the Bournemouth services of the Southern Region, excessive buckling forces would be generated on the curved stretches of the West Coast main line north of Carnforth. Neither was the arrangement of the diesel-powered HST acceptable (that of having a power car at each end of the train). Experiments had shown that the collection of current from two pantographs on one train was not satisfactory at speeds of 125 mph (200 km/h) and more, with the existing overhead equipment. Quite apart from these considerations the elimination of the driving cab from the power car enabled equipment to produce 5,500 hp to be built in, without exceeding the severe weight limitation imposed of 69 tonnes. When two power cars are used the equipment on both would be fed from the one pantograph.

With the power cars in the middle the passenger accommodation on either side had to be completely self-contained, with first and second class seating and catering facilities in each half. The formation of a high-power prototype APT is thus: driving trailer, one second class intermediate trailer, one second/catering trailer, one unclassified trailer (for catering service), one first class intermediate

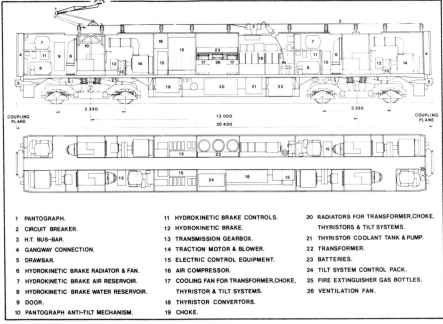

| 1 PANTOGRAPH. | 11 HYDROKINETIC BRAKE CONTROLS. | 20 RADIATORS FOR TRANSFORMER,CHOKE, |
| --- | --- | --- |
| 2 CIRCUIT BREAKER. | 12 HYDROKINETIC BRAKE. | THYRISTORS & TILT SYSTEMS. |
| 3 H.T. BUS–BAR. | 13 TRANSMISSION GEARBOX. | 21 THYRISTOR COOLANT TANK & PUMP. |
| 4 GANGWAY CONNECTION. | 14 TRACTION MOTOR & BLOWER. | 22 TRANSFORMER. |
| 5 DRAWBAR. | 15 ELECTRIC CONTROL EQUIPMENT. | 23 BATTERIES. |
| 6 HYDROKINETIC BRAKE RADIATOR & FAN. | 16 AIR COMPRESSOR. | 24 TILT SYSTEM CONTROL PACK. |
| 7 HYDROKINETIC BRAKE AIR RESERVOIR. | 17 COOLING FAN FOR TRANSFORMER,CHOKE, | 25 FIRE EXTINGUISHER GAS BOTTLES. |
| 8 HYDROKINETIC BRAKE WATER RESERVOIR. | THYRISTOR & TILT SYSTEMS. | 26 VENTILATION FAN. |
| 9 DOOR. | 18 THYRISTOR CONVERTORS. | |
| 10 PANTOGRAPH ANTI–TILT MECHANISM. | 19 CHOKE. | |

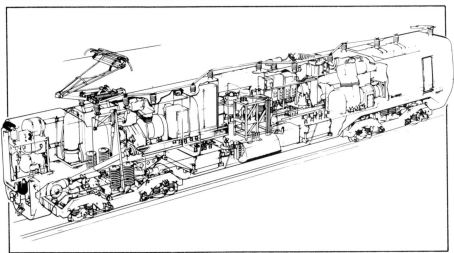

**Top** *General arrangement of power car.* **Above** *APT-P power car.*

trailer, one van trailer with first class seating, and then the two power units. The second half of the train is a duplicate of the first, but marshalled in the reverse order. The low powered version, with only one power car, and not called upon to run at more than 125 mph (200 km/h), would have a shorter formation. What is termed the 'stretched' version, having a total of 14 vehicles in addition to the two power cars, would have two additional second class intermediate trailer cars. The seating arrangement follow those of the HST cars. In the trailer seconds there are seats for 64 passengers at tables for four, plus an additional

*One of the power cars of the APT-P* (British Railways).

eight, two each side of the partition dividing the smoking and non-smoking sections. The trailer firsts have tables for four on one side of the gangway, and for two on the other. Accommodation for both classes is notably spacious.

Dealing now with the 'power to pull', as it is sometimes referred to, the so-called low powered version, with one power car and 11 trailers, represents the longest train that can be hauled up the Shap and Beattock inclines, and it would be limited to a nominal maximum speed of 125 mph (200 km/h). Even with this limitation, however, it is estimated that the time from Euston to Glasgow, with one stop at Preston could be cut to 4 hours 5 minutes. Of course, a certain amount of recovery time would have to be included in a commercial schedule, but this is indicative of the saving in journey time that the APT tilting principle makes possible. It is interesting to see how the capacity of a single APT power car compares with that of the very efficient class '87' electric locomotives which are doing such excellent work on the West Coast main line. The tractive effort of the two is approximately equal at 81 mph (130 km/h), and at the nominal rated maximum of the class '87' 100 mph (160 km/h) the APT is definitely superior. It will, of course, be appreciated that the class '87' is virtually a mixed traffic unit, employed in fast freight service as well as high speed passenger service, whereas the APT power car is purely for passenger duty.

Although the tilting mechanism of the APT is provided primarily in the interests of passenger comfort it is applied also to the power cars, involving the anti-tilt mechanism on the pantograph referred to in the previous chapter. When the experimental gas turbine powered APT was built, conventional DC electric traction motors were used as a matter of expediency, to get the experimental train built as quickly as possible. These motors were axle-hung, and involved a heavy unsprung weight that was unacceptable beyond the earliest experimental stages. The main thing at that time was to prove the practicability of the tilting principle. For the prototype APT the traction motors are mounted in the power car body. This has meant using a flexible drive to accommodate the differential movement of body and bogie when tilting takes place. The arrangement is shown in the drawing on page 98, and consists of the well-tried principle of the Cardan shaft, having universal couplings at each end. There is a similar drive on to each of the four axles of a power car, the traction motors each having a capacity of 1,000 horse-power continuous rating.

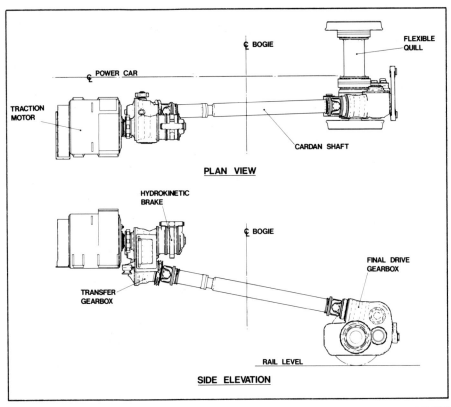

PLAN VIEW

SIDE ELEVATION

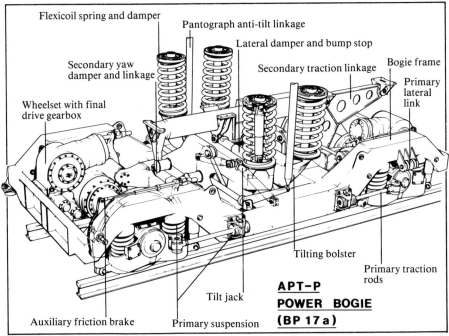

Flexicoil spring and damper

Pantograph anti-tilt linkage

Lateral damper and bump stop

Secondary yaw
damper and linkage

Secondary traction linkage

Bogie frame

Primary
lateral
link

Wheelset with final
drive gearbox

Tilting bolster

Primary traction
rods

Tilt jack

Auxiliary friction brake

Primary suspension

APT-P
POWER BOGIE
(BP 17 a)

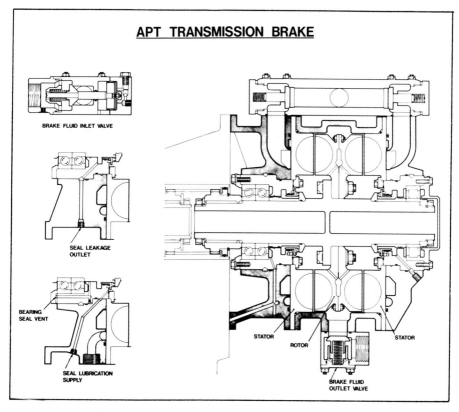

**Above left** *APT-P transmission.* **Left** *APT-P power bogie.* **Above** *APT transmission brake.* **Below** *APT trailer axle brake.*

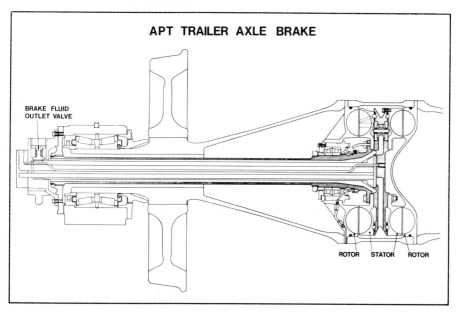

The general layout of the equipment on the power bogie is shown at the bottom of page 98, and the disposition of the primary and secondary suspensions, together with the damping devices, can be seen. The layout is complicated by the necessity for the pantograph anti-tilt linkage, the tilting bolster, and the tilt jacks. The top drawing on page 98 showing the Cardan shaft connection from the traction motor to the final drive gear box on the axle, shows also the location of the hydrokinetic brake, which is shown in detail at the top of page 99. While the hydrokinetic principle is used on the brakes throughout the APT the method of application on the power cars is quite different from that on the rest of the cars in the train. Needless to say the braking performance is of the very first importance because it is essential that the APT must be able to stop from its maximum speed of 156 mph (250 km/h) in the same distance as taken by conventional locomotive hauled trains from their maximum speed of 100 mph (160 km/h), for which many hundreds of miles of colourlight signalling have been installed, not only on the West Coast main line, but now over most of the main line network of Great Britain.

The hydrokinetic brake uses the principle of the water turbine, in reverse. It provides a very attractive alternative to any form of direct friction brake, either of the on-tread type which at the speeds involved would produce excessive temperatures, or of the disc type. The hydrokinetic brake has a freedom from wear that results in much reduced maintenance costs. On the power cars the brake unit is mounted on the shaft of the traction motor, the arrangement being shown in the drawing (top, page 99), while on the axles of the trailer cars it forms an integral part of the axle itself, as shown in the drawing below. In both cases the braking effect is produced by churning water between the vanes of rotating and static turbines. The water is cooled after the stop in external radiators. In applying the principle of the water turbine to the braking of a high speed train every care has been taken to build in all the safety features that have been established over the past hundred years and more, in railway braking techniques. As shown in the diagram the brake is applied by admitting air pressure into the fluid reservoir from an air reservoir connected to the train pipe, and the air pressure is controlled by an electro-pneumatic valve. There is one of these on each axle, and they are all connected electrically to the driver's brake controller. It is important to appreciate that the hydrokinetic brake is in operation only at high speed; as deceleration proceeds a conventional form of brake comes automatically into effect.

Except at the leading and trailing ends of the train all the passenger cars are articulated in their suspension. Thus the driving trailer car at the leading end has a four-wheeled bogie under the nose, but the following trailer cars have their ends supported on a common bogie. It will be recalled that this principle was used by Sir Nigel Gresley on the LNER 'Silver Jubilee' train in 1935. On a maximum power APT, with two power cars and 12 trailers, there are only 16 bogies (instead of 24 if each vehicle had two bogies in the conventional manner). This makes possible a considerable saving in weight. The bogies are a major source, the 'drag' effect, and this design not only reduces that component of the train resistance but also the cost. Recalling the very lively riding of the 'Silver

**Top right** *One of the articulated trailer cars of the prototype APT* (British Railways). **Centre right** *The bogie and mounting of one articulated car* (British Railways). **Right** *Interior of the driving cab of the APT-P* (British Railways).

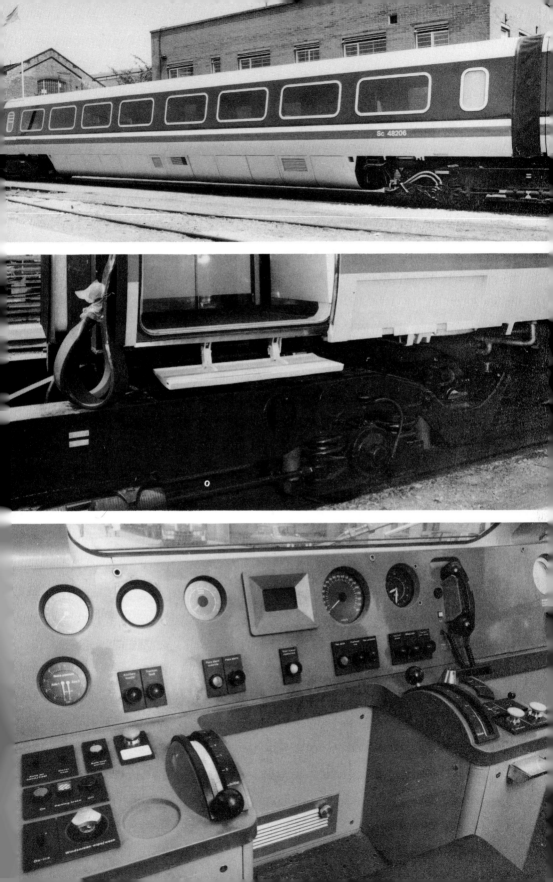

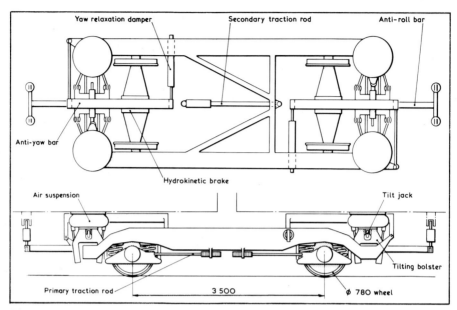

*The BT 11 articulated bogie provides independent suspensions for adjacent vehicle bodies.*

Jubilee' train when it was first put on, the thought of articulated coaches brings back one or two hectic memories. But the research staff of British Railways have applied the most scientific principles to the examination of every conceivable factor that could influence the steady and comfortable riding of the new trains, with results that were very successful on the gas turbine powered experimental train.

It must also be remembered that the tilting principle has to be incorporated in the connection between body and bogie in this articulated assembly. The accompanying drawing shows how the intermediate trailer bogie provides independent suspension for adjoining vehicles. The tilting mechanism is quite independent. While one could conceivably imagine this leading to a differential tilt action on two adjoining coaches, it would be so small as to be unnoticeable. What is important, however, is that tilting must be related to the lateral acceleration forces experienced by the passengers. The length of a 12-car train, with two power cars is 321 yards (294 metres), and at a speed of 100 mph (160 km/h) there would be a difference of about seven seconds between the time of the front and rear of the train entering upon a curve. Thus it was necessary that the tilting mechanism on every single bogie in the train should be free to react independently.

The top drawing opposite shows the general scheme of things on an intermediate trailer car. It will be seen that the primary suspension is by helical springs but, as in the case of the HST cars, the secondary suspension is by air springs. The separate tilting bolster at each end will be noted. The second of the drawings shows the end trailer bogie, which is used at the leading end of the driving trailer car, and at the inward end of the van trailer, next to the power cars. This has a single tilting mechanism in the centre, and a single pair of air springs for the secondary suspension. This drawing also shows clearly how the

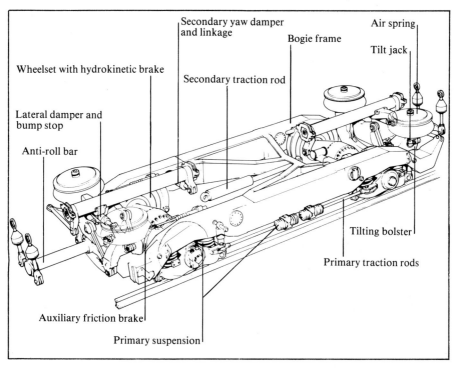

Above *APT-P intermediate trailer bogie.* Below *APT-P end trailer bogie.*

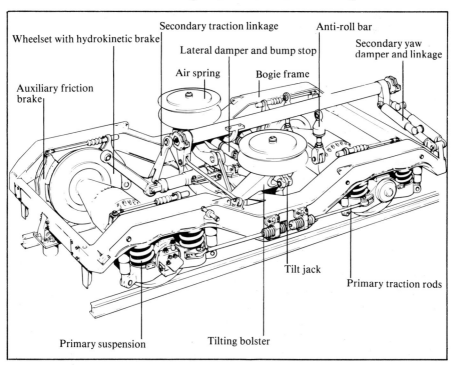

hydrokinetic brake forms an integral part of the axle and wheel set assembly.

In the previous chapter the methods of compensating the effect of higher centrifugal forces on curves for the passengers were described. There is, of course, another side to this, because the greater forces on curves due to higher speeds are transmitted in full to the track. This was a situation that lay outside conventional experience—that of a train running round curves at a far higher speed than that provided by the normal super-elevation. To say it lay outside conventional experience was perhaps not quite true, if one can believe some of the stories that were circulating at the time of the 'Race to the North' in 1895. It was then said that on certain sections the relaying gangs were out day after day correcting curve alignments that had been pushed out of true by the unprecedented speeds of the racing trains! But a paper read before the Institution of Mechanical Engineers in 1976 by Messrs D. Boocock and M. Newman contains this significant passage:

'The track is held in position mainly by friction between sleeper and ballast. However, tests have shown that instead of there being simply a threshold force at which gross permanent deformation is initiated, all lateral rolling loads cause some hysteresis . . . [colloquially a hangover effect] resulting in some sideways creep of the track. The creepage rate increases with load and diminishes as the track is consolidated with traffic after tamping. Acceptable performance tends to be determined by maintenance rather than safety criteria'—which seems a scientific way of explaining exactly what had to be done in 1895!

In studying this particular situation British Railways were very fortunate in having the test track of the Nottingham-Melton line on which to make experiments, and a curve of 0.71 miles (1.15 km) radius (57 chains) was used for a long series of runs at speeds up to 121 mph (195 km/h), which produced conditions corresponding to a 12 degree cant deficiency. Tests were carried out with the track repeatedly tamped, and in various degrees of consolidation of the ballast. Measurements were taken of track displacement, and of bogie lateral forces and track lateral forces, and these tests have established confidence for the future in running a fleet of APTs, with a designed 9 degree cant deficiency as discussed in the previous chapter. The design features of the train, with unsprung and bogie weights that are low in comparison with the supported weight of the car body ensure that the steady sideways forces, plus the sudden dynamic forces resulting from track imperfections are minimised relative to the axle load. The cars themselves are very light in relation to their length and seating capacity thus:

| Description | Length metres | Tare Weight tonnes | Class | No of Seats |
|---|---|---|---|---|
| Driving trailer | 21.5 | 34.6 | 2nd | 52 |
| Intermediate trailer | 21.0 | 23.0 | 2nd | 72 |
| Catering trailer | 21.0 | 26.4 | 2nd | 28 |
| Intermediate trailer | 21.0 | 23.8 | 1st | 47 |
| Van trailer | 21.1 | 31.2 | 1st | 25 |
| Power car | 20.4 | 69.3 | — | |

One always felt that G.J. Churchward, on the Great Western had done well to keep the weight of his handsome 70 ft 'concertina' stock down to 33 tons for an 80-seater third; but now an APT intermediate trailer 'second', with 72 seats, weighs no more than 22.5 Imperial tons. Moreover the modern car has far more in the way of passenger amenities. It was noticeable that when Collett built his

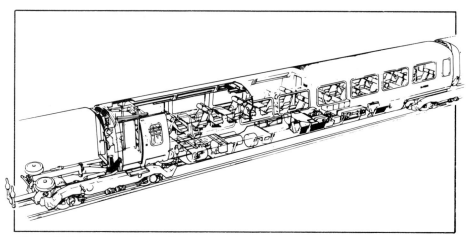

**Above** *APT-P intermediate trailer car.*

**Below** *APT second class trailer car trim cross section.*

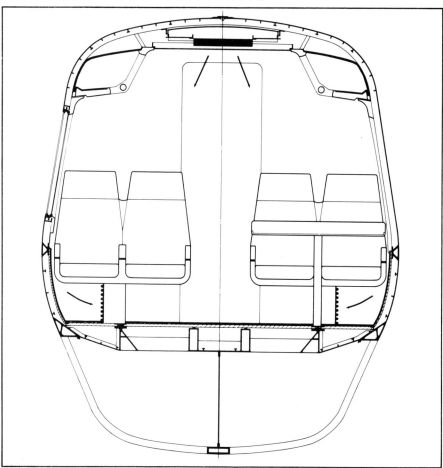

own version of the 70 ft stock on the Great Western, and added a number of refinements, the tare weight went up to 38 tons. It is especially gratifying that despite the over-riding need to keep weight to the minimum, the coach interiors are still very spacious, with the seating not only to acceptable, but to much appreciated standards.

In the 'race' to provide passenger train services that are fully competitive with road and air transport there is naturally keen interest in what other countries are doing, in the 125 mph (200 km/h) and over field. The French, in particular, seem to be turning a complete somersault in their philosophy towards high speed travel, in planning their new TGV trains on the Paris-Lyons route not only to carry both first and second class passengers, but to involve no supplementary charges for high speed, as has previously been done all over Europe on TEE trains. In what they have aptly called 'the democratisation of travel', however, the coach interiors have been arranged airline style with the seats close behind one another with sufficient room between only to allow a retractable tray for the meals served at one's seat. The spacious interiors of the APT, with seats arranged at tables for four are a great and satisfying contrast.

The details of construction of the light-weight APT trailer cars are very interesting. The underlying principle in design was to provide stiffness rather than strength, and the bodies are in aluminium alloy throughout. Extensive use is made of extruded sections of commercial grade aluminium, of the shapes shown in the following drawing, which gives their varying thicknesses. The cross-sectional drawing of the car shows clearly where these extruded sections

*APT-P trailer car extrusions.*

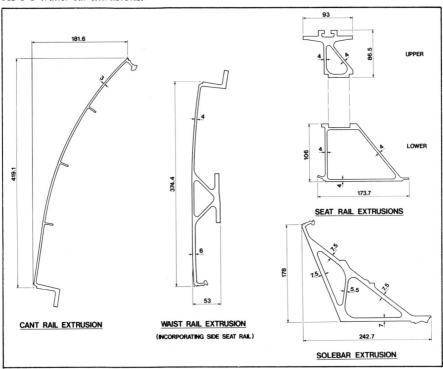

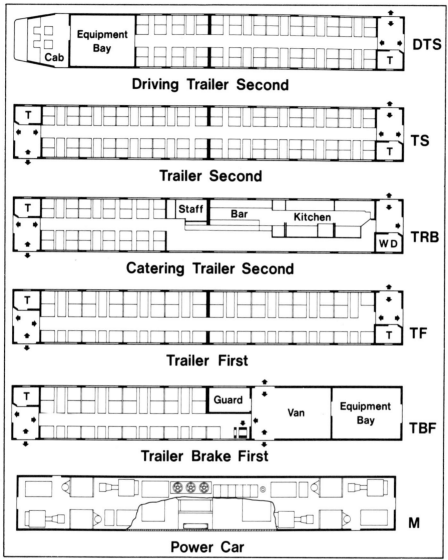

*Layout of APT-P vehicles.*

are located. They all run from end to end of the vehicle, and between them make up the outer profile. The power cars are made of a light-weight steel construction. Special interest naturally centres around the details of the articulation. That used on the experimental gas turbine powered APT, involving a spherical pivot between adjacent vehicle bodies, was not satisfactory, and on the pre-production prototype cars a modified form has been used that allows for relative movements between vehicle ends. The passenger doors are located in diagonally opposite corners of each vehicle—one wide door on each side—as shown in the accompanying diagram. The trains are vestibuled throughout, though passengers would not be permitted to pass through the power cars.

There is no need for them to do this because each half of the train is self-contained so far as catering and other facilities are concerned.

Although the electric APT is being introduced on the Euston-Glasgow route, the potentialities of the train on important routes where, because of the curvature, the HST could not be used with advantage, were shown in striking fashion by a test run made with the experimental gas turbined-powered APT from St Pancras to Leicester. The fastest timings of today over this 99 miles (160 km) are 80 minutes, after deduction of recovery time, and are made by diesel-electric locomotives of type 4 capacity, and subject to a maximum speed of 90 mph (145 km/h); but particularly between St Albans and Luton, and from a point about 54 miles (86 km) north of London there are numerous curves that lower the maximum permitted speed to 74.5 mph (120 km/h) quite apart from the more severe restrictions imposed at the major junctions of Wellingborough and Market Harborough. Under present track configuration at these two latter points even the APT was required to slow down to 78 and 81 mph (125 and 130 km/h), as compared to 62 and 56 mph (100 and 90 km/h) with ordinary trains.

The accompanying diagram shows a speed graph of the APT test run, superimposed upon one of the speeds required from an ordinary locomotive hauled train maintaining the present schedule. The test run showed a saving of 22 minutes, on this journey of 100 miles (160 km), with speed not exceeding 125 mph (200 km/h), except from one brief peak at 135 mph (218 km/h). As the graph shows, however, the APT was handicapped at the start out of London, by track restrictions for the first 6 miles (10 km). It can be envisaged also that it could prove well worth while to make investments in track re-alignment at Wellingborough and Market Harborough. It has many times been demonstrated how the slowing down and re-acceleration from permanent speed restrictions affects fuel consumption, and the wear and tear of braking equipment. Even with these limitations, however, a saving of 22 minutes on a journey of 100 miles (160 km), with the raising of average speed from 75 to 103 mph (120 to 165.5 km/h) is an attractive business proposition.

*Speed profiles of London to Leicester journey, showing improvement demonstrated by APT-E relative to present-day service.*

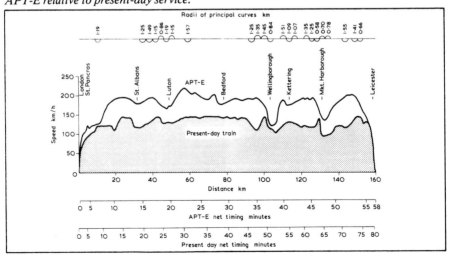

**Chapter 11**

# Planning the future services

Planning the ideal timetable has always been a favourite occupation for a certain erudite group of railway enthusiasts. There is a temptation to regard the professionals as a collection of somewhat reactionary individuals whose motto is: 'for Heaven's sake leave it alone'. Whatever the situation may have been in the days of conventional timetables, in which a start-to-stop average speed of 62 mph (100 km/h) was the hall-mark of a top class express train, it has long ceased to be the case today, when timetabling has become a scientific exercise, in which those responsible have to take into account a number of technical features of train performance, and signalling. In Chapter 3 of this book, dealing particularly with the planning around the high speed train services that are now well established on the Western Region, and are steadily becoming so on the East Coast main line, I have emphasised some of the complexities that arise when a number of extra-fast trains have to be implanted into a timetable network that already includes a very mixed pattern of service, consisting of varying grades of passenger trains, fast, medium, and mixed freight, and in the environs of large cities a host of local passenger services, themselves of a prestigious quality.

In the Eastern and Scottish Regions, although the authorised quota of 32 HSTs was available early in 1979 the development of the full programme of train service improvement was seriously delayed by the disastrous collapse of the roof in Penmanshiel Tunnel, between Berwick and Dunbar. This led to complete severance of railway communication between Berwick and Edinburgh, and diversion of certain through services via Carlisle. The full service of HST sets from Kings Cross to the West Riding, Newcastle and Scotland, at 125 mph (200 km/h) standards of running is now planned for May 1980. Particularly in respect of the business services morning and evening it will be one of the most remarkable timetables ever offered to the travelling public. In recent years we have become used to the hourly 'flights' of 100 mph electric trains on the West Coast main line, and to the running of the Bristol and South Wales HSTs five minutes behind each other from Paddington; but then look at the morning procession from Kings Cross all running at 125 mph (200 km/h):

|                              |                       |
| ---------------------------- | --------------------- |
| 07.25 to Middlesbrough       | 08.00 to Edinburgh    |
| 07.35 to Newcastle           | 08.05 to Hull         |
| 07.45 to Leeds and Bradford  |                       |

All these trains will call at Stevenage, to collect the extensive clientele driving their cars from a wide area in the northern residential districts. Then they will 'fly' northward at 125 mph (200 km/h).

*The 11.35 Kings Cross to Newcastle, at York, May 1979; the locomotive on the centre road is Class '31' diesel-electric No 31 252 (Patrick Kingston).*

The habits of business travellers in making early starts has now become thoroughly established in Great Britain, and one can recall with amusement the leisurely starting times of the isolated prestige trains of the 1930s—10 am both by the up 'Silver Jubilee' from Newcastle, and by the down 'Bristolian' from Paddington. Now, men of affairs require to be at, or near their *destination* by 10.00 hours! The sequence of arrivals at Kings Cross is no less remarkable than the departures roughly two hours earlier, thus:

| | |
|---|---|
| 09.23 from Leeds | 09.56 from Middlesbrough |
| 09.39 from Leeds | 10.04 from Newcastle |
| 09.50 from Hull | 10.08 from Bradford |

The last named travels direct via Wortley Junction, not entering Leeds at all.

During the day the pattern of service is that there is a train every hour between London and Edinburgh, and similarly between London and Leeds, but that while many of these trains make long non-stop runs others call at many of the intermediate stations. It is interesting to see that the Middlesbrough HSTs turn off the East Coast main line at Northallerton, stopping there and at Eaglescliffe. Peterborough has already come into the HST picture, as destination, intermediately, of the fastest scheduled diesel run in the world, by the 08.00 and 09.05 departures from Kings Cross, on the 1979-80 timetable, both of which run the 48.7 miles (78 km) from Stevenage in $27\frac{1}{2}$ minutes start to stop, an average of 106.25 mph—or in the now familiar metric notation, 172 km/h. This is a pretty sharp timing, even allowing for the favourable start from the site of the old station at Stevenage down to Three Counties.

With the present allocation of 32 HSTs it has not been possible to change all the trains over to the new stock, and some of the hardest running will be required on some of the trains that pick up at a number of intermediate stations and then feed into HSTs further down this line. There is the case of the present 16.05 to York, which calls at Stevenage, Huntingdon, Peterborough, Grantham, Newark and Retford to reach Doncaster only eight minutes ahead of the 16.50 HST 'flier' to Leeds, and then continuing, with a stop at Selby, to reach York six minutes ahead of the 17.00 'Scotsman'. These are very close timings and require some hard running on the part of the locomotive hauled train, and smart station working intermediately. In the May 1980 timetable the timings will be equally close, and if not maintained liable to cause severe reaction, and headaches for the regulators!

The down early evening succession from Kings Cross also includes some close scheduling, as from May 1980, as follows:

| | |
|---|---|
| 15.45 to Bradford, direct, via Wortley | 16.45 to Middlesbrough |
| 15.50 to Leeds | 16.50 to Leeds |
| 16.00 to Edinburgh | 17.00 to Edinburgh |
| 16.05 to York (locomotive hauled) | 17.05 to Hull |

All except the 16.05 are to be worked by HST sets, and this latter train will have to do some hard running to keep its booked timings, and get to York ahead of

*Picturesque rear-end view of a Kings Cross-Edinburgh HST on the Ganwick curve, between Hadley Wood and Potters Bar* (Brian Morrison).

the 16.45. At the time of writing, application has been made for another seven sets, which would enable the very fast intermediate workings, like the 16.05 down from Kings Cross to be HST operated. There is also a proposal for a Kings Cross-Sheffield HST, via Retford, which would fulfil a much needed want, until the time comes for a St Pancras-Sheffield APT.

The Penmanshiel Tunnel emergency has led to some unexpected HST workings of the Anglo-Scottish services. During the summer of 1979 three Kings Cross-Edinburgh services in each direction have been worked via Carlisle, and northward over the Caledonian route. These have been the 08.00, 15.00 and 16.00 departures from Kings Cross, and 07.57, 08.57 and 12.52 departures from Waverley. It was very creditable to be able to book an overall time of 6 hours 10 minutes from Kings Cross to Edinburgh via this route, with stops at York, Darlington, Newcastle and Carlisle. Of course the Newcastle-Carlisle section cannot be run at anything like normal HST speed. The fastest time scheduled between the two cities was 74 minutes, representing an average of no more than 49 mph (79 km/h). Over the West Coast main line the timings of the diverted HSTs have naturally had to fit in with the ordinary workings over that route. The fastest booking was that of the 12.52 up from Waverley, allowed 88 minutes for the 101.6 miles (161 km) to Carlisle, while the 15.00 down from Kings Cross was scheduled 91 minutes for the same run. These average speeds of 68 and 66 mph (109.8 and 106.3 km/h) were extremely good, seeing that the line beyond Carstairs had not been upgraded to the same extent as had the electrified line to Glasgow. Certain runs with HST sets over this route are discussed in Chapter 15.

The new Middlesbrough service is an interesting example of timetable planning, to secure good utilisation of the trains. The early morning 07.25 from Kings Cross results in an arrival on Teesside at a time when there would be no justification in a return run to London after a reasonably short turn-round time; so the set is worked light to Newcastle to provide stock for one of the regular up expresses. Similarly a set from Newcastle is worked light to Middlesbrough in the early afternoon to provide the stock for the up evening flier from Teesside to Kings Cross. Taken all round, the introduction of the HSTs on to the Eastern Region and Scottish Region, in the accelerated timetable of May 1980, is making a most profound impact, though as previously emphasised the track geometry of the line is favourable towards the HST, and the remarkable service improvement, as on the Western Region, is not likely to be repeated on many other main lines of British Railways. In this chapter I am very much concerned with the future generally; and that future would seem to lie with the APT rather than the HST.

At the moment, of course, financial authorisation has gone no farther than the prototype—the pre-production version—which is to be introduced in regular

**Top right** *Rear view of an HST from Weston-super-Mare leaving Didcot for Paddington. Trains pass through Didcot at the full 125 mph. Note the yellow line on the platform marking the limit beyond which it is not safe to stand when a non-stopping train passes through* (Patrick Kingston).

**Centre right** *A down HST passing Didcot at the full line maximum speed of 125 mph* (Patrick Kingston).

**Right** *Arrival of a well-patronised HST at Platform 7, Paddington. Two more HSTs are at platforms 5 and 6* (Patrick Kingston).

revenue earning service on the West Coast main line in 1980. But a great deal of forward thinking has centred around the general introduction of this type of train, not only on the West Coast main line, but on other routes, where the market potential would appear to be particularly favourable. At the same time it must be emphasised that the construction and commissioning of a fleet of APTs would represent a very substantial financial investment, and in consequence the launching of APT-P in 1980, is a prototype exercise not only in respect of all the technical features of the train, which have been discussed in some detail in the two previous chapters, but also in its presentation to the travelling public. The engineers have produced a superb pre-production job. It has next to be sold in a highly competitive market.

Even though the target service between Euston and Glasgow promises an accelerated overall time of between 45 and 60 minutes, it would not bring the journey time down to the three-hour norm, below which railway service becomes highly competitive with inland air service, and therefore very special care would have to be taken to make the accelerated service something 'special'. That it would be just another train, albeit a considerably faster one, was not considered enough inducement to justify the higher capital investment. At management level it has been realised for some time that all too frequently customer relations on British passenger trains leave much to be desired. The installation of loudspeaker systems, whereby announcements can be made to passengers, in case of any unusual occurence, or purely items of routine information, has greatly improved matters, though not all guards, or restaurant car stewards, have a felicitous way of putting information across—nor could they reasonably be expected to have. Their training, and normal duties do not extend to the art of being polished announcers. With the APT however there are certain factors that are likely to make customer relations even more vital than merely the job of giving a good impression.

The reception given by the public to the pre-production APT is all important. At the outset it was considered essential to have approximately the same amount of passenger accommodation as on the ordinary 'Electric Scots', normally 11 coaches. Then, as discussed in the preceeding chapter, technical considerations demanded the use of two power cars to maintain the full accelerated schedule, and for other technical reasons the power cars had to be located at mid-train. It was not admissible for passengers to pass through the power cars, except in cases of emergency, and so all facilities on the train would require duplicating. With separate catering in both halves the make up required to be 12 instead of 11 cars. This formation, which is something entirely new in British railway working, was clearly going to require the most careful passenger-relations technique. Imagine the feelings of a late-comer arriving on the train seconds before the departure signal was given, boarding the last coach, intending to make his way forward, and finding his way barred beyond the sixth coach. With all seats taken at the rear end he would have to stand to Preston, even though there could well be plenty of unused accommodation in the forward section of the train.

Senior railway officers have expressed it to me that the time is coming when it will be necessary to have signalling for passengers at the principal stations, not as a means of herding them to and fro like so many cattle, but to give clear, pleasant, and unmistakable directions for boarding the special high speed trains. With APT-P the situation will be quite different from that at Paddington

*After the passengers have gone the number plates are swung upwards to give access for platform servicing* (Patrick Kingston).

or Kings Cross where the HSTs are boarded with the nonchalance usually devoted to a commuter train. With APT-P reservation will be obligatory, and if not made beforehand seats will be allocated by a reservation clerk on passing through the barrier. This will ensure that no one boards at the rear end, intending to walk forward, and comes to a dead end at the power cars. On the train itself a 'Train Captain' is proposed, to have overall charge of all railway staff on board, including catering, and to be responsible for all matters concerning passenger relations.

The injection of the prototype APTs into the ordinary timetable has posed a number of problems, quite apart from the formation of the trains themselves, passenger relations and such like. It has been mentioned in Chapter 3 how a train with a maximum speed of 125 mph (200 km/h) would take the timetable space of four running at 100 mph. The problem to the timetable planner would be far easier if provision had to be made—as we all hope it will have to be eventually—for a whole fleet of 125 mph (200 km/h) trains. But at present it is only a very few, and it is vital, at this 'selling' stage that they run punctually. It is equally vital that in giving the APT a clear road other services are not disrupted. The now well-established tradition for early-start business express trains will be followed in the case of the down Euston-Glasgow APT, which will be despatched immediately ahead of the first 100 mph 'flight'. This so far as the intensively used London-Rugby section is concerned will avoid problems of the APT catching up the rearmost members of a preceeding flight inconveniently early.

It is not likely, however, that the train formations of the APT-Ps will be followed when the production batches are authorised. The 14-vehicle set is not only very long for present day operating functions, and the duplication of all catering facilities expensive, but the fact that the power units being in the centre means that the passenger accommodation is unduly stretched out. Not all passenger platforms on the West Coast main line are as long as those at Preston and Carlisle, and in certain cases the 14-vehicle set would overlap the platform ends, with all the attendant complications of moving passengers forward from the rear, or backwards from the front to enable them to alight. Furthermore, experience elsewhere in operating a frequent, high quality, very fast business service has shown that relatively small coach formations are adequate. It is certainly true that more elaborate restaurant facilities are needed on Anglo-Scottish trains than on the commuter-line runs from London to Bristol, and the South Wales cities, and it is now thought that 10-car formations will be adequate for the production APT sets. This would avoid the need for using two power units, and a single unit could be located at one end of the train.

The production APTs would remain, however, single consist trains. The power units would remain at one end. Some years ago, when the Southern Region electrification to Bournemouth was planned, concern was felt in some quarters as to the wisdom of keeping the power unit at one end, and in one direction propelling a long, heavy and fast train from the rear. In actual practice no disadvantages have been revealed, at speeds up to 100 mph and so far as the APT is concerned there will be plenty of experience with propelling on the prototype because, with the twin power cars in the middle, one part of the train is always being propelled. With the 10-car APT, and a single power car at one end, all problems over passenger guidance are avoided and there will be no trouble with platform overlapping at the shorter stations.

*HSTs in the West Country: on July 4 1979, first day of revenue earning service west of Taunton, an eastbound train, seen from the rear, takes the curve into Totnes* (Brian Morrison).

# Chapter 12

# Maintaining the trains

The foregoing chapters have described in some depth the conception, the investment policy, and the experimental, prototype, and production engineering that has launched these splendid, indeed epoch-marking, new trains into everyday traffic on the busiest railway network of the world. A mere ten years ago the service now offered to the public would have appeared simply breathtaking—venturesome to the last degree—not only in the speed, but in the intense utilisation made of the new trains. In view of the investment involved the utilisation would necessarily have to be high; and, taken all round, an extremely high standard of service has been achieved.

That the HSTs are diesel powered has tended to obscure the fact that they *are* new trains—not quite so new perhaps as their predecessors, which were involved in the transition from steam to diesel, but definitely new in that they have a fixed consist. Some readers will no doubt be ready to point out to me that we did have the fixed consist 'Blue Pullman' trains; but whatever their consist their introduction was a pretty ghastly blunder. While the fixed consist concept came from the very origin of the HST project it was originally not quite so 'fixed', as it has since become. The trailer cars in the prototype HST were designed to be interchangeable with the locomotive hauled Mark III stock. Consequently they had buffers and drop-head buckeye couplers, and each car had its own electrical power supply. The individual motor-alternators were installed to supply either 800 volts DC or 800 volts single-phase AC for supplying the electrical equipment on each car. Then however, with the object of reducing weight, it was considered better to have a three-phase 800 volt supply direct from the power cars, and having made this variation from the standard Mark III coaches the designers of the production HST went two steps further, and eliminated the buffers and the buckeye couplers. The HST trailer cars then became something different from all other British Railways coaching stock.

The production HSTs were thus established as completely self-contained sets, something quite apart from the ordinary locomotives and coaches. The very important decision was then taken that they should have entirely separate maintenance depots. It was not merely a case of avoiding the costly mistake, born out of hurried decisions, of having mixed breeds in the same shed: new diesels amid the inevitable dirt and smoke of a steam shed. The HST depots were designed to deal with the entire train as a unit and the equipment was planned to deal with all the day-to-day maintenance requirements of power cars and trailers alike, and so positioned in the depot that the whole train could be dealt with simultaneously. On the Western Region, where the first production

*Old Oak Common Maintenance Depot. Connecting a 'shore' supply of electricity* (British Railways).

HSTs went into intense regular service in 1977, two new depots were built. It is important to point out, however, that the need was not felt to have these in a completely standardised form. Geographical conditions dictated the difference in layout between the depots of Old Oak Common, and St Philips Marsh. That at Old Oak, like the great steam shed that has long since disappeared, is single-ended, whereas that at St Philips Marsh is a through depot.

These two original HST maintenance depots were designed to service the 27 trains providing the London-Bristol, and London-South Wales high speed service. The working strategy can perhaps be more readily appreciated by reference to the procedure at St Philips Marsh. A total of 14 trains are allocated to the depot, to fulfil 10 diagrams, one of which is worked jointly with Old Oak. The Bristol diagrams include a number of workings between Paddington, Cardiff and Swansea. There is, as yet, no HST maintenance depot in South Wales. Every train in service is subjected to what is known as the 'A' examination every two days, either at St Philips Marsh or Old Oak, and this means that each depot has to examine five trains every night. The HSTs provide an exclusively daytime service, and so all the regular scheduled examinations have to be made during the night. A target time of $3\frac{1}{2}$ hours is allowed for examination, cleaning both inside and out, and the execution of any light repairs. In the case of proprietary equipment as, for example, air-conditioning sets, no attempt is made to repair or adjust *in situ*; the whole unit is removed and a duplicate inserted.

The depot at St Philips Marsh is on historic ground. Collectively, Bristol in steam days had the largest accumulation of locomotives on the Great Western Railway, and as at Crewe on the London and North Western, the passenger and freight units were segregated: at Bath Road, for the former, and St Philips Marsh. It was, however, only from the avoiding line that the large collection of engines outside the latter could be seen, from those Saturdays-only reliefs to the West of England that were diverted clear of Temple Meads station and stopped beside 'The Marsh' to change engines, or to reman. Today no trace of the big steam shed remains, but the location of the HST depot, as shown on the accompanying sketch plan, enabled it to be made a through shed. It is just long enough to accommodate the standard Western Region HST sets, consisting of two power cars and seven trailers and, with three roads, three trains can be dealt with simultaneously. There is no time to spare with five trains to be serviced during the night hours.

When I was privileged to pay a visit, during the day time, only one train was on the depot. This was receiving more extensive repairs of a kind taking longer than could be attended to during the night but not for complete overhaul. For the latter the HSTs go to Derby, and there they are split up. The power cars go into the old locomotive works, and the trailer cars into Litchurch Lane carriage works. In the summer of 1979 the additional sets for the Paddington-West of England service began to go into traffic. An entirely new maintenance depot is under construction at Plymouth, Laira, and this will be different from both Old Oak and St Philips Marsh, in being on a much more comprehensive scale. It will

*St Philips Marsh HST depot.*

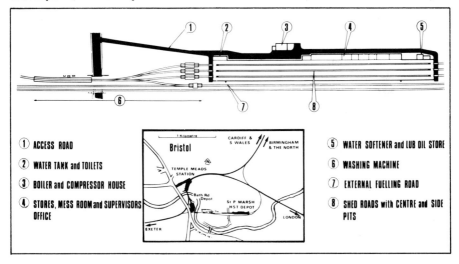

*Refuelling in the depot at Old Oak Common* (British Railways).

deal, in entirely separate sections, both with HSTs and conventional diesel electric locomotives. Until this is ready the Penzance HSTs will be maintained from St Philips Marsh and Old Oak. At the time of writing the Bristol and South Wales HSTs are averaging 800 to 1,000 miles *a day*—in excess of 250,000 miles (400,000 km) a year. That is the kind of duty for which maintenance is required.

With the first intensive revenue earning service of HSTs concentrated on the Western Region it was no more than natural that their weak points, as well as their magnificent overall reliability, should have become noticed in that region; and the resulting experience was surveyed in a comprehensive paper presented to the Railway Division of the Institution of Mechanical Engineers in December 1978 by S.R.D. Power, Chief Mechanical and Electrical Engineer, Western Region. Reliability has taken on a new dimension with the introduction of the HSTs. Any time a technical defect results in the train being delayed for more than five minutes it is recorded as a 'failure'. The record of the HSTs on the Bristol and South Wales services of the Western Region is remarkable against this most exacting standard. At the time Mr Power presented his paper the sets in service were showing an average of 12,400 miles (20,000 km) each per casualty, and with increasing experience the trend was improving. The number of complete failures have been very few; this is partly due to there being two separate power cars, each capable of working the train. Although one power car would not be capable of working the train punctually on those sections of the line where speeds of 125 mph (200 km/h) are required, a power car of 2,250 hp with 7-trailer cars, and a power car *dead* is capable of an excellent performance. It is important to note that even in these conditions it is better to operate the service with half normal power than to substitute a class '4' diesel-electric locomotive, either of class '47' or class '50', with an 8-car train. The loss of time would be less with a half-power HST set.

Since the HSTs were introduced on the Bristol service I have had more than 70 runs in each direction between Bath and Paddington, and only once, and then as far back as February 1977, have I experienced a case of running with only one of the power cars operating. The defect developed after we had started, because the time from Paddington to Southall, 8 minutes 30 seconds was normal for that period, and it was not until we passed on to the line then released for 125 mph (200 km/h) that we did not run up to standard. Even so, the average speed from Southall to Didcot was 98 mph (158 km/h), and we passed Swindon, (125 km), in 50 minutes 56 seconds from the start. Signal checks delayed the conclusion of the run, but the limited extent to which the train was handicapped on this occasion is shown by a comparison with a run I logged three weeks later on the same train when Swindon was passed in 45 minutes 25 seconds in what was then considered fairly exceptional time. So far as my own travelling records are concerned, this one very minor 'failure', represents one in about 16,250 miles (26,250 km) of travel.

Emphasising that the HSTs are run at speeds of 25 per cent greater than conventional trains it is not surprising that a number of mechanical defects have revealed themselves in the course of this high-speed running and very intensive

*Bounds Green depot—one of the HST power cars being serviced* (Brian Morrison).

*Heaton depot, Newcastle: a complete HST being serviced* (British Railways).

use. The remarkable thing is that they have been so few. As has befitted so spectacular an advance in service requirements the greatest care has been taken to investigate all casualties. A Service Problems Committee under British Railways Board chairmanship meets regularly to examine reports of defects, and any discernable trends—whether particular forms of failure are getting more, or less—and how these could be related to the practice in main workshops and service depots. In this, of course, the operating experience of the Eastern Region has been added to that of the Western, since the early summer of 1978. In such way a co-ordinated approach to troubles can be made. Before making any detailed reference to some of the troubles that have occurred, I think enough has been written so far to underline the extreme care in maintenance that lies behind the successful operation of the High Speed Trains.

The running of the prototype train, under severe and prolonged tests, brought to light a number of weak features that were corrected on the production trains, but others developed under the normal, albeit intense, service conditions. One of these was the age-old problem of core shifting in the cylinder heads, which led to fractures. Robert Stephenson had it, in casting the cylinders for the *Rocket,* while an undetected failing in the same way led to the downfall of the *Sans Pareil* in the Rainhill trials of 1829. It was also one of the contributory factors in the collapse of the first Tay Bridge. Fractures in the cylinder heads of the HST engines revealed insufficient wall clearances in the port areas, and an improved foundry technique has since been adopted to ensure exact location of the cores, and maintenance of wall thickness exactly at the designed figure. Another contributory factor towards cylinder head fractures was traced to the presence of coolant in the lubricating oil, and damage to the turbo-charger thrust bearing has been caused by the oxidizing effect, in certain conditions, of the anti-freeze liquid.

The traction motor flexible drive was a highly original design, but despite this, and the severity of the usage, the defects that have been apparent are notably few. It has been found desirable, for example, to improve the lubrication of the gearbox bearings, and to permit a longer period in service between attention to lubrication, the oil capacity has been increased by some 50 per cent, from 0.5 to 0.7 gallons (2.3 to 3.4 litres). Oil weirs, with oil priming holes, have been added so that the bearings are no longer totally dependent upon splash lubrication. It is sometimes thought that the railway traction machinery is a relatively 'rough job' compared to what is necessary in aircraft and high grade automobile practice. Of course the widespread introduction of diesel locomotives has needed changed techniques, but in the case of the HST, precision engineering is required at all points, and the standard of finish on the flexible drive links had to be improved.

In his paper Mr Power reported:
'The gearbox torque reaction link couples the gearbox to the bogie frame transom. The bushes at both upper and lower positions are of the bonded rubber type which depend on adequate axial load in the securing pins to provide the necessary friction grip between the central metal sleeve of the bush and the lugs of the gearbox or transom, thus ensuring that any movements are absorbed by the rubber. After several months in service, a lower securing pin fractured and the subsequent examinations revealed high wear rate between the head end of the pin and the bush in the gearbox lug. To eliminate the problem, the pins have been machined with tapered heads to which are fitted tapered split collets. The collets take up any clearance that exists between the pin and the bush and wear on the metal interfaces is prevented.'

The disc brakes are one of the most vital operating features of the HST, enabling stops to be made from 125 mph (200 km/h) in the same distance as that taken by the conventional locomotive-hauled trains from 100 mph. Thus, no modification was needed to the modern signalling on lines equipped for 100 mph maximum speeds. A heavy application, with disc brakes, inevitably causes some smell, and some of it was transmitted via the air-intake shutters to the coach interiors. Largely through the efforts of certain journalists, whose sole job in life seems to be to find fault, this defect was magnified out of all proportion, and having found nothing else to grumble about they 'plugged' it for all it was worth. In all probability none save the most fastidious of passengers would otherwise have noticed it; but attention having been drawn the complaints duly came in, and something had to be done about it. The first alteration was to arrange for the intake shutters to close during a brake application. This made a big improvement; but it is typical of the meticulous attention given to any adverse passenger reaction that steps are being taken to eliminate the smell at its source, by a changed design of brake block.

While it is, of course, the power cars with their sophisticated and intricate layout of machinery that are subjected to the most severe service conditions, the trailer cars are those in which the passengers form their impressions, and the brains packed into the bogie design and suspension have already been emphasised, in Chapters 7 and 8. The trailer cars are fitted with the BT 10 bogie, which is the production version of the BT 5 used on the prototype HST. Now the BT 10 is also used on Mark III locomotive-hauled coaches, and it was the fracture of an axlebox on one of the latter that led to a re-design, also of course for HST. As previously described the axlebox is designed to provide the anchorage points for the various springs and, through the principle of a swinging arm, to ensure accurate wheelset alignment. Following the fracture on a locomotive-hauled coach the axleboxes on the entire HST fleet came under immediate scrutiny and, with a number of vehicles taken out of service, a very stringent series of tests was made to examine under both static and running conditions the stress distribution in the housing that had fractured. Strain gauges were fitted at all the stress points leading to the actual line of fracture and, as a result, a deeper section was evolved using the latest computer techniques.

So far I have referred only to Western Region practice and experience. The Eastern Region situation, together with the associated activities in Scotland, are at once more widespread and complicated. There are two groups of activities to be provided for, the London-Newcastle-Scotland, and the London-West Riding. Servicing depots, on the lines of those at Old Oak Common and St Philips Marsh have been established at Bounds Green (London Area); Neville Hill (Leeds); Heaton (Newcastle) and Craigentinny (Edinburgh). As in the Western Region the HSTs provide purely daytime service, and overnight stabling covers the routine servicing for sets as follows, Bounds Green 8; Neville Hill 7; Heaton 4; Craigentinny 4; with 2 others stabled, but not serviced, at Aberdeen. Of these East Coast depots two (those at Neville Hill and Heaton) are on the site of former large steam sheds, but Craigentinny, on the main line less than 3 miles (5 km) each of Edinburgh (Waverley) and Bounds Green, are entirely new. Bounds Green is the furthest of any, so far, from one of the main starting points of HST service, and is on the Enfield line, about midway between Wood Green and Palmers Green, some 6 miles (10 km) out of Kings Cross. The East Coast depots are built to accommodate trains of 8-trailer and two-power cars. When the North-East to South-West HST service is introduced these will have 7-trailer cars, and will be maintained by the Western Region, probably from the new Laira depot. As discussed in Chapter 11, it is planned to have HST services from Kings Cross to Hull, and Kings Cross to Sheffield, via Retford. These will be maintained from Neville Hill, as are already those terminating at Harrogate and Bradford.

*An HST passing through one of the high speed cleaning plants at Heaton* (British Railways).

# Chapter 13

# Fulfilment—some fine runs

Few train services, anywhere in the world, have been the subject of more intense planning than the HSTs of British Railways, whether it be in the many engineering disciplines, in timetable scheduling, or in the many ways in which the rolling stock and the service as a whole has been designed to attract public patronage. It is all the more gratifying therefore that, taken for all in all, the day to day running of the trains has sustained a very high degree of reliability. I have been able, personally, to appreciate the service on the Paddington-Bristol route from several angles. As a passenger travelling for business purposes the speed, frequency, and punctuality of the trains, and the smoothness of the riding is valuable in time saving, and in the opportunities it gives for attention to many matters en route. As an engineer I find the sustained excellence of the coach riding, quietness, and equable temperature deserving of high praise, while as one who has made a practice of logging the running of trains for more than 50 years the performance of the HSTs forms a most fascinating study. In the previous chapter I referred to the consistent reliability of the trains on which I

*Just at the end of '125' area: a Bristol to Paddington HST passing Acton, where more restricted speed begins* (Brian Morrison).

have travelled since the HST service was first introduced from Paddington, and now in this present chapter, and the following one, it is time to look at the train running in more detail.

While the great majority of my runs have been made in the Western Region I have travelled to a considerable extent on the East Coast main line, and also on some interesting occasions when the HSTs have been diverted from their regular routes. The landslip near Wootton Bassett in 1977 resulted in some diversions via Trowbridge and the Berks and Hants line, while the blockage of Penmanshiel Tunnel, between Berwick-on-Tweed and Dunbar, which had such a catastrophic effect on East Coast services during so much of the year 1979 led to some of the Kings Cross-Edinburgh HST workings being diverted via Carlisle, and the former Caledonian main line to Edinburgh. I was fortunate in being able to see some of these diverted workings. Quite apart from ordinary passenger services one or two special runs must be mentioned, as showing both the build-up to regular working and the demonstration on special advertised runs of what the new trains can do.

Brief mention has been made earlier of the runs made with the prototype HST, before what the theatrical world would describe as an 'invited audience'. This round trip was made from Kings Cross to Darlington and back on August 2 1973. Between Kings Cross and York, in each direction, the special was limited to the maximum speed then allowed over the line, namely 100 mph; but between York and Darlington we had a fine demonstration of speed in each direction. Fortunately, from the viewpoint of spectacular performance, the speedometer was reading slightly low, so that when this indicated '125' to the driver we were actually doing nearly 128 mph. The interesting thing about this demonstration run is that in the very week that I was writing this chapter I travelled by the 08.00 Edinburgh express from Kings Cross, and with the usual 8-coach set we made almost identical times, until the special, in 1973 made its demonstration stop just north of Otterington. From the following comparison it will be agreed that what was shown as an exhibition run to that invited audience is now a commonplace occurrence.

## HST north from York

| Date | 2-8-73 | 13-7-79 |
|---|---|---|
| Formation | 7 cars | 8 cars |
| Distance | Actual | Actual |
| Miles | m  s | m  s |
| 0.0  YORK | 0  00 | 0  00 |
| 5.0  *Milepost 5* | 5  24 | 5  25 |
| 9.0  *Milepost 9* | 7  33 | 7  30 |
| 11.0  *Milepost 11* | 8  32 | 8  30 |
| 13.0  *Milepost 13* | 9  29 | 9  29 |
| 15.0  *Milepost 15* | 10  26 | 10  26 |
| 19.0  *Milepost 19* | 12  19 | 12  21 |
| 22.2  Thirsk | 13  49 | 13  54 |
| 26.0  *Milepost 26* | 15  35 | 15  42 |
| — | brake stop | pass |
| 30.0  NORTHALLERTON | — | 17  34 |

On that exciting August 2, however, the special arrangements provided for some extra fast running southbound from Darlington to York and although, as the tabulated details show, we did not exceed the nominal '125' as far as Northallerton the train was then driven considerably faster from there onwards and we reached a maximum of 137 mph (219 km/h) before Thirsk. There was an easing back to 123 mph afterwards for a short time, and then came a second acceleration to a top speed of $131\frac{1}{2}$ mph. Here is the log of the run:

## HST Demonstration Run, August 2 1973

| Distance Miles | | Actual m  s | Average speed mph |
|---|---|---|---|
| 0.0 | DARLINGTON | 0 00 | — |
| 2.6 | *Croft Spa* | 3 41 | — |
| 5.2 | *Eryholme* | 5 20 | 94.5 |
| 7.1 | *Milepost 37* | 6 22 | 110.3 |
| 9.1 | *Milepost 35* | 7 24 | 116.2 |
| 11.1 | *Milepost 33* | 8 21 | 126.3 |
| 13.1 | *Milepost 31* | 9 19 | 123.4 |
| 14.1 | NORTHALLERTON | 9 47 | 128.5 |
| 17.1 | *Milepost 27* | 11 09 | 132.0 |
| 19.1 | *Milepost 25* | 12 02 | *136.0 |
| 21.9 | Thirsk | 13 18 | 132.5 |
| 23.1 | *Milepost 21* | 13 50 | 134.8 |
| 25.1 | *Milepost 19* | 14 48 | †124.4 |
| 33.1 | *Milepost 11* | 18 35 | 127.2 |
| 36.1 | *Milepost 8* | 20 00 | 127.0 |
| 38.1 | *Milepost 6* | 20 55 | 130.9 |
| 40.1 | *Milepost 4* | 21 50 | 130.9 |
| 44.1 | YORK | 27 37 | |

* Maximum speed 137 mph. † Minimum speed 123 mph. In this chapter I am quoting all distances in miles, as the metric system has not yet been extended to the actual measurements of length along the track.

*Paddington-South Wales HST at full speed near Pangbourne. Note the superb track* (British Railways).

The original production HSTs were built at Derby, but before they were sent to take up revenue earning service on the Western Region they were put through full speed commissioning trials, and for this purpose the York-Darlington section of the East Coast main line was used. To get a completely unhindered run, the northbound starts were made from Milepost 2, north of York, near Skelton signal box. From there the trains were driven at high speed to various points north of Danby Wiske where test stops were made. An engineer who travelled on the test trains, Mr J.N.D. Proudlock, kindly gave me details of a number of these runs. One of the most interesting and significant features of these runs was their remarkable uniformity. Naturally the acceleration from rest was more rapid than would be possible over the curved exit from York station, and a speed of 100 mph was regularly attained in about $3\frac{1}{4}$ minutes from the start. On three successive runs the time to Northallerton was 15 minutes 20, 27 and 13 seconds, the actual timing point there being 27.99 miles (45 km) from the point of departure. The maximum speed attained on any of these runs was 132 mph (211 km/h). The average speeds over the 24 miles (38 km) from Tollerton to Danby Wiske varied between the very narrow limits of 126.1 and 126.7 mph (201-203 km/h). As an example of acceleration in ideal conditions the following log is interesting. The gradients are rising very slightly from Alne northwards.

### Typical HST commissioning run

| Distance | | Actual | Speeds |
|---|---|---|---|
| Miles | | m  s | mph |
| 0.0 | Milepost 2 | 0 00 | — |
| 3.54 | Beningbrough | 3 20 | 102 |
| 7.75 | Tollerton | 5 37 | 120 |
| 9.18 | Alne | 6 20 | 124 |
| 11.35 | Raskelf | 7 23 | 126 |
| 14.07 | Pilmoor | 8 42 | 125 |
| 16.04 | Sessay | 9 38 | 128 |
| 20.24 | Thirsk | 11 35 | 131 |
| 24.54 | Otterington | 13 39 | 125 |
| 27.99 | Northallerton | 15 27 | 128 |
| 31.76 | Danby Wiske | 17 13 | 131 |
| 37.75 | Milepost $39\frac{3}{4}$ | 20 28 | STOP |

The distances quoted above are those of the exact spots at which the engineers took their timings. The average speed, start to stop, over this relatively short distance was 108.8 mph (174 km/h).

The general introduction of the HST sets began with the Western Region timetables of October 4 1976, and in the following January I was able to title my monthly article in *The Railway Magazine* 'The Massive Western Speed-up'. From that time there were 11 'Inter-City 125' trains in each direction between Swansea and Paddington and about half that number from Bristol, via Bath. It was on the South Wales route that I had my first experiences in the driving cabs of these trains, in both cases on trains booked non-stop between Paddington and Newport. The 13.00 down was then allowed 96 minutes to cover the 133.4 miles (213 km); but that timing included $11\frac{1}{2}$ minutes recovery time, so that if running up to full recovery standard a time of no more than $84\frac{1}{2}$ minutes could be expected—an average of 95.5 mph (153 km/h). The publicly advertised time of the Paddington-Newport non-stops is now 89 minutes. At the time I made my trips, however, there were still some locations where speed had to be reduced, and these restrictions have now been removed. All in all it was a very impressive first experience.

**Above** *The first of the Western Region production sets, No 253 001, during trials, running on 'slab track' near Derby* (British Railways).

**Below** *The 09.45 Swansea to Paddington HST crossing the River Usk viaduct on leaving Newport* (Brian Morrison).

First of all, the driving controls are without question the simplest I have ever seen. Conveniently placed to the driver's right and left hands respectively are two small levers, controlling the power and the brakes. The former works in a sector plate marked with five positions. On the Western Region it was interesting to see that once maximum speed was attained on the level (or slightly rising sections), trains with 7-trailer and two-power cars, did not need full power, with the lever in the fifth notch, to sustain it. With the Eastern and Scottish Region trains, having 8-trailer cars, it was originally intended to have slightly uprated power cars having 2,500 hp each, instead of 2,250; but this has not eventuated and, in consequence, on the level stretches the East Coast sets are more frequently working at full power to maintain maximum line speed. The accompanying table gives full details of my first run in the driver's cab of an HST. In explanation of the speeds it needs only to be added that the line is virtually level to Didcot and then very gradually rising to a summit point at the 80th milepost. The gradients are nowhere steeper than 1 in 754, and on this a speed of 125 mph could be sustained with the lever in the 4th notch. The various speed restrictions then in effect are noted on the log, but I must add that the '125' did not begin until the 13th mile (21st km) out of Paddington. Now it begins only $4\frac{1}{2}$ miles (7 km) out.

## Western Region, 13.00 Paddington-Newport

| Distance Miles | Sched min | Actual m  s | Speeds mph | Distance Miles | Sched min | Actual m  s | Speeds mph |
|---|---|---|---|---|---|---|---|
| 0.0 PADDINGTON | 0 | 0 00 | — | — | | pws | 87 |
| — | | sig stop | — | 71.5 *Shrivenham* | | 47 56 | — |
| 3.3 *Old Oak West* | | | | 77.3 Swindon | 51 | 51 21 | *97 |
| *Junc* | | 6 16 | 90 | 80.0 *Milepost 80* | | 52 56 | 105 |
| 5.7 Ealing Broadway | | 7 54 | 90 | 82.9 *Wootton Bassett* | | | |
| 9.1 Southall | 8 | 10 10 | | *Junc* | 54 | 55 10 | *70 |
| — | | pws | 30 | 89.7 *Little Somerford* | | 59 18 | 122 |
| 13.2 West Drayton | | 14 03 | 110 | 100.0 *Badminton* | 64 | 64 43 | 108/ |
| — | | sigs | 40 | | | | 115 |
| 16.2 Langley | | 16 06 | — | 104.6 *Chipping* | | | |
| — | | pws | 20 | *Sodbury* | | 67 13 | 102 |
| 18.5 SLOUGH | 13 | 19 07 | 78 | — | | sigs | 45 |
| 24.2 Maidenhead | 16 | 22 30 | 117 | 111.8 BRISTOL | | | |
| 31.0 Twyford | | 25 50 | 125 | (PARKWAY) | $72\frac{1}{2}$ | 72 55 | — |
| 36.0 READING | 25 | 28 53 | *79 | — | | sig stop | |
| 41.5 Pangbourne | | 32 12 | 117 | 116.6 *Pilning* | | 78 30 | 94 |
| 44.7 Goring | | 33 48 | 126 | — | | — — | *75 |
| 53.1 DIDCOT | 36 | 37 50 | 125 | 123.6 SEVERN | | | |
| 56.5 *Steventon* | | 39 27 | 127 | TUNNEL JUNC | $82\frac{1}{2}$ | 83 56 | *70 |
| — | | pws | 97 | 128.8 *Milepost 154†* | | 88 04 | 75 |
| 66.5 *Uffington* | | 44 55 | 121 | 133.4 NEWPORT | 96 | 93 12 | |

\* Permanent speed restrictions
† Mileage via Gloucester

The South Wales direct line, via Badminton, is entered upon at Wootton Bassett over a junction with a speed limit then of 70 mph. After that the ruling gradient is everywhere 1 in 300 as far as Bristol Parkway: downhill to Little Somerford, uphill continuously at that inclination to Badminton, and then down again to Parkway. Full power was used after taking the junction at Wootton Bassett, except to observe a brief restriction to 110 mph through the Alderton Tunnel, between Hullavington and Badminton. There is no more high speed running after Parkway, which was passed practically on time, despite the

*An HST from the West entering Paddington, but the platforms are thronged with spectators to see the steam King George V backing down to work the 'Paddington 125' excursion train (G. Silcock).*

various checks experienced on the way down. Speed must be restrained through the Severn Tunnel, and a maximum of 75 mph (120 km/h) is all that was then allowed along the estuarine flats between Severn Tunnel Junction and Newport. But with recovery time in the schedule we were $2\frac{3}{4}$ minutes early on arrival. I estimate that the various checks had cost a full 9 minutes in running leaving us with a net time of about 84 minutes—just about equal to maximum recovery standard, and an average speed of 95.5 mph (153 km/h). It is important to appreciate that this high average was made despite the initial limitation in speed leaving London, and various other restrictions that have been relaxed. Except on the 1 in 300 gradient of the Badminton line full power was used only to accelerate to the maximum of 125 mph (200 km/h), and then the power lever was moved back to avoid exceeding that speed.

There is no doubt that once they were fully accustomed to the new trains the drivers enjoyed their high speed running, so much so that when there was time to be made up, and signals were clear, some of them indulged occasionally in considerably faster running. There was, indeed, what a very senior engineer once described to me as 'a 140 club'. While exhilarating to a recorder, and at the same time a manifestation of the power capacity of the trains and the enterprise of their crews, it was not really desirable to run these high speed units at so much above their rated maximum speed and, as explained later, a regulating device has since been added that limits the speed, in practice, to no more than about 128 mph (205 km/h). The fastest I personally noted, on a run from Chippenham to Paddington in the autumn of 1977, has been 136 mph (218 km/h). It was made at a time when there were a number of restrictions on the line, but, as a study of the accompanying log will show, we 'flew' to some purpose, and in the aggregate $41\frac{1}{4}$ miles (66 km) we covered in 18 minutes 38 seconds, at an average of 133.5 mph (214 km/h).

## Western Region, Chippenham-Paddington

| Distance Miles | | Actual m s | Average Speeds mph | Distance Miles | | Actual m s | Average Speeds mph |
|---|---|---|---|---|---|---|---|
| 0.0 | CHIPPENHAM | 0 00 | — | 52.5 | *Milepost 41½* | 31 43 | 110.4 |
| — | | pws | — | — | | pws | (60) |
| 11.1 | *Wootton Bassett* | 11 09 | — | 55.5 | *Milepost 38½* | 34 04 | 76.6 |
| 14.0 | *Milepost 80* | 12 48 | 105.2 | 57.0 | *Milepost 37* | 34 59 | 98.2 |
| — | | sigs | — | 58.0 | READING | 35 43 | 81.8 |
| 16.7 | SWINDON | 14 39 | 87.6 | 61.0 | *Milepost 33* | 37 38 | 94.3 |
| 22.5 | *Milepost 71½* | 17 49 | 109.8 | 63.0 | *Milepost 31* | 38 43 | 110.5 |
| 25.0 | *Milepost 69* | 19 00 | 126.4 | 66.0 | *Milepost 28* | 40 13 | 120.0 |
| 27.5 | *Milepost 66½* | 20 08 | 132.2 | 73.0 | *Milepost 21* | 43 24 | 131.7 |
| 30.0 | *Milepost 64* | 21 15 | 134.5 | 75.5 | SLOUGH (18¼) | 44 32 | 132.0 |
| 33.5 | *Milepost 60½* | 22 49 | 135.5 | 77.75 | *Milepost 16¼* | 45 33 | 132.5 |
| 37.5 | *Milepost 56½* | 24 38 | 132.1 | 80.75 | *Milepost 13¼* | 46 53 | 135.0 |
| 40.0 | *Milepost 54* | 25 46 | 132.2 | 83.0 | *Milepost 11* | 47 54 | 132.5 |
| 40.9 | DIDCOT | 26 11 | — | 85.0 | *Milepost 9* | 49 07 | 98.8 |
| 42.5 | *Milepost 51½* | 26 53 | 134.5 | 88.0 | *Milepost 6* | 51 09 | 88.6 |
| 45.5 | *Milepost 48½* | 28 15 | 132.0 | 92.0 | *Milepost 2* | 54 09 | 80.0 |
| 49.25 | *Milepost 44¾* | 29 57 | 132.2 | 94.0 | PADDINGTON | 57 30 | — |

It is extraordinary how anti-speed sentiments recur over the ages, and letters appear in the press today just as they did at the time of Rainhill, the Race to the North, in 1895, and with the steam-hauled streamlined trains of the 1930s. At the very time I was writing this chapter a letter appeared in *The Railway Magazine,* thus: 'Supersonic flight now occurs in the air: but excessive speed *on land* occurs on metal rails, and a feeling of mental and cardiac distress is experienced. The writer, for example, finds the 125 HSTs very tiring (although a smooth ride) and that a slower speed of 60 to 80 mph is more restful and natural for human rhythms, and would choose any other type of Inter-City, locomotive hauled, in preference to the High Speed sets—which are too fast to see station names, and produce an effect of being pulled backwards through a prickly hedge, gagged, bound and asphyxiated!'

Poor fellow! He must be one in tens of thousands who feel that way, and by way of a counterblast may I quote a paragraph I myself wrote in *The Railway Magazine* for March 1977: 'Following on with details of a few recent runs, all of my own timing, I feel impelled to give some general impressions in addition to technical details. For instance I joined the 19.05 from Paddington at Reading one Saturday evening, when it was crowded with passengers who had evidently been on a pre-Christmas shopping spree in London. There were family parties, with children quietly playing with newly acquired toys, their elders dozing off after a strenuous day; desultory conversations, occasional visits to the buffet, and no one within my own observations giving one thought to the way they were being whirled homeward. Why should they? The coaches were warm and cosy. It was dark outside, and the sights, sounds, and other evidences of travel were practically non-existent'. Even if it had been daylight I cannot imagine that any of those passengers would have distressed themselves trying to read the names of such stations as remain, and in any case, for the benefit of the distracted gentleman from Bradford-on-avon the Western Region has obligingly still retained speed restrictions through Reading and Swindon!

**Opposite** *'Paddington 125': the steam hauled excursion leaving abreast of the 11.20 HST to Bristol* (G. Silcock).

For the record, on that pre-Christmas night, from a start at Reading we passed Uffington, 30.5 miles (49 km), in 17 minutes 50 seconds, speed having risen by then to 128 mph (205 km/h); but a number of speed restrictions followed, and the remaining 40.4 miles (65 km) to Bath took 27 minutes 40 seconds. The total time for the 70.9 miles (113 km) from Reading was thus no more than $45\frac{1}{2}$ minutes, giving a start to stop average of 93.5 mph (150 km/h). Nowadays, while the restriction to 100 mph through Swindon remains, the line is cleared otherwise for 125 mph up to the eastern end of Box Tunnel. Thereafter the limit is 90 mph up to the approaches to Bath. In that same article I also wrote: 'How the HST sets will stand the pace remains to be seen, but my own experience of the first three months has been uniformly impeccable . . . .' It still is, after three years! And I add ' . . . as an engineering job and a superb operating innovation one can imagine the shades of Brunel, Gooch, and the other great men who launched the GWR on its remarkable saga crowding to the lineside to cheer'.

The Jeremiah from Bradford-on-avon, who wishes to see a reversion to 60 mph travel, would no doubt have been pleased to see the Bath and Bristol HSTs diverted from their normal route, for some time in 1977—and consequently slowed down—because of the landslip on the main line between Dauntsey and Wootton Bassett. Seriously however, the diversions were of great interest as they followed a considerable mileage of the West of England main line, on which HSTs were introduced in limited numbers as from October 1979. The diverted trains had to make their way among other traffic, particularly on the busy stretch of line between Bathampton Junction and Westbury, where in any case speeds are severely limited because of the many curves. The first of two journeys, the logs of which are set out in detail, represents about the best one could expect, with maximum speeds of 63 to 65 mph (101-104 km/h) between the very severe restrictions at Bathampton, Bradford Junction, and Heywood Road. The very rapid accelerative capacity of the HSTs was used to great advantage in recovering from these checks, and enabled the remarkably good time of $28\frac{3}{4}$ minutes to be made for the first 24.5 miles (39 km), from Bath to Lavington.

*A striking shot outside Paddington, with the 09.50 from Bristol arriving as the 11.20 to Bristol gets under way* (Brian Morrison).

## Western Region, Bath-Reading (via Berks & Hants line)

| Distance Miles | | Actual m s | Speeds mph | Distance Miles | | Actual m s | Speeds mph |
|---|---|---|---|---|---|---|---|
| 0.0 | BATH | 0 00 | — | 49.9 | Hungerford | 47 15 | *60 |
| 2.3 | *Bathampton* | 3 25 | — | 52.9 | Kintbury | 49 44 | 82 |
| — | | — — | 64 | — | | pws | 20 |
| 6.4 | *Limpley Stoke* | 8 15 | *53 | 58.3 | NEWBURY | 55 38 | — |
| 9.4 | Bradford-on-Avon | 11 23 | 63 | 61.8 | Thatcham | 58 38 | 90 |
| — | | — — | *20 | 64.6 | Midgham | 60 55 | *72 |
| 12.7 | TROWBRIDGE | 16 42 | — | 66.6 | Aldermaston | 62 20 | 90 |
| 16.8 | *Heywood Road Junc* | 23 07 | *65/15 | — | | pws | 30 |
| 24.5 | *Lavington* | 28 45 | 92 | 69.6 | Theale | 65 53 | — |
| 30.3 | *Patney* | 32 36 | 90 | — | | — — | 90 |
| 36.1 | Pewsey | 36 17 | 94 | 73.5 | *Southcote Junc* | 69 05 | |
| 41.3 | *Savernake* | 39 55 | *60 | — | | sigs | |
| 45.0 | Bedwyn | 43 15 | *90/70 | 75.4 | READING | 73 17 | |

* Permanent speed restrictions

## Western Region, Paddington-Bath (via Berks & Hants line)

| Distance Miles | | Actual m s | Speeds mph | Distance Miles | | Actual m s | Speeds mph |
|---|---|---|---|---|---|---|---|
| 0.0 | PADDINGTON | 0 00 | — | 61.5 | Hungerford | 45 38 | *20 |
| 3.3 | *Old Oak West Junc* | 4 32 | 85 | 66.4 | Bedwyn | 51 32 | 75 |
| 5.7 | Ealing Broadway | 6 06 | 95 | 70.1 | *Savernake* | 55 01 | *60 |
| 9.1 | Southall | 8 10 | 100/91 | 75.3 | Pewsey | 58 22 | 97/92 |
| 13.2 | West Drayton | 10 45 | 100 | 81.1 | *Patney* | 62 02 | 96/93 |
| 18.5 | SLOUGH | 13 27 | 122½ | 86.9 | *Lavington* | 65 39 | 97½/90 |
| 24.4 | Maidenhead | 16 12 | 130 | 93.0 | *Milepost 93* | 69 36 | 97 |
| 31.0 | Twyford | 19 23 | 126 | 94.8 | *Heywood Road Junc* | 71 28 | *15 |
| 34.0 | *Milepost 34* | 20 51 | 121 | — | | — — | 75 |
| 36.0 | READING | 22 41 | *40 | 98.9 | TROWBRIDGE | 78 00 | *20 |
| 37.9 | *Southcote Junc* | 25 42 | — | 102.2 | Bradford-on-Avon | 83 14 | 60 |
| 41.8 | Theale | 28 18 | *90/62 | 105.2 | *Limpley Stoke* | 86 40 | |
| 46.8 | Midgham | 32 23 | *94/74 | 106.3 | *Milepost 3 (ex-Bathampton)* | 88 56 | sig stop |
| 53.1 | NEWBURY | 38 31 | 45 (sigs) | | | | |
| — | | — — | 95 | | | | |

* Speed restrictions

By that time we were going at the normal maximum speed of the West of England main line and, although checked for permanent way work at both Hungerford and Theale, passed Southcote Junction, 73.5 miles (117.5 km) from Bath in 69 minutes 5 seconds. On a westbound run made about the same time on the express then leaving Paddington at 17.03 hours, I had the experience of passing Bradford-on-Avon in no more than 83 minutes 14 seconds for the 102.2 miles (163.5 km), a start to pass average of 74 mph (118 km/h). This included a heavy permanent way slack at Hungerford, in addition to the drastic slowings necessary for the junction at Heywood Road, and Trowbridge. There was some very fast running on certain sections, including some slight bending of the rules. Before we turned off the Brunellian main line at Reading there was a maximum speed of 130 mph (208 km/h) at Maidenhead and then, while the rising section of the Berks and Hants line to Savernake was beset with a number of checks, we had a fast run down through the Vale of

Pewsey, several times touching 97 mph (155 km/h). The train rode with extreme smoothness, and when we turned on to the Trowbridge line at Heywood Road Junction the average speed from the start was almost 80 mph (128 km/h). Passing Limpley Stoke in, what is for me, a record time of 86 minutes 40 seconds from Paddington it seemed that we should reach Bath in about 94 or 95 minutes; but we had caught up a local train, and were checked by signals throughout the concluding stages. The log shows what excellent work had been done up to that point. On another run during the same diversion period, when I was travelling behind one of the class '47' diesel-electric locomotives, we were unchecked after Heywood Road, and from there ran to the stop at Bath in 24 minutes 27 seconds. Had the HST been able to do likewise we should have reached Bath in 95 minutes.

On Saturday May 7 1977, the Western Region made history by scheduling for the first time in Great Britain a train booked to average more than 100 mph. This was a special excursion named the 'Inter-City 125 Jubilee Special', from Bristol to Paddington and back, making the run of 117.6 miles (188 km), via Badminton, in $70\frac{1}{2}$ minutes eastbound, and 70 minutes on the return. Actually both runs were made comfortably within these schedules, the actual time being 68 minutes 23 seconds and 67 minutes 35 seconds, respective average speeds from start to stop of 103.3 and 104.4 mph (165 and 167 km/h). In both directions the line was kept completely clear, and the train was run up to maximum line speed—sometimes just a little more. By that time the '125' was permitted as far east as milepost $4\frac{1}{2}$ (Acton yard) and full advantage was taken of this to make a very fast approach to Paddington, with no more than 5 minutes 21 seconds for the last 5.7 miles (9 km) inwards from Ealing Broadway. The speed on both runs was maintained at a remarkably even level, with no greater variation than between 123 and 126 mph (197 and 201 km/h) for 30 miles (48 km) between Shrivenham and Pangbourne, and between 124 and 127 mph (198 and 203 km/h) from Milepost 27 and Ealing Broadway. On the return journey it was the same, with a twice attained maximum of 128 mph (205 km/h).

**Chapter 14**

# Fulfilment—East Coast and West Riding

On the East Coast main line the HSTs did not get off to such a good start as they did on the Western Region. The route itself needed a good deal more attention than did the wonderful straight and level lines of Brunel; but the new trains of the '254' series, with eight trailer cars, were ready in sufficient numbers for an introduction to be made in the late spring of 1978. I have seen the new schedules criticised as being too venturesome in their striking accelerations, having regard to the amount of work still to be done on the line; but they included a generous amount of recovery time. If some of the HST Anglo-Scottish services suffered unduly from out-of-course slacks, there was sufficient running of a very first class character to indicate what can be expected, in daily performance, when the service has finally settled down. But the East Coast route became dogged with the direst misfortune in March 1979 by the complete blockage of the line at Penmanshiel Tunnel, near to the summit point between Berwick and Dunbar.

The collapse of the tunnel roof, causing the death of two workmen who were engaged in the enlargement of the interior profile, proved of such a nature that the decision was taken in April to close the tunnel altogether and build a diversion line. Tenders were invited on April 27 and the successful contractor, Sir Robert McAlpine & Sons, began work on May 8. With modern machinery and an immense sense of urgency the work was carried with such speed that the new line was reopened to traffic on August 20. As can well be imagined, the closing of the line between Berwick and Dunbar created an immense problem in handling the East Coast traffic. The circumstances of 1948 were recalled, when storms of unprecedented severity and violence led to the destruction of many bridges and culverts, and several major washouts between Berwick and Dunbar on the afternoon of August 12 1948. At the time of that disaster which, by the greatest good fortune, was not accompanied by any loss of life on the railway, the flood water was running at no more than 4 ft (1.2 m) below the crown of the arch in Penmanshiel Tunnel. While the line was completely breached in so many places, all through traffic had to be diverted, and at that time it was possible to do this from Tweedmouth Junction, via Kelso, to join the Waverley Route at St Boswells. In this recent emergency, however, both these lines had been closed and diversions had to be made via Carlisle.

This created problems of its own, because the enginemen normally operating the passenger train services on the West Coast Route, with 25 kV electric locomotives, had no experience of handling HSTs and it was not until there had been time and opportunity for a number of the regular HST drivers from

*Bradford Exchange: two HSTs alongside* (British Railways).

Haymarket shed to learn the road down to Carlisle that a few HST workings between Kings Cross and Edinburgh via Newcastle and Carlisle could be operated. Nevertheless, as in the case of the Western Region diversions over the Berks and Hants line described in the previous chapter, these workings between Newcastle and Edinburgh have given an even broader picture of HST working, and some highly interesting performance, even if the speed on certain sections was necessarily much slower than that normally expected where HSTs are concerned.

The inaugural run, on May 8, 1978 of 'The Flying Scotsman' as an HST was unfortunate. The scheduled time for the 392.7 miles (628 km) from Kings Cross to Edinburgh was 292 minutes inclusive of a two minute stop at Newcastle, but we were slowed for engineering work at no less than *thirteen* places. Worse than this we were, in addition, twice brought to a stand from adverse signals. The engine crews tried hard, but the odds were against them. Between Kings Cross and Newcastle the delay amounted to $22\frac{1}{2}$ minutes in running, but $9\frac{1}{2}$ minutes were recovered by loco and we were 13 minutes late into Newcastle. The honours on that inaugural day rested with the up 'Talisman', which made a splendid run. It can be summarised as follows:

| Section | Distance miles | Schedule min | Actual m s | Net time min |
|---|---|---|---|---|
| Edinburgh-Newcastle | 124.4 | 104 | 95 18 | 93 |
| Newcastle-Darlington | 36.0 | $31\frac{1}{2}$ | 30 45 | $30\frac{3}{4}$ |
| Darlington-Peterborough | 155.9 | 112 | 111 38 | 104 |
| Peterborough-Stevenage | 48.8 | 34 | 33 45 | 31 |
| Stevenage-Kings Cross | 27.6 | $22\frac{1}{2}$ | 24 45 | $22\frac{3}{4}$ |
| TOTAL | 392.7 | 304 | 296 11 | $281\frac{1}{2}$ |
| Average running speed mph | — | 77.5 | 80 0 | 83.6 |

In the first weeks of HST operation the running over the magnificent racing stretch from York to Darlington was severely hindered by permanent way work giving the engineers absolute possession of the down main line in the neighbourhood of Thirsk in the middle of the day, with diversion to the slow line for part of the way. But there was no mincing matters on the southbound line, and the accompanying table gives details of two very fast runs. The first of these, on the up 'Talisman', showed an average speed of 126.3 mph (202 km/h) over the 24.5 miles (39 km) from Northallerton to Beningbrough, but the actual approach and passage through York was slow—in fact the second run, on the 17.30 up from Newcastle, actually stopped in York station in a few seconds less time than the 'Talisman' took to pass. This second run was a remarkable one, showing a start-to-stop average speed of 103 mph (165 km/h) over this relatively short distance of 44.1 miles (70.5 km).

## HST runs: Darlington-York

| Train | | 'Talisman' | | 17 30 ex-Newcastle | |
|---|---|---|---|---|---|
| **Distance**<br>**Miles** | | **Time**<br>m   s | **Average**<br>**Speed**<br>mph | **Time**<br>m   s | **Average**<br>**Speed**<br>mph |
| 0.0 | DARLINGTON | 0 00 | — | 0 00 | — |
| 2.6 | *Croft Spa* | 3 02 | — | 2 53 | — |
| 5.2 | *Eryholme* | 4 36 | 99.5 | 4 27 | 99.5 |
| 10.4 | *Danby Wiske* | 7 20 | 113.4 | 7 13 | 122.7 |
| 14.1 | NORTHALLERTON | | | | |
| 17.5 | *Otterington* | 10 47 | 126.4 | 10 40 | 127.3 |
| 21.9 | Thirsk | 12 52 | 126.7 | 12 42 | 129.7 |
| 26.1 | *Sessay* | 14 50 | 127.7 | 14 37 | 131.5 |
| 30.7 | *Raskelf* | 17 05 | 122.7 | 16 49 | 125.2 |
| 34.4 | *Tollerton* | 18 49 | 127.4 | 18 31 | 130.5 |
| 38.6 | *Beningbrough* | 20 47 | 127.7 | 20 30 | 126.7 |
| 42.5 | *Skelton Junc* | 22 47 | 116.7 | 22 23 | 124.1 |
| 44.1 | YORK | 25 50 | PASS | 25 47 | STOP |

*During the time of the Penmanshiel Tunnel blockage: the 08.57 Edinburgh to Kings Cross diverted via Carlisle, here seen passing Wylam (David H. Allen).*

*The 07.40 Kings Cross to Newcastle in August 1978 in picturesque country north of Durham* (David H. Allen).

On the down road all my earlier runs were checked in one way or another, between York and Darlington, but the 14.00 and 16.00 departures from Kings Cross, booked non-stop to Darlington in 161½ minutes, ran over the section north of York when the work-train had gone home for the day, and thus experienced no more than a routine slowing, instead of a diversion on to the slow line. When the HSTs were first put on, both these trains were non-stop to Darlington. The former has since been accelerated to run the 232.3 miles (372 km) from Kings Cross in 146 minutes, a splendid average of 95.5 mph (153 km/h), while the 'Talisman', calling at both Doncaster and York, and one of the trains diverted via Carlisle in the emergency timetable of May 1979, was booked to reach Darlington in 158 minutes. Two runs made in the summer of 1978 gave arrivals at Darlington in 158½ and 158 minutes, 3 and 3½ minutes early. The former run experienced three signal and four permanent way checks, and the second, four permanent way checks and a dead stand for signals. 'The Flying Scotsman' was allowed 155 minutes to pass Darlington. On the inaugural run, when I was a passenger, we passed through in 164¾ minutes and, on a later occasion, when I was riding in the driving cab our time was 166 minutes 12 seconds. Delays accounted for 19 minutes on the first trip and 18½ minutes on the second, leaving net running times of 145¾ and 147¾ minutes, both around the 95 mph (152 km/h) mark. On the run on 'The Flying Scotsman' when I was in the driver's cab the delays as far as Darlington amounted to no less than 29 minutes, leaving a net time of 137¼ minutes. This train had 16 minutes recovery time in the schedule between Kings Cross and Darlington, thus expecting a run in 139 minutes if working to maximum recovery standard. We did nearly two minutes better than this with a start to pass average of 102 mph (163 km/h), without the slightest excess over 125 mph (200 km/h) anywhere.

While the Scottish HST service was very much upset in 1979 by the Penmanshiel Tunnel blockage some excellent services have been run between Kings Cross and the cities of the West Riding. The 'Leeds Executive', for example, runs non-stop over the 185.8 miles (297 km) in 2 hours 8 minutes, while the 'Bradford Executive' leaving Kings Cross only five minutes later, covers the 156 miles (250 km) to its first stop at Doncaster in 98 minutes, at 95.5

mph (153 km/h) start to stop. The Bradford HST then calls only at Wakefield and New Pudsey, taking the direct line at Wortley Junction instead of going into Leeds. I had an interesting run on the 13.50 departure from Kings Cross which calls intermediately at Wakefield, but takes only five minutes longer to Leeds than the non-stop 'Executive' leaving London two hours later. We began well, passing Peterborough 76.4 miles (122 km), in $45\frac{1}{4}$ minutes in spite of a slowing for permanent way at New Barnet. But then we were subject to what appeared to be an operating error. A slower train was allowed to take the main line ahead of us, and it was not until Little Bytham, by which time it had delayed us for six minutes, that it was crossed over on to the slow line. A severe permanent way check was also experienced north of Newark so that, despite some rousing spurts up to 125 mph (200 km/h) intermediately, we took exactly 103 minutes to pass Doncaster, 156 miles (250 km). The net time was, however, no more than $91\frac{1}{2}$ minutes an average of $102\frac{1}{2}$ mph (164 km/h) from the start.

The line from Doncaster to Leeds was never exactly a speedway, with sharply undulating gradients, and the frequent incidence of speed restrictions because of colliery subsidences. On this trip, we had two 20 mph (32 km/h) slowings soon after passing Doncaster, and although we were doing 90 mph (144 km/h) on passing South Elmsall the 8.7 miles (14 km) from Doncaster to that station had taken $11\frac{1}{4}$ minutes and there was yet another slowing to 35 mph (56 km/h) after we had just topped the '100' near Nostell. So the last 11.2 miles (18 km) from South Elmsall into Wakefield took 10 minutes 20 seconds making a total of 124 minutes 32 seconds for the 175.9 miles (281 km) from Kings Cross. The actual average speed, inclusive of all checks, was 85 mph (136 km/h) but the net time was no more than 107 minutes, against 113 minutes scheduled, showing the excellent net average speed of 98.8 mph (158 km/h).

The 9.05 departure from Kings Cross, which carries the HST service through to Harrogate, in 3 hours 4 minutes for the 204.2 miles (327 km) (66.4 mph (106 km/h) average), shares (with the 08.00 to Edinburgh) the fastest start to stop booking that has yet been scheduled on British Railways, being required to run the 48.8 miles (78 km) from Stevenage to Peterborough in $27\frac{1}{2}$ minutes, an average of 106.5 mph (170 km/h). So far I must confess I have not yet seen this

*Down East Coast HST at King Edward Bridge Junction. Another picturesque rear end view as the train enters upon the bridge and crosses to Newcastle* (David H. Allen).

*A southbound HST passing Durham, with a magnificent view of the cathedral* (British Railways).

very sharp timing kept. On a run with the 08.00 train we passed Fletton Junction, 47.4 miles (76 km) from Stevenage, in 26 minutes 22 seconds but the approach to the platform at Peterborough involves a crossover movement from the through line, with delayed clearance of the junction signal in accordance with present signalling and operating practice on British Railways. So, the last 1.4 miles (2 km) took 2 minutes 40 seconds, and the time from Stevenage was 29 minutes 2 seconds. Had we been able to approach as the Western Region HSTs do at Chippenham, in the westbound direction, we should have arrived in a little under 28 minutes. But it is a very sharp timing, there being sections of line, round the Offord curves, and across the Fens at Holme, where speed was still limited to 100 mph.

When compelled to travel on Sunday one does not ordinarily expect any very fast running; but as in so many other respects the HSTs are changing that too. Twice in the summer of 1979 I travelled by the 11.48 express from Leeds to Kings Cross. This originates at Bradford, and reverses direction at Leeds. On both occasions departure was delayed and there were numerous checks en route. The timing certainly is not so fast as the weekday flyers; but even so 2 hours 38 minutes including three stops is good going for a run of 185.8 miles (297 km), a scheduled overall average speed of 70.6 mph (133 km/h). On both occasions, however, we ran so well that we were waiting for time before leaving Peterborough, and our total running times were $135\frac{1}{2}$ and $142\frac{1}{2}$ minutes, inclusive of all checks. On the first occasion we ran very fast up from Peterborough and, with none of the checks the driver was anticipating, arrived in Kings Cross nine minutes early—on a Sunday! On the second run we should have been dead on time, but for a check in the immediate approach to the terminus.

In the opening paragraphs of this chapter I referred to 'great expectations' for the East Coast HST service, and even before the troubled summer of 1979 was ended I had some experience of really splendid running on the Anglo-Scottish trains. The very thorough 'spade-work' on the track that was still in progress at the time of the first introduction of HSTs has paid off handsomely and, on a return trip from Kings Cross to Newcastle and back at the beginning of August, apart from the slowing over the embankment subsidence site at Relly Mill, just south of Durham, we had only two permanent way cautions going north, and only one southbound. I was very interested to observe the running of the sharply timed 14.00 hours from Kings Cross which, at that time, had been accelerated to run the 232.3 miles to Darlington in 146 minutes. The two permanent way checks, at Muskham, north of Newark, and at Danby Wiske were both severe, and the driver who opened the ball, from Kings Cross, ran splendidly from the start to get some time in hand. I think it was the first time I have ever covered more than 100 miles in the first hour out of the London terminus, on the East Coast route. As will be seen from the accompanying log we actually covered $106\frac{1}{4}$ miles (170 km) in the exact hour and, while it does not compare for distance with the Inter-City 125 Jubilee Special run by the Western Region, when Bristol Parkway, 111.75 miles (179 km) from Paddington, was passed in 60 minutes 36 seconds, the start out of Kings Cross is considerably more restricted. It is not until one is past Stevenage that an East Coast train can really get going.

## HST 14.00 hours Kings Cross-Darlington

| Distance Miles | | Actual m  s | Speeds* mph | Distance Miles | | Actual m  s | Speeds* mph |
|---|---|---|---|---|---|---|---|
| 0.0 | KINGS CROSS | 0  00 | — | 138.6 | RETFORD | 81  58 | 122/100 |
| 2.5 | Finsbury Park | 4  08 | — | 143.9 | *Ranskill* | 84  41 | 123 |
| 5.0 | Wood Green | 5  56 | 97 | 147.7 | *Bawtry* | 86  53 | 80 (slack) |
| 9.2 | New Barnet | 8  26 | 102 | 152.5 | *Milepost* $152\frac{1}{2}$ | 90  01 | 100 |
| 12.7 | Potters Bar | 10  28 | 105 | — | | sigs | |
| 17.7 | Hatfield | 13  17 | 107/103 | 156.0 | DONCASTER | 95  06 | sig |
| 25.0 | Knebworth | 17  20 | 120 | | | 95  26 | stop |
| 27.6 | Stevenage | 18  41 | 100 | 163.0 | *Moss* | 101  55 | 102 |
| 31.9 | HITCHIN | 21  05 | 124 | 166.0 | *Balne* | 103  31 | 116 (max) |
| 35.8 | *Three Counties* | 22  56 | $126\frac{1}{4}$ | 174.4 | SELBY | 108  18 | — |
| 41.1 | Biggleswade | 25  32 | 128 | 184.0 | *Naburn* | 114  46 | 106 |
| 51.7 | St Neots | 30  33 | 122 | — | | sigs | 5 |
| 56.0 | *Offord crossing* | 32  46 | 109 | 188.2 | YORK | 120  15 | — |
| 58.9 | HUNTINGDON | 34  18 | 111 | 189.8 | *Skelton Junc* | 122  30 | 67 |
| 62.2 | *Milepost* $62\frac{1}{4}$ | 36  05 | 114 | 193.7 | *Beningbrough* | 125  08 | 102 |
| 69.4 | *Holme* | 39  59 | 120/95 | 197.9 | *Tollerton* | 127  25 | 113 |
| 76.4 | PETERBOROUGH | 43  52 | 103 | 201.6 | *Raskelf* | 129  14 | 121 |
| 79.5 | *Werrington Junc* | 45  40 | 116 | 206.2 | *Sessay* | 131  29 | 125 |
| 84.9 | *Tallington* | 48  20 | 122/120 | 210.4 | Thirsk | 133  28 | 126 |
| 92.2 | *Little Bytham* | 51  57 | 125 | 214.7 | *Otterington* | 135  32 | 126 |
| 100.1 | *Stoke summit* | 56  17 | 100 | 218.2 | NORTHALLER- | | |
| 105.5 | GRANTHAM | 59  30 | eased | | TON | 137  10 | 127 |
| 106.25 | *Milepost* $106\frac{1}{4}$ | 60  00 | 95 | — | | pws | — |
| 120.1 | NEWARK | 67  53 | 120 | 227.1 | *Eryholme* | 145  14 | 106 |
| — | | pw slack | 15 | 229.7 | *Croft Spa* | 146  38 | 111 |
| 127.4 | *Crow Park* | 75  32 | — | 232.3 | DARLINGTON | 151  14 | — |
| 131.9 | *Tuxford* | 78  21 | 106/100 | | | | |

Net time $137\frac{3}{4}$ minutes

* By stop watch, at or near stations and mileposts noted.

Despite the permanent way slowing north of Newark we had covered $152\frac{1}{2}$ miles (244 km) in the first $1\frac{1}{2}$ hours out of London, but the delay at Doncaster was a bad one and cost us a full five minutes in running. In these latitudes, however, there had developed a very strong side wind, which must have made some effect on our running on the exposed level stretches north of Shaftholme Junction and we were brought almost to a stand by adverse signals in the approach to York. But we made some grand speed onwards to Northallerton averaging 123 mph for 24.5 miles (39 km) and eventually reached Darlington in $151\frac{1}{4}$ minutes after delays that had cost us $13\frac{1}{2}$ minutes. The net time of $137\frac{3}{4}$ minutes showed an average speed of 101.2 mph (162 km/h). There is some recovery time in the schedule north of Darlington, and, although we had the severe slowing over the subsidence site at Relly Mill, the final 36 miles (57.5 km) into Newcastle were covered in $30\frac{3}{4}$ minutes, and the arrival was only one minute late.

I found the working over the division route via Carlisle very interesting. Although the very maximum speed allowable is only one instead of two miles a minute, the high tractive power of HSTs makes it possible to run at maximum line speed regardless of the intermediate gradients. The line speeds, apart from fairly numerous intermediate restrictions at a lower level, are 55 mph (88 km/h) from leaving Newcastle to a point near Haydon Bridge; 60 mph (96 km/h) up the rest of the climb to the level plateau, near Low Row, and then no more than 50 mph (80 km/h) throughout the long descent to Carlisle. A train like the 15.00 hours from Kings Cross to Aberdeen which, during the Penmanshiel emergency, left Newcastle for the west at 18.22, seemed to be timed right up to the limit of the road in having only $74\frac{1}{2}$ minutes for the 60.2 miles (96 km) to Carlisle. On the eastern part of the run, for example, the 16.8 miles (27 km) from Blaydon to Hexham were allowed no more than $19\frac{1}{2}$ minutes, an average of 51.7 mph (83 km/h) inclusive of regular speed restrictions to 35 mph (56 km/h) at Blaydon, and west of Wylam, and 30 mph (48 km/h) through Hexham. With a temporary engineering slack to 20 mph (32 km/h) at Stocksfield we dropped $1\frac{1}{2}$ minutes on this section. I had the privilege of a cab

*Rear-end of the 12.10 Edinburgh to Kings Cross, diverted via Carlisle, passing under the picturesque gantry carrying the signal box at Hexham, on the cross country journey to Newcastle (David H. Allen).*

*An HST arriving at York from the north* (Brian Morrison).

pass, and saw that the train was being very skilfully handled, accelerating rapidly to 55 mph (88 km/h) after each restriction.

Beyond Hexham there was a very long restriction to 20 mph (32 km/h) over track where there had been a freight train derailment; but after Haydon Bridge, on continuously rising gradients, we had some 60 mph running although, because of the checks, we had dropped six minutes in all, on the allowance of 43 minutes for the 37.2 miles (59.5 km) to Haltwhistle. There are some tempting stretches of downhill grades after passing Low Row and it seemed extraordinary to see an HST restrained to no more than 50 mph! But 'orders are orders', and in any case this leisurely descent gave time for an appreciation of the wide vistas over the Border country. There was three minutes' recovery time between Brampton and Carlisle and, despite a signal check, we arrived in Carlisle five minutes late. The net time was about 73 minutes. In travelling east on the following day, as a passenger, by the 10.02 train from Aberdeen, and leaving Carlisle at 14.23, I could appreciate that during this emergency the eastbound run was the easier of the two. The long permanent way check between Haydon Bridge and Hexham affected only the westbound line and, of course, an HST could make light of the gradients between Carlisle and Low Row.

Quite apart from traction performance, however, in fine sunny weather the leisurely cross-country run formed a delightful interlude in an otherwise fast journey. The visibility was very clear, and the countryside looking its best. I noted the energetic interest in it taken by a Japanese tourist who sat opposite to me at lunch, who was jumping up taking innumerable photographs through the window. I did just the same when I was travelling in his country! For the record, we took 19 minutes 20 seconds to climb the 13.9 miles (22 km) to Low Row, and then covered the next 35.7 miles (57 km) to Prudhoe in 39 minutes 35 seconds. Only once I noted a speed as high as 63 mph (101 km/h) and the speed restrictions through Hexham and Stocksfield were accurately observed. Running into the industrial area we passed Blaydon, 56.2 miles (90 km), in 66 minutes 37 seconds, but then being a little ahead of time we experienced signal checks and eventually took 77 minutes 49 seconds to the stop in Newcastle, where we were just over two minutes early.

The continuation to Kings Cross gave me some of the finest running I have yet clocked with an HST on the East Coast Route. To fit in a suitable path the train had a wait of 14 minutes at Newcastle, but followed on with a timing of 3 hours 19 minutes to London inclusive of four stops. Detailed logs of some of the fastest spells of running are included in this chapter, but the summary details give a good overall impression.

## 15.57 hours HST: Newcastle-Kings Cross

| Distance Miles | | | Public Time | Actual | Min late |
|---|---|---|---|---|---|
| 0.0 | Newcastle | | 15 57 | 15 57 | RT |
| — | | | — — | pw check | |
| 36.5 | Darlington | arr | 16 26 | 16 30 | 4½ |
| | | dep | 16 27 | 16 34 | 7 |
| 44.1 | York | arr | 16 59 | 17 00½ | 1½ |
| | | dep | 17 01 | 17 05 | 4 |
| — | | | — — | sig check | |
| 32.2 | Doncaster | arr | 17 30 | 17 35½ | 5½ |
| | | dep | 17 32 | 17 38 | 6 |
| 79.6 | Peterborough | arr | 18 24 | 18 25½ | 1½ |
| | | dep | 18 26 | 18 28 | 2 |
| | | | | pw check | |
| 76.4 | Kings Cross | arr | 19 16 | 19 17 | 1 |

Time lost by checks 13 minutes          Time regained by loco 18¼ minutes

Overtime at stations (heavy traffic) 6¼ minutes

The schedule includes recovery time on certain sections, but in any case to arrive only one minute late after a succession of delays costing 19½ minutes in all was a highly commendable performance, having particularly in mind the fast schedule in itself. The booked running times add up to 202 minutes for the run of 268.8 miles (430 km), an average of exactly 80 mph (128 km/h), but the net running times total up to no more than 183½ minutes, an average of 88 mph (141 km/h). The run from Darlington to York in making up most of the seven minute late start was quite a classic in itself: not quite so fast as those detailed on page 139, but even so yielding an average speed of 127 mph (203 km/h) over the 28.5 miles (45.5 km) from Northallerton to Skelton Junction. The time over the 44.1 miles (70.5 km) was 26 minutes 25 seconds start to stop, exactly 100 mph.

# HST 17.32 hours Doncaster-Peterborough

| Distance Miles | | Actual m s | Average Speed mph | Distance Miles | | Actual m s | Average Speed mph |
|---|---|---|---|---|---|---|---|
| 0.0 | DONCASTER | 0 00 | — | 46.3 | *Barkston South Junc* | 28 37 | 108.5 |
| 4.7 | *Rossington* | 5 13 | — | 50.5 | GRANTHAM | 31 05 | 102.5 |
| 8.3 | *Bawtry* | 7 31 | 94.0 | 55.9 | *Stoke summit* | 34 30 | 95.1 |
| — | | pw slack | — | 59.0 | *Milepost 97* | 36 15 | 106.5 |
| 12.1 | *Ranskill* | 9 59 | 93.0 | 62.0 | *Milepost 94* | 37 44 | 121.0 |
| 17.4 | RETFORD | 12 53 | 109.8 | 65.0 | *Milepost 91* | 39 08 | 128.7 |
| 22.0 | *Milepost 134* | 15 19 | 113.0 | 69.0 | *Milepost 87* | 41 01 | 128.0 |
| 24.1 | *Tuxford* | 16 24 | 116.0 | 71.1 | *Tallington* | 42 00 | 128.2 |
| 29.6 | *Carlton* | 19 38 | 100.2 | 74.0 | *Milepost 82* | 43 23 | 126.8 |
| 33.2 | *Bathley Lane* | 21 22 | 124.0 | 76.5 | *Werrington Junc* | 44 35 | 125.0 |
| 35.9 | NEWARK | 22 51 | 124.0 | 79.6 | PETERBOROUGH | 47 47 | |
| 40.6 | *Claypole* | 25 28 | 108.3 | | | | |

The accompanying log shows details of the excellent run from Doncaster to Peterborough, again showing the driver's persistent efforts to regain lost time. There were no temporary slowings enforced on this section; the restrictions below the line maximum speed of 125 mph (200 km/h) are those in regular operation, such as the '80' over Bawtry viaduct, and slight slowings for curves that have not yet been brought up to 125 mph standards. Otherwise we had a completely clear road, and the driver made the most of it, to arrive in Peterborough only 1½ minutes late after the delays that had led to a late start from Doncaster. We did very well also on the final stage, regaining a minute on the fast schedule of 50 minutes for the 76.4 miles (122 km) to Kings Cross in spite of a check for permanent way work south of Hitchin. The Eastern Region may well be proud of train running of this kind, showing how admirably the fine new equipment is being put to excellent purpose.

*An Edinburgh to Kings Cross HST passing Doncaster, with the offices of the famous Great Northern Railway locomotive works as a background* (G.S. Cutts).

# Chapter 15

# The HSTs in Scotland

The temporary rearrangement of the East Coast services during the period of the Penmanshiel Tunnel blockage brought a most interesting extension of HST activities, as referred to in earlier chapters of this book, and I had the privilege of riding in the driving cab on a non-stop run from Carlisle to Edinburgh. In Caledonian days such workings were relatively few. Instinctively one looks back to the time of the 1888 Race to the North, and to the stirring exploits of the famous 4-2-2 locomotive No 123; while within my own personal recollection the Edinburgh portion of the 10 am up Anglo-Scottish service to Euston was booked non-stop over the $100\frac{1}{2}$ miles (160 km) from Princes Street to Carlisle in the level two hours. I saw it several times coming into Carlisle, usually a few minutes before time, and headed by a Pickersgill 4-4-0. Even though it carried through coaches for Liverpool, Manchester and Birmingham, as well as for Euston, it rarely loaded to as much as 300 tons.

*Edinburgh in 1890.*

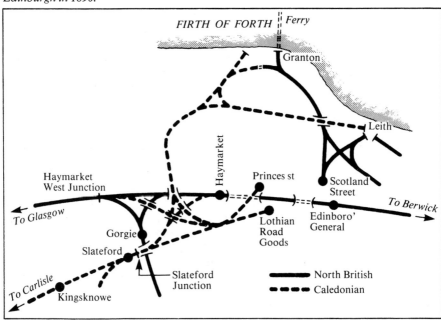

*A northbound HST drawing near to Berwick-on-Tweed, with the lonely Northumberland coast as a background* (D. Haviland).

In addition to its own terminal station in Edinburgh, the Caledonian had a comprehensive series of connections with the North British lines. After nationalisation, in 1948, there was clearly a good deal of overlapping of facilities, and in due course arrangements were made to route the Liverpool and Manchester services over the connection from Slateford Junction to Haymarket, and so into Waverley; and it was over this link that the diverted HSTs were run. These connections date back to the times before the Forth Bridge was constructed, when the Edinburgh, Perth and Dundee Railway had its terminus at Scotland Street, and 'Waverley', according to a map in an early edition of the Railway Clearing House book of junction diagrams, reproduced herewith, was known as Edinboro' General, with the spelling that justifiably infuriated all good Scots! Enough of ancient history, however. As will be appreciated from the map, Waverley is a little further from Carlisle than the now-closed Princes Street was, exactly one mile (1.6 km), making a run of 101.6 miles (162.5 km). I travelled in the driving cab of the 19.39 from Carlisle, which had an advertised time of 91 minutes to Edinburgh, though the working time is one minute less. The two drivers, from Haymarket depot, were both named Henderson, while the inspector who came with us, J. Dick, was an old footplate friend of mine. As always I was made very welcome in the cab.

Over the Caledonian line, as far as the Carstairs junction, these diverted HSTs were timed at the same speed as the 'Electric Scots', and running to the same line maximum speeds. Thus we had 40 minutes to cover the 57.8 miles (92 km) to Abington, with an average of 89.5 mph (143 km/h) over the 49.2 miles (79 km) from Gretna Junction. After negotiating the sharply curved Strawfrank and Dolphinton Junctions in the neighbourhood of Carstairs the timing was a good deal easier, with a maximum permitted line speed of 75 mph (120 km/h) and a useful piece of recovery time between Midcalder and Stateford Junctions. Because of the delays experienced in coming across country from Newcastle we left Carlisle four minutes late; but immediately getting away in characteristic HST style we were soon into the high 'nineties' when we had to slow for a long permanent way repairs slack, extending for rather more than a mile. This brought us to the head of the Solway Firth at no more than 20 mph (32 km/h); but although we had to regain speed from an altitude of little more than sea level, gradients of 1 in 200 were no handicap to an HST. With the engines working on four notches out of the five on the controller we quickly accelerated to 90 mph.

Although part of the line between Lockerbie and Beattock is subject to a line maximum speed of 100 mph, our driver aimed to keep the speed at around 90, and once we were up the second length of 1 in 200 gradient, to where Castlemilk signal box used to be, he was using no more than two notches on the controller. The permanent way check before Gretna had cost a full four minutes in running, but the sharp point-to-point timings over this part of the line precluded any appreciable regaining of time. At Beattock, travelling at 91 mph (145.5 km/h), the controller was put over to the 'full' position, and we made a very impressive ascent of the famous bank. At first the speed was sustained unvaryingly at 90 mph but on the upper reaches where the curves can be something of a hindrance there was some slight falling off, but as can be seen from the log a little over half a minute was gained on schedule on the bank. In the descent of Upper Clydesdale, apart from a brief 97 mph (155 km/h) before Elvanfoot the speed was maintained at around 90 mph and there was a slight signal check prior to the usual slow approach to the signals controlling the diverging route at Strawfrank Junction. But with the aid of recovery time the four minutes lost by the initial check at the Solway had now been regained. After recovery from that check, however, we had run the 58.3 miles (93 km) from Quintinshill to Thankerton in 39 minutes 6 seconds at an average speed of 89.5 mph (143 km/h).

In turning on to the Edinburgh line at Strawfrank Junction I am always reminded of gallant little '123' running the racing train in 1888. Unlike the West Coast main line to Glasgow, climbing is not finished at Strawfrank when bound for Edinburgh because the road is almost continuously adverse for the next nine miles up to Cobbinshaw, where the altitude is 880 ft (268 m) above sea level, as compared to 1,015 ft (309 m) at Beattock summit. Of course, with an HST it is the line limit of maximum speed rather than gradients that govern the rate of progress, and in recovering from the very severe slowing round the Strawfrank curves we took 10 minutes 24 seconds to climb the nine miles to Cobbinshaw. After that the descent is continuous all the way to Slateford Junction, at 1 in 100 nearly to Midcalder Junction, and then varying between 1 in 120 and 1 in 220. In 1888, on her fastest run, the little 4-2-2 No 123, with her four coaches, almost

*Across the Border—a southbound HST on the cliffs just south of Burnmouth in September 1978* (D. Haviland).

*The down 'Flying Scotsman' arriving at Edinburgh Waverley* (Brian Morrison).

exactly equalled our time from Strawfrank up to Cobbinshaw, and again down as far as Currie Hill—quite an extraordinary correspondence, showing a time of 22 minutes 14 seconds from Strawfrank against our 22 minutes 10 seconds. There was no correspondence in the manner of the final approaches to Edinburgh, for whereas we went slowly round the curves from Slateford Junction and through the Haymarket tunnel, little '123' roared in like the proverbial bomb, taking no more than 5 minutes 35 seconds for the last 5.5 miles (9 km) from Currie Hill into Princes Street. On the HST, with the aid of further recovery time, we were able to make an exactly punctual arrival in Waverley, with a net time of 82 minutes from Carlisle, 74.5 mph (119 km/h) average.

Returning from Scotland I travelled passenger by the 12.52 from Waverley. In this direction the rising gradients to Cobbinshaw were no handicap, and on the long 1 in 100 from Midcalder Junction we were doing 70 mph for most of the way. But with the restriction on line maximum speed our initial time of 32 minutes 22 seconds for the 28.4 miles (45 km) from Waverley to Strawfrank Junction does not show so spectacular an improvement upon earlier days as the HSTs can produce elsewhere. For example, in the last years of the Caledonian Railway the 10 am express from Princes Street to London Euston was allowed 41 minutes. Once on to the West Coast main line we really began to *run,* and the 59.9 miles (96 km) from Thankerton to Gretna Junction were covered in 39 minutes 12 seconds at an average of 90.4 mph (144.5 km/h). By Lockerbie, indeed, we were getting confortably ahead of time and the speed was distinctly eased down. As it was we arrived in Carlisle $3\frac{3}{4}$ minutes early, and allowing for the permanent way check at Midcalder the net time was only $81\frac{1}{2}$ minutes, a start to stop average of 75 mph (120 km/h).

In Scotland I had the interesting experience of travelling by HST in both directions between Edinburgh and Aberdeen, northbound in the driving cab. These runs went some way towards answering the question as to what kind of service improvement will be possible with HSTs over routes where their full high speed potential cannot be developed. For there is no question of being able to run at 125 mph or at 100, or anywhere near it. So why, it might be asked, use HSTs at all? With the changing of almost the entire daytime East Coast service south of Edinburgh over to the new trains it would, of course, be most inconvenient not to run the through services to Aberdeen with them, and the Edinburgh-Aberdeen line represents a northern counterpart to the practice of running the West of England HSTs through to Penzance. The line west of Plymouth is similarly handicapped in respect of the allowable maximum line speed. Despite all its hindrances to sustained fast running, however, the East Coast main line north of Edinburgh is a fascinating route to ride, especially as it always brings to me memories of footplate work going back to 1935, to North British 'Atlantics', Gresley 'Pacifics' and 2-8-2s, 'Green Arrows', and their less distinguished successors. So, on arrival in Edinburgh by the 15.00 hours from Kings Cross, it was in the keenest of anticipation that I walked the length of the HST, to what had been the rear cab, to be greeted by another old footplate friend, Inspector L. Duncan, of Aberdeen, and to meet Driver Tulloch.

It was now well after nine in the evening but, at the beginning of August, still broad daylight. Fortunately, too, the lowering skies and heavy rain that had dogged our running through the Border country had given way to a calm and clear evening that gave marvellously long vistas over the country, with its majestic succession of broad estuaries, picturesque coastal stretches and distant glimpses of hill ranges to the west. The first stretch, delightful though it is scenically, is the most slack-infested of all. This is reflected in that $31\frac{1}{2}$ minutes are allowed, start to stop, for the opening run of 25.9 miles (41 km) to Kirkcaldy. The day 'Aberdonian' of 1978 was booked 36 minutes here, while the Gresley 'Pacifics' were expected to keep almost as good time with loads up to 480 tons tare. We reached 75 mph (120 km/h) beside the Edinburgh airport at Turnhouse and then, with thoughts of the Firth of Forth ahead, it was strange

*An HST on the Forth Bridge* (British Railways).

to see directly in line with the track one of the towers, not of Sir Benjamin Baker's classic viaduct but of the new road bridge. It is not until one is passing Dalmeny that the three great cantilevers come into view. Speed is limited to 40 mph (64 km/h) across the bridge,—still, surely, the most magnificently proportioned of any in the whole world.

Speed was allowed to rise briefly to 50 mph (80 km/h) on the steep descent from North Queensferry, and then came the slack of 30 mph (48 km/h) through the Inverkeithing curves and junctions. Immediately beyond comes the sharp rise to Dalgetty, mostly at 1 in 94½, and here we had a brief flash of HST brilliance. I recalled a Gresley 'Pacific' here, not even holding the 28 mph (45 km/h) with which she had passed Inverkeithing, falling back at one point to 23 mph (37 km/h). Then there was the class '47' diesel, that fought back to 49 mph (78 km/h) on the climb; but the HST, on four notches out of five on the controller swept up to 58 mph (93 km/h) and then had to be restrained a little to observe the '50' over Dalgetty summit. Then there came restrictions to 45 mph (72 km/h) through Aberdour, 25 mph (40 km/h) at Burntisland, and 30 mph (48 km/h) through Kinghorn Tunnel. Meanwhile the prospects across the Firth of Forth, to where the lights of Leith and Edinburgh were already twinkling in the soft evening light, were delightful and we saw far down the Lothian coast to North Berwick Law and the Bass Rock. Between the slacks, as the accompanying log shows, speed was quickly worked up to 60 mph and we were a little behind time at Kirkcaldy, 32 minutes 25 seconds from Edinburgh. Station work was heavy, and we left 3¾ minutes late; but on the continuing run through Fife the capacity of the HST was shown off to excellent effect, where the 33.3 miles (53 km) on to Dundee are allowed 40½ minutes. It is true there are several intermediate speed restrictions, to 55 mph (88 km/h) at Cupar and Leuchars Junction, to 35 mph (56 km/h) at Ladybank Junction, and prolonged caution in the approach and crossing of the Tay Bridge; but there are opportunities for some good speed elsewhere.

## HST : 21.17 Edinburgh-Dundee

| Distance Miles | | Sch min | Actual m s | Speeds mph | Distance Miles | | Sch min | Actual m s | Speeds mph |
|---|---|---|---|---|---|---|---|---|---|
| 0.0 | EDINBURGH- | | | | 5.0 | *Thornton Junc* | | 6 00 | 64/60* |
| | WAVERLEY | 0 | 0 00 | — | 7.4 | *Markinch* | | 8 20 | 65 |
| 1.2 | Haymarket | | 2 52 | — | 9.0 | *Lochmuir* | | 9 58 | 60 |
| 6.5 | *Turnhouse* | | 7 50 | 75 | — | *Kingskettle* | | — — | 78 |
| 9.5 | Dalmeny | | 10 37 | 40* | 13.2 | Ladybank Junc | | 13 56 | 36* |
| 11.3 | North Queensferry | | 13 17 | 40*/50 | 16.4 | *Springfield* | | 16 08 | 75 |
| 13.2 | INVERKEITHING | | 15 45 | 28* | 18.7 | Cupar | | 18 40 | 55* |
| 16.1 | *Dalgetty* | | 19 25 | 58/50* | — | *Dairsie* | | — — | 75 |
| 17.4 | Aberdour | | 20 55 | 45*/50 | 25.0 | LEUCHARS JUNC | | 23 58 | 55* |
| 20.1 | BURNTISLAND | | 24 40 | 18*/60 | — | *St Fort* | | — — | 65 |
| 22.7 | Kinghorn | | 28 18 | 29*/62 | 30.6 | *Tay Bridge South* | | 29 58 | — |
| 25.9 | KIRKCALDY | 31½ | 32 25 | — | 32.5 | *Esplanade* | | 33 36 | — |
| 2.1 | *Dysart* | | 3 25 | 58 | 33.3 | DUNDEE | 40½ | 36 08 | — |

\* Speed restrictions

We began vigorously, accelerating to 58 mph (93 km/h) up the 1 in 100 to Dysart, but then went easily down, and through the Thornton junctions. I have also been faster with a '47' class up the ensuing climb to Lochmuir; but from there onwards we fairly romped along. I think that before the coming of the HSTs it must have been very rare to attain even time from the start anywhere

Left *An HST heading north taking the curve from the Tay Bridge past Dundee Esplanade station (now closed).* (British Railways).

Right *An APT test train standing on the loop line at Lockerbie station, September 20 1979* (D. Haviland).

between Edinburgh and Dundee; but on this trip we did so shortly after Cupar while, despite the subsequent slowings we were still inside even time at Tay Bridge South, 30.6 miles (49 km) from Kirkcaldy in 29 minutes 58 seconds. And what a prospect over the firth at 10.30 pm on this summer evening! It was still light enought for me to read my watches without switching on the light in the cab, while ahead of us, as we rolled across the lengthy bridge, the waterfront of Dundee was stretched out for miles in a galaxy of twinkling lights. We took 6 minutes 10 seconds to cover the 2.7 miles (4 km) across the bridge and down the grade into Dundee Tay Bridge station, but our time of 36 minutes 8 seconds from Kirkcaldy brought us slightly ahead of time, having made a start-to-stop average speed of 55 mph (88 km/h).

Where the HSTs are concerned it is always a case of comparing present with past, and on the line between Edinburgh and Dundee one comes up against the hair-raising run of Driver Joe McGregor on the last night of the 1895 race, with the Holmes 4-4-0 engine No 293. On this HST run of mine if, for comparative purposes, the effect of the Kirkcaldy stop is deducted we are left with a non-stop time of 66 minutes for the 59.2 miles (95 km) from Waverley to Dundee. Yet, believe it or not, the time in the early hours of August 22 1895 was 59 minutes! There is no doubt that in the thrill and venturesome spirit of the race, the curves were taken at speeds that would be intolerable today. In view of the theoretical considerations over the APT discussed in Chapter 9 of this book it would perhaps be correct to say that the speeds of 1895 on the North British line were not *unsafe;* it was merely that they were very uncomfortable for those paggengers who were on the racing train! In present conditions, to go much' faster than we did over the North British line, an APT would be needed.

The level stretch along the coast from Dundee to Arbroath was by tradition one of the least interesting parts of the journey. Drivers would drift along at 55 to 60 mph (88 to 96 km/h) however vigorously they had steamed their engines

elsewhere; but now all is indeed changed. The opening run through the tunnel, and up the sharp incline to Camperdown Junction was of necessity slow, but once up on to the level we quickly swept up to line maximum speed. This was the first time I had been in the driving cab of an HST after dark, and I was interested to see the effect of the headlight—only the left hand one being normally used. It lit up the mileposts clearly, and I would have been able to clock the speeds easily, had not the accuracy of the speedometer rendered any independent check unnecessary. The power of the HST also made the sharp switchback section between Arbroath and Montrose look like a straightforward level road, with the driver skilfully controlling the engines so as to climb the steep inclines at 65 to 70 mph (104 to 112 km/h) sometimes briefly using full power, but equally taking care not to exceed 70 mph on the equally steep descents. The time of 13 minutes 20 seconds start to stop was quite a record for me over this run of 13.7 miles (22 km). The diesel timing in 1978 was 16 minutes.

Both the concluding stretches were delayed by severe permanent way slacks, first a long one to 20 mph (32 km/h) in the neighbourhood of Fordoun, and then a shorter one, also to 20 mph, shortly after leaving Stonehaven. But having regard to the steeply uphill start out of Montrose, and the need to reduce speed over historic Kinnaber Junction, it was something of a feat to pass Laurencekirk in less than even time—10 miles (16 km), in 9 minutes 38 seconds having climbed the 1 in 100 gradient of the Marykirk bank at a steady 75 mph (120 km/h). But because of the permanent way check we were four minutes late into Stonehaven, 26 minutes 12 seconds from Montrose instead of the very sharp 22 minutes for this 24.5 miles (39 km); the final timing of 23 minutes for the concluding 16.2 miles (26 km) into Aberdeen includes some recovery time, however, and once we had observed the 20 mph (32 km/h) speed order, on the ascent to the cliffs overlooking the North Sea, we went hard and recovered all but a single minute of the lost time. Our total running time, inclusive of the speed restrictions

*An APT test train coming from Beattock in the neighbourhood of Lockerbie. The placid grazing of the cows suggest there is no environmental disturbance from the train dashing by at 125 mph!* (D. Haviland).

enforced, was 146 minutes 9 seconds for the 130.6 miles (209 km) from Edinburgh to Aberdeen, showing a running average of 53.5 mph (85.5 km/h) including the time inevitably consumed in the slowing down and accelerating periods from five intermediate stops. The diesel schedule times of 1978 added up to 165 minutes.

The impressive capacity of the HST over a route of so many physical difficulties was shown perhaps even more strikingly on my return journey from Aberdeen, by the 10.02 train, on which I travelled right through to Kings Cross as a passenger. The immediate start out of Aberdeen is hampered a little because there is a speed limit of 50 mph as far as Cove Bay (Milepost 236) while the speed restriction over Stonehaven viaduct applied also to the southbound line; but the restart, up the Fetteresso bank provided an interesting comparison with

*The down 10.00 HST train from London approaching the new cutting of Penmanshiel on the diversion line. The cutting leading to the now blocked tunnel can be seen in the left background. This picture shows clearly the exhaust deflector plates now being fitted to prevent the nose ends of the power cars, and the windscreens, being fouled by exhaust gases* (D. Haviland).

*The up 15.15 HST train Edinburgh to Kings Cross in the new cutting on the line circumventing the blocked Penmanshiel Tunnel, September 23 1979* (D. Haviland).

the performance of steam and diesel locomotives. The bank is mostly at 1 in 100, with a brief easing to 1 in 423 past the site of the now-removed Dunnottar signal box. The top of the bank is at Milepost $220\frac{1}{4}$ (from Carlisle by the former Caledonian Route), 4.7 miles (7.5 km) from the Stonehaven start. Steam locomotives, with their normal maximum loads used to take $9\frac{1}{2}$ to $9\frac{3}{4}$ minutes to clear that milepost, with ex-Caledonian 4-4-0s, Midland compounds, North British 'Atlantics' and the big Gresley 2-8-2s giving very consistent results. Then, in 1978, one of the '47' class diesel electrics, worked at full power throughout, set up a new record so far as I was concerned in passing that critical milepost in 6 minutes 57 seconds, at 53 mph (85 km/h). The steam locomotives were usually doing about 35 mph (56 km/h). Then came the HST; she was quickly up to 60 mph (96 km/h), went on accelerating all the way up, and topped the gradient at 72 mph (115 km/h) in 5 minutes 33 seconds from the start at Stonehaven. There was no restriction at Fordoun on the up line, and we passed Craigo 19.8 miles (31 km) in a mere 18 minutes from the start. Even though a slowing to 15 mph (24 km/h) was required at Kinnaber Junction we still reached Montrose in less than even time.

The exhilarating running continued to Dundee. We quickly accelerated to 60 mph on the 1 in 88 ascent out of Montrose and ran fast and uniformly over the undulations thence to Arbroath, while on the final stretch along the coast we had a most exhuberant sprint, with an average speed of 77 mph (123 km/h) over 14 miles (22 km) from Elliott Junction, before the very slow entry, through the tunnel to Tay Bridge station. As the log overleaf shows we had another fast run on the continuation through Fife, and arrived outside Edinburgh a little before they were ready for us. The running times in this direction totalled up to 145 minutes 12 seconds, again showing a substantial improvement on any previous scheduling. A typical very good run at the height of the steam era, with the North British and the Gresley types at the peak of their achievements, gave a total time of 183 minutes. Of course it can be argued that there *ought* to be a big improvement, seeing that the HSTs have an engine horsepower of 4,500 to haul a trailing load of no more than eight cars, with a tare weight of around 280 tons. It is, however, not a case of straight comparisons where such a difficult route as that from Edinburgh to Aberdeen is concerned.

To the limited extent to which they have so far been used, the HSTs have made a striking impact upon Scottish railway operating. So far as possible running times are concerned, one looks back inevitably to the records of the 1895 race, when the fastest East Coast time was 8 hours 40 minutes for the 524 miles (888 km) from Kings Cross to Aberdeen. It is remarkable, however, to

# HST : 11.27 Dundee-Edinburgh

| Distance Miles | | Actual m s | Speeds mph | Distance Miles | | Actual m s | Speeds mph |
|---|---|---|---|---|---|---|---|
| 0.0 | DUNDEE | 0 00 | — | 33.3 | KIRKCALDY | 34 38 | — |
| 2.7 | *Tay Bridge South* | 5 03 | — | 2.1 | *Seafield* | 2 38 | |
| 4.6 | *St Fort* | 7 03 | 71½ | 3.2 | Kinghorn | 3 56 | 61/27* |
| 8.3 | LEUCHARS JUNC | 10 26 | 55* | 5.8 | BURNTISLAND | 7 55 | 22* |
| 11.6 | *Dairsie* | 13 19 | 77½ | 8.5 | Aberdour | 11 37 | 50 |
| 14.6 | Cupar | 16 06 | 52* | — | *Dalgetty* | — — | 60 |
| 16.9 | *Springfield* | 18 08 | 77 | 12.9 | INVERKEITHING | 16 43 | 29* |
| 20.1 | *Ladybank Junc* | 20 06 | 49* | 14.6 | North Queensferry | 19 20 | 40 |
| — | *Kingskettle* | — — | 75 | 16.4 | Dalmeny | 23 05 | — |
| — | *Falkland Road* | — — | 65* | 19.4 | *Turnhouse* | — — | 76½ |
| 24.3 | *Lochmuir* | 24 52 | 56* | 24.7 | Haymarket | 29 53 | — |
| 25.9 | *Markinch* | 26 23 | 69/63 | — | | sig stop | — |
| 28.3 | *Thornton Junc* | 28 47 | 58* | 25.9 | EDINBURGH-WAVERLEY | 35 18 | |
| 31.2 | *Dysart* | 31 51 | — | | | | |

\* Speed restrictions

record that during the emergency of 1979 the 15.00 hours HST from Kings Cross was booked into Aberdeen at 23.54, including 29 minutes standing time at the *ten* intermediate stops, as well as having 37.4 miles (60 km) farther to go. Whereas the 'racer' of 1895 had the most preferential treatment, the booked running time of the 15.00 of 1979 was only 505 minutes, for a journey of 567 miles (907 km). Furthermore this included the 60 miles (96 km) of very slow running between Newcastle and Carlisle, as discussed in the previous chapter. The 10.02 up from Aberdeen was allowed 9 hours 14 minutes to Kings Cross, with 12 intermediate stops and, on my own journey, the total running time inclusive of all checks was 488 minutes 14 seconds for the distance of 560.7 miles (897 km), an average of 69 mph (110 km/h). The overall average, inclusive of all stops, and an arrival in London one minute late was 60.8 mph (97 km/h). These are impressive figures and show what can be done on lengthy journeys by the HSTs even though some parts of the route may be subject to much restricted speed.

# HST : 19.39 Carlisle-Edinburgh

| Distance Miles | | Sch min | Actual m s | Speeds mph | Distance Miles | | | Actual m s | Speeds mph |
|---|---|---|---|---|---|---|---|---|---|
| 0.0 | CARLISLE | 0 | 0 00 | — | 52.6 | *Elvanfoot* | | 40 23 | 97/85 |
| 2.2 | *Kingmoor Box* | | 3 09 | 77 | 57.8 | *Abington* | 40 | 43 49 | 93 |
| 5.5 | *Milepost 5½* | | 5 29 | 97 | 63.2 | *Lamington* | | 47 21 | 90 |
| — | | | pw slack | 20 | 66.9 | *Symington* | | 49 46 | 88/91 |
| 8.6 | *Gretna Junc* | 7 | 10 31 | 69 | 68.5 | *Thankerton* | | 50 51 | 95 |
| 10.2 | *Quintinshill* | 8 | 11 45 | 82 | — | | | sigs | |
| 13.0 | *Kirkpatrick* | | 13 42 | 90 | 73.2 | *Strawfrank Junc* | 55½ | 55 15 | 15 |
| 16.7 | *Kirtlebridge* | | 16 11 | 95/86 | 79.1 | *Auchengray* | | 62 49 | 72 |
| 22.7 | *Castlemilk* | | 20 15 | 90 | 82.2 | *Cobbinshaw* | | 65 39 | 65 |
| 25.8 | LOCKERBIE | 18 | 22 15 | 92 | 85.3 | *Harburn* | | 68 23 | 75 (max) |
| 31.0 | *Milepost 31* | | 25 43 | 86 | 89.3 | *Midcalder Junc* | 71 | 71 56 | 53/50 |
| 34.0 | *Milepost 34* | | 27 46 | 94 | 90.5 | Midcalder | | 73 05 | — |
| 37.0 | *Milepost 37* | | 29 43 | 90 | 95.1 | Currie Hill | | 77 25 | 75 |
| 39.7 | *Beattock* | 27 | 31 33 | 91 | 97.6 | Kingsknowe | | 79 43 | — |
| 42.0 | *Milepost 42* | | 33 05 | 90 | 98.9 | *Slateford Junc* | 85 | 81 10 | — |
| 44.0 | *Milepost 44* | | 34 24 | 90 | 100.2 | Haymarket | 87 | 83 30 | — |
| 46.0 | *Milepost 46* | | 35 47 | — | 101.6 | EDINBURGH-WAVERLEY | 90 | 86 05 | — |
| 48.0 | *Milepost 48* | | 37 13 | 83 | | | | | |
| 49.7 | *Summit* | 34½ | 38 29 | 80 | | | | | |

## HST : 12.52 Edinburgh-Carlisle

| Distance Miles | Actual m s | Speeds mph | Distance Miles | Actual m s | Speeds mph |
|---|---|---|---|---|---|
| 0.0 EDINBURGH-WAVERLEY | 0 00 | — | 43.8 *Abington* | 43 11 | 91 |
| 1.4 Haymarket | 2 53 | — | 49.0 *Elvanfoot* | 46 38 | 95 |
| 2.7 *Slateford Junc* | 5 05 | — | 51.9 *Summit* | 48 40 | 85 |
| 4.0 Kingsknowe | 6 25 | 64 | 55.6 *Milepost 46* | 51 07 | — |
| 6.5 Currie Hill | 7 45 | 64 | 59.6 *Milepost 42* | 53 50 | — |
| — | pw check | 20 | 61.9 *Beattock* | 55 17 | 95/90 |
| 11.1 Midcalder | 13 57 | — | 67.1 *Wamphray* | 58 41 | 100 |
| 12.3 *Midcalder Junc* | 16 13 | 53 | 75.8 LOCKERBIE | 64 12 | 88/92 |
| 19.4 *Cobbinshaw* | 22 43 | 70/65 | — *Castlemilk* | — — | 88 |
| 22.5 *Auchengray* | 26 00 | 72 (max) | 84.9 *Kirtlebridge* | 70 15 | 90 (max) |
| 28.4 *Strawfrank Junc* | 32 22 | 25 | 88.6 *Kirkpatrick* | 72 51 | 86 |
| 33.1 *Thankerton* | 36 35 | — | 93.0 *Gretna Junc* | 75 47 | eased |
| 34.7 *Symington* | 37 40 | 101 | 99.4 *Kingmoor Box* | 80 37 | — |
| 38.4 *Lamington* | 39 51 | 97 | 101.6 CARLISLE | 84 17 | — |

Schedule 88 minutes. Net time 81½ minutes.

## HST : 22.32½ Dundee-Aberdeen

| Distance Miles | Sch min | Actual m s | Speeds mph | Distance Miles | Sch | Actual m s | Speeds mph |
|---|---|---|---|---|---|---|---|
| 0.0 DUNDEE | 0 | 0 00 | — | 13.7 MONTROSE | 13 | 13 20 | — |
| 0.7 *Camperdown Junc* | | 2 35 | — | 2.6 *Kinnaber Junc* | | 3 40 | — |
| 4.0 Broughty Ferry | | 6 23 | 75 | 4.7 *Craigo* | | 5 40 | 77/70 |
| 6.4 Monifieth | | 8 17 | 76 | 10.0 *Laurencekirk* | | 9 38 | 75 |
| 9.3 Barry Links | | 10 32 | 76 | 13.3 *Fordoun* | | 12 51 | |
| 10.9 Carnoustie | | 11 50 | 78 | — | | pw slack | 20 |
| 15.6 *Elliott Junc* | | 15 88 | — | 19.0 *Carmont* | | 20 22 | 75/60* |
| 17.0 ARBROATH | 19 | 18 00 | | 24.5 STONEHAVEN | 22 | 26 12 | — |
| — | | — — | 63 | — | | pw slack | 20 |
| 6.2 *Inverkeilor* | | 5 14 | 70 | 8.0 *Portlethen Box* | | 7 40 | 80/65 |
| — *Lunan Bay* | | — — | 65 | — | | — — | 80 |
| — *Milepost 26¼* | | — — | 70 | 15.6 *Ferryhill Junc* | | 18 23 | — |
| 11.6 *Usan Box* | | 10 05 | — | 16.2 ABERDEEN | 22 | 20 04 | — |

* Speed restriction

## HST : 10.02 Aberdeen-Dundee

| Distance Miles | Actual m s | Speeds mph | Distance Miles | Actual m s | Speeds mph |
|---|---|---|---|---|---|
| 0.0 ABERDEEN | 0 00 | — | 19.8 *Craigo* | 17 58 | 72 |
| 3.1 *Milepost 238* | 5 04 | 50* | 21.9 *Kinnaber Junc* | 20 46 | 15* |
| 5.1 *Milepost 236* | 7 19 | 50* | 24.5 MONTROSE | 24 10 | — |
| 7.1 *Milepost 234* | 9 07 | — | 2.2 *Milepost 28½* | 3 30 | — |
| 11.6 Muchalls | 12 43 | 75 | 3.7 *Milepost 27* | 5 00 | 60 |
| — | pw slack | 20 | 7.5 *Inverkeilor* | 8 16 | 75/68 |
| 16.2 STONEHAVEN | 18 20 | | 9.7 *Milepost 21* | 10 03 | 77½ |
| 0.9 *Milepost 224* | 2 06 | — | — | slack | — |
| 1.9 *Milepost 223* | 3 07 | — | 13.7 ARBROATH | 15 36 | — |
| 2.9 *Milepost 222* | 4 02 | 66 | 1.4 *Elliott Junc* | 2 22 | 75 |
| 3.9 *Milepost 221* | 4 55 | — | 6.1 Carnoustie | 5 55 | 82/75 |
| 4.7 *Milepost 220¼* | 5 33 | 72/65* | 10.6 Monifieth | 9 23 | 82 |
| 11.2 *Fordoun* | 11 03 | 75/82 | 13.0 Broughty Ferry | 11 15 | 76½ |
| 14.5 *Laurencekirk* | 13 39 | 70* | 16.3 *Camperdown Junc* | 14 40 | — |
| — | — — | 80½/69* | 17.0 DUNDEE | 17 40 | — |

* Speed restrictions

# Chapter 16

# Gala days on the Western

Early in April 1979 I had a telephone call from the Western Region at Bristol, telling me that an attempt was to be made on the world record for a start-to-stop average speed by a diesel powered train, and asking if I would be free to join them and log the running. I am afraid that if I had any other engagements for the morning in question they would have been tactfully pushed to one side; for when the Western Region, like its predecessor the Great Western Railway, is set upon record breaking what are other commitments! My mind went back to earlier occasions when distinguished manipulators of the stop-watch were invited to join special runs. There was July 14 1903, for example, when Charles Rous-Marten and the Rev W.J. Scott joined the Royal advance portion of the down 'Cornishman', and logged a record run to Plymouth made by the 4-4-0 engine *City of Bath*. Then there was June 5 1932 when, with the engine *Tregenna Castle*, a world record was made with the 'Cheltenham Flyer' duly logged by Cecil J. Allen and Humphrey Baker. They both proved to be outstanding occasions but, in their way, vastly different from what was planned for April 10 1979.

The HSTs on the Bristol and South Wales services, like the great majority of fast express trains on British Railways today have recovery times included in their schedule to provide for punctual arrival at destinations on those occasions when maintenance work on the line necessitates the imposition of temporary speed restrictions over certain sections. The 09.20 from Paddington, for example, which is booked to run the 94 miles (150 km) to Chippenham in $57\frac{1}{2}$ minutes start to stop has $4\frac{1}{4}$ minutes of recovery time between Didcot and Swindon. Thus, if running up to 'full recovery standard', as it is termed, the train would reach Chippenham in 53 minutes, making a start-to-stop average speed of 106.3 mph (170 km/h) instead of the scheduled 98 mph (157 km/h). During that particular week in April there was no engineering work on the line programmed, and the train would have a clear run; but there was another factor to be considered. Leaving Paddington only five minutes ahead was another HST, non-stop to Newport, and running to the same point to point times as far as the bifurcation, at Wootton Bassett. In the ordinary way, with no permanent way slowings in prospect that train would have been justified in easing down after Didcot was passed and taking advantage of the recovery time in the schedule. This, of course, would have reacted back on to the 09.20 and involved the latter in signal checks. So if record running was to be made the pre-planning had to be more comprehensive.

There was a parallel here to June 5 1932. The 'Cheltenham Flyer' then left

Swindon at 3.48 pm and was due in Paddington at 4.55 pm. Ahead of it, joining the main line from the Berks and Hants line at Reading, was the up Cornish Riviera Express due into Paddington at 4.45 pm. If, as was hoped, the 'Cheltenham Flyer' was breaking records there was every chance of the 'Limited' blocking her in the final stages. So a locomotive inspector was put on, with instructions to see that the famous holiday train from the west ran well ahead of time. He, and the engine crew made no mistake about it, because they got in seven minutes early. So, also on April 10 1979, an inspector was put on to the 09.15 South Wales HST with instructions to see that its crew ran up to full recovery standards as far as Wootton Bassett. Although the planning was thus very careful from the operating point of view, not a hint that anything spectacular was being attempted was made public and I, personally, was sworn to secrecy. There is nothing worse than announcing special intentions and then, if things do not work out, having to explain why afterwards!

That not even a suppressed air of expectancy prevailed at Paddington that morning is evident from a letter I received from America sometime afterwards, from Mr F.M. Bragg, of Richmond, Virginia. He wrote: 'I was in Europe and UK the first two weeks of April of this year trying to cover as much mileage on my Eurail and Britrail passes as possible and still leave a little time for sightseeing. On April 10 I planned to go to Dublin, Ireland, leaving Paddington Station sometime around 09.00 for Fishguard, thence to Rosslare Harbor, etc. At about 08.00 on that date I was consulting with the travel agent in Paddington who informed me that rail transportation from Rosslare Harbor to Dublin was very uncertain and that I had better go by way of Holyhead. The train for Holyhead was to leave from Euston at 10.00. As I had plenty of time to get to Euston I loitered about the platforms at Paddington filming the activity, etc, and might very well have unknowingly included you in some of my scenes. Of course, I knew nothing of the attempt to break the world speed record and

*A high level view of an HST outside Paddington* (Brian Morrison).

would not have noticed anything unusual about the activity that morning'.

Just before starting time a little group of Western Region men and I slipped into some reserved seats in the rearmost coach of the train, having noted that the critical 09.15 for South Wales had left on time. Knowing what HSTs have done in the past, if for nothing higher than my own recordings of maximum speeds in ordinary service up to 136 mph (217.5 km/h), I just wondered if something really special was to be attempted on this occasion; but the whole essence of this particular enterprise was to be strict observance of the speed limits—and in any case, as mentioned in an earlier chapter of this book, apparatus has now been added that automatically cuts off the power if speed exceeds a small margin above 125 mph. In all my recent travelling on both Western and Eastern Region HSTs the maximum speed has not exceeded 128 mph. One of the most remarkable features of HST performance, however, is its astonishing consistency, so much so that for some time prior to April 10 1979, I had ceased to take note of the individual power cars used on the trains by which I travelled; and on what proved to be a record breaking morning our time to passing Reading was no more than 17 seconds faster than on my last previous run down from London, on March 23 1979. On that occasion we had reached Chippenham in exactly 56 minutes in spite of a long and severe slowing for permanent way work, which had absorbed all our 4½ minutes recovery time. The net time on this earlier occasion was no more than 51½ minutes, which was an average speed of 109.3 mph. If we bettered this, as my Western Region friends hoped we should do, it would not be a case of making a world record for diesel, but for any form of rail traction. The Japanese on their much publicised Skinkansen line have a train averaging 110 mph from Nagoya to Skizouka; and if the 09.20 from Paddington that morning could better the net time of my run of March 23 by no more than a single minute it would be an outright world record.

## The Western Region World Record run
## 09.20 HST Paddington-Chippenham April 10 1979

| Distance Miles | | Sch min | Actual m s | Average Speeds mph | Dist Miles | | Sch min | Actual m s | Average Speeds mph |
|---|---|---|---|---|---|---|---|---|---|
| 0.0 | PADDINGTON | 0 | 0 00 | — | 44.75 | Goring | | 25 29 | 123.0 |
| 2.0 | *Milepost 2* | | 3 14 | — | 48.5 | Cholsey | | 27 18 | 123.4 |
| 3.25 | *Milepost 3¼* | | 4 10 | 80.6 | 51.5 | *Milepost 51½* | | 28 45 | 124.0 |
| 5.7 | Ealing Broadway | | 5 37 | — | 53.1 | DIDCOT | 31 | 29 31 | — |
| 6.0 | *Milepost 6* | | 5 48 | 100.9 | 56.5 | Steventon | | 31 09 | 124.8 |
| 7.5 | *Milepost 7½* | | 6 36 | 112.5 | 60.5 | *Milepost 60¼* | | 33 04 | 124.8 |
| 9.0 | Southall (MP 9) | 8½ | 7 21 | 120.0 | 64.0 | *Milepost 64* | | 34 45 | 124.8 |
| 11.0 | *Milepost 11* | | 8 19 | 124.0 | 66.5 | Uffington | | 35 57 | 125.0 |
| 13.25 | West Drayton | | 9 24 | 124.5 | 69.0 | *Milepost 69* | | 37 08 | 126.3 |
| 16.25 | Langley | | 10 50 | 125.4 | 71.5 | Shrivenham | | 38 20 | 125.0 |
| 18.5 | SLOUGH | 13 | 11 55 | 124.5 | 73.75 | *Milepost 73¾* | | 39 25 | 124.5 |
| 21.0 | Burnham | | 13 07 | 125.0 | 76.0 | *Milepost 76* | | 40 36 | 114.0 |
| 24.2 | Maidenhead | 16 | 14 39 | 125.0 | 77.3 | SWINDON | 47½ | 41 24 | 97.6 |
| 27.0 | *Milepost 27* | | 16 00 | 124.4 | 80.0 | *Milepost 80* | | 42 57 | 104.3 |
| 29.0 | *Milepost 29* | | 16 57 | 126.2 | 83.0 | Wootton Bassett | | | |
| 31.0 | Twyford | 19 | 17 54 | 126.2 | | (MP 83) | 51 | 44 27 | 120.0 |
| 33.0 | *Milepost 33* | | 18 52 | 124.1 | 85.0 | *Milepost 85* | | 45 25 | 124.2 |
| 35.0 | *Milepost 35* | | 19 51 | 122.1 | 87.75 | Dauntsey | | 46 45 | 123.8 |
| 36.0 | READING | 21½ | 20 33 | 85.8 | 91.0 | *Milepost 91* | | 48 18 | 125.8 |
| 38.5 | *Milepost 38½* | | 22 15 | 88.3 | 92.75 | *Milepost 92¾* | | 49 10 | 121.0 |
| 41.5 | Pangbourne | | 23 54 | 109.0 | 94.0 | CHIPPENHAM | 57½ | 50 31 | — |

Naturally there was a good deal of suppressed excitement in our little party that morning, as we began ticking off the miles, and slowly but steadily drew ahead of the earlier run. On such an important occasion I took a very detailed record, which is reproduced herewith. From this it will be seen that we reached 100 mph at Ealing Broadway, 5.7 miles (9 km) out of the terminus, and 120 mph by Southall. After that a most meticulous observation of the line maximum speed of 125 mph was made, and the average speed for the 26 miles (41.5 km) between mileposts 9 and 35 was 124.7 mph (199.5 km/h). Then came the speed restriction to 80 mph through the station at Reading, and we were back to 123 mph (197 km/h) by Goring, a little over eight miles (13 km) farther on. Again there was a punctilious observance of the speed limit, but by Didcot we were 1½ minutes ahead of time, and the prospects of a world record seemed to be coming within our grasp. Up the slight gradients through the Vale of the White Horse we averaged a shade over the '125', but the driver slightly overdid the speed restriction through Swindon. Instead of 100 mph he came down to a little over 90, but even so we were six minutes early. From the summit of the line, at milepost 80, there used to be the great racing ground for steam locomotives, and it was as the foot of the Dauntsey bank that I clocked my highest ever with the Great Western 'King' class 4-6-0, 102½ mph (164 km/h). With the HST that morning it was no different from any other part of the journey, the speed being just fractionally over the '125', but there was a tearing finish to a very smooth stop in Chippenham—50 minutes 31 seconds from Paddington—and a world record average speed of 111.6 mph (178.5 km/h) from start to stop.

Then all reticence on behalf of Western Region disappeared. The intercom on the train told passengers all about it. The loud speakers on Chippenham station told arriving and waiting people, while at Bath, when the approach of the train was announced, the fact that earlier in its journey a world record had been made was also included in the broadcast. The fact that it had been done in so

*After the record run; the author photographed with the two drivers at Bristol.*

unobtrusive a manner, so much as a matter of course, set the occasion apart
from other record runs on other parts of British Railways. There was no
sensationally bad riding of the coaches to cause acute apprehension by railway
staff, as on the Invitation Run of 'The Silver Jubilee' in September 1935; no
smashing of crockery, as on the too-rapid entry into Crewe by the 'Coronation
Scot' in 1937, no damage to the locomotive, as with *Mallard* in 1938. On the
HST one lady passenger was so unimpressed by the occasion that she
complained to the train staff about the long wait at Chippenham, where we had
arrived seven minutes early!

It is naturally interesting to speculate as to how the overall average speed
might have been pushed up had we bent the rules slightly. In the course of my
ordinary travelling I have frequently noted maximum speeds of 128 mph (205
km/h) quite apart from that occasion in 1977, referred to in Chapter 13, when
an eastbound Western Region train ran up to 136 mph (217.5 km/h) twice
between Swindon and Paddington. If, for sake of argument, the 09.20 of April
10 1979, had averaged 128 mph (205 km/h) instead of 124.7 mph (199.5 km/h)
between mileposts 9 and 35, and again through the Vale of the White Horse, the
overall time would have been cut by another half minute, and the average
brought up to nearly 113 mph (181 km/h). As comparison will naturally be
made with the Japanese Shinkansen, which is virtually free from any speed
restrictions between stopping stations, it is interesting to check the effect of the
two permanent restrictions on the Paddington-Chippenham run. If, instead of
slowing to 80 and 100 mph at Reading and Swindon respectively, one could
maintain full line speed throughout, no more than $1\frac{1}{2}$ minutes would be saved.
Though slowing to 80 mph is a big reduction from 125 mph the capacity of the
HST for acceleration afterwards is such that the effect of the slack is
surprisingly small.

To raise the limit at a station like Reading is a matter not only of track
alignment. In the down direction the non-stopping HSTs pass through a
platform line, and a platform often thronged with passengers. While safety
from trains passing at maximum speed can be reasonably assured at stations like
Slough, Maidenhead, and Didcot, by the provision of yellow lines on the
platform edges to mark the limit of safety, this could not be done at a very busy
station like Reading; and as I have shown the time that would be saved by
raising the speed limit would scarcely be worth while. So far as Reading is
concerned, as if to show that the run of April 10 1979 was no mere flash in the
pan, the Western Region marginally beat their own and the world record on
Friday April 27. On that day the 17.20 from Paddington, which normally runs
non-stop to Chippenham, was required to make a special stop at Reading. From
the restart the 58 miles (93 km) to Chippenham were covered in 31 minutes
10 seconds start to stop, showing an average speed of 111.68 mph (178.68
km/h). I was not a passenger myself on that occasion, but the run was logged by
a regular traveller who is a fully experienced observer. For 54 miles (86 km) of
that run the average speed was a shade over 120 mph.

September 27 seems to be a recurring red letter day for railway record
breaking. In 1825 it saw the opening of the Stockton and Darlington Railway,
and in 1935 the sensational 'Invitation Run' of Britain's first streamline train
the LNER 'Silver Jubilee', when the unprecedented maximum speed of $112\frac{1}{2}$
mph (180 km/h) was attained. Then, in 1979, the Western Region of British
Railways chose that same date for a record-breaking Invitation run of a

# HST Demonstration run September 27 1979
# 11.05 Exeter-Paddington

| Distance Miles | | Sch min | Actual m s | Average Speeds mph | Distance Miles | | Sch min | Actual m s | Average Speeds mph |
|---|---|---|---|---|---|---|---|---|---|
| 0.0 | EXETER | | | | 86.45 | Lavington | | 62 36 | 92.7 |
| | (ST DAVIDS) | 0 | 0 00 | — | — | | | pw slow | — |
| 1.25 | Cowley Bridge | | | | 94.55 | Woodborough | 70¼ | 70 19 | 63.0 |
| | Junc | | 2 04 | 36.3 | 103.35 | Savernake | | 76 07 | 91.0 |
| 3.70 | Stoke Canon | | 4 04 | 73.5 | 107.00 | Bedwyn | 79¼ | 79 13 | 70.6 |
| 8.40 | Hele | | 7 10 | 91.0 | 119.90 | Hungerford | | 83 06 | 75.7 |
| 14.80 | Tiverton Junc | | 11 46 | 83.5 | 120.35 | NEWBURY | 89½ | 89 03 | 85.2 |
| 19.90 | Whiteball Box | 15½ | 15 03 | 93.2 | 128.65 | Aldermaston | | 94 53 | 85.4 |
| 23.65 | Wellington | | 17 36 | 88.2 | 135.60 | Southcote Junc | | 99 42 | 86.6 |
| 30.75 | TAUNTON | 23 | 22 22 | 89.4 | 137.45 | READING | 104¼ | 102 16 | 43.2 |
| 38.65 | Athelney | | 27 45 | 88.0 | 142.45 | Twyford | | 105 48 | 84.9 |
| 47.95 | Somerton | | 33 48 | 92.2 | 149.20 | Maidenhead | | 109 09 | 120.9 |
| 53.45 | Keinton | | | | 155.00 | SLOUGH | 114¼ | 111 56 | 125.0 |
| | Mandeville | | 37 31 | 88.8 | 160.20 | West Drayton | | 114 25 | 125.6 |
| 58.30 | CASTLE CARY | 42 | 40 50 | 87.7 | 167.70 | Ealing Broadway | | 118 02 | 124.4 |
| 66.95 | Witham | | 47 07 | 82.6 | — | | | pw slow 60 mph | |
| 71.20 | Blatchbridge Junc | *arr* | 50 13 | 82.3 | 172.20 | Westbourne | | | |
| | | *dep* | 51 12 | — | | Park | | 121 40 | — |
| 73.20 | Clink Road Junc | | 53 44 | 47.4 | 173.50 | PADDINGTON | 130 | 124 10 | — |
| 78.85 | Heywood Road | | | | | NET TIME: 119¼ min. | | | |
| | Junc | 57 | 57 41 | 85.8 | | | | | |

different kind. Guests from Cornwall and Devon, joining at stations where the
'Cornish Riviera Express' stops, were taken for a high speed trip to Paddington
and back, as a preliminary to the substantial acceleration of the service which
came into effect on the following Monday.

This special train, which left Penzance at 08.25, was timed to cover the 305
miles (488 km/h) to London, Paddington, in 4 hours 50 minutes, 41 minutes
faster than the accelerated time from October 1 onwards. The almost
continuous curvature on the line in Cornwall and South Devon was not suitable
for very fast running in the normal HST style; but the Special did extremely well
to cover the 131.5 miles (210 km) from Penzance to Exeter in 155½ minutes,
inclusive of seven stops at stations to take up guests, and a brief stop for adverse
signals outside Plymouth. The running time from Penzance to Exeter was 148¾
minutes, a fine average, over such a route, of 53.1 mph (85 km/h).

Then came the non-stop run of 173.5 miles (277.5 km/h) from Exeter to
Paddington, booked in 130 minutes, at an average speed of 80 mph (128 km/h).
In comparing this with some of the very fast runs made by the HST sets
elsewhere the speed limits imposed over the whole of the line west of Reading
must be borne in mind. Actually, despite a stop for adverse signals at Blatchbridge Junction, at the entrance to the Frome bypass line, and a temporary
speed restriction to 20 mph (32 km/h) near Lavington the run was made in 124
minutes 10 seconds, to complete the journey from Penzance in the truly record
time of 4 hours 43 minutes an overall average speed of 64.7 mph (103.5 km/h).
In the greatest days of steam on the 'Cornish Riviera Express' the time was 6½
hours, with two fewer stops.

On the more spectacular part of the run on September 27 1979, the effect of
the permanent speed restrictions at present in force can be appreciated by some
of the average speeds. Over one of the least affected lengths, between Stoke

Canon and Castle Cary, the average was 89.3 mph (143 km/h). Then the stop at Blatchbridge and the slowing at Lavington lowered the average between Castle Cary and Savernake to 77 mph (123 km/h), while the downhill stretch from Savernake to Southcote Junction did not produce a higher average than 82 mph (131 km/h) because of the many intermediate slowings for curves. Once on to the Bristol main line, however, the $25\frac{1}{4}$ miles (40 km) from Twyford to Ealing Broadway were dashed off at an average of 124.3 mph (199 km/h).

Mr P.G. Barlow, Train Planning Officer of Western Region, to whom I am indebted for the detailed log and other information on the run, estimates that the delays experienced cost approximately 5 minutes, leaving a net running time from Exeter to Paddington of $119\frac{1}{4}$ minutes. This average of 87.5 mph (140 km/h) is remarkable seeing that so much of the distance is limited to an overall maximum speed of 90 mph (144 km/h). It gives pleasurable anticipations of what is likely to be achieved over this route, when the track improvements referred to in Chapter 3 of this book are completed; gala days on the Western indeed!

# Chapter 17

# 'Watch out! APT about'

For the title of this chapter I have taken the heading of a panel in a special traffic notice issued by Scottish Region in June 1979. This followed an earlier notice advising staff that from February 18 1979, the road tests of the prototype APT would begin on the former Caledonian main line between Glasgow and Carlisle. While the technologists of the Chief Mechanical and Electrical Engineer's department had a vast amount of observation to do in respect of the running of the train, and the behaviour in full speed service of the numerous novel features of design and construction, it hardly needs to be added that the train itself, and its physical reaction to the track and its geometry, is only one facet of the highly complex business of introducing such an innovation. There is the safety of men working on the line. Since the electrification of the West Coast main line between Weaver Junction and Glasgow the men whose duties take them on to the track have been accustomed enough to speeds of 100 mph but the increase to 125 mph made it necessary to issue special precautionary notices, and I am permitted to quote the relevant passage from that of June 1979, thus:

### 'Watch out! APT about

#### between Carlisle and Glasgow Central via Beattock.

From 18 February 1979 the Advanced Passenger Train will commence running on the Carlisle—Glasgow Central via Beattock line at speeds up to 125 mph.

Staff must exercise the utmost vigilance when walking the track and observe the provisions of the 'Safety Code for Track Walking' (BR2999/12).

Attention is specially drawn to the reduced time which will be available from staff sighting an APT and clearing to a point of safety.

A place of safety is one which will allow 2.5 m (8′ 3″) clearance from the track.

If unable to reach a place of safety in time staff must lie down in the cess.

In areas of limited clearance the following additional safeguards are provided:-

1. Where refuges are not provided, the extent of limited clearance will be denoted by blue and white chequered plate lettered "Warning—No Refuges".

2. Where clearance is limited on both sides of the line, refuges or hand-rails are normally provided, at 40 metre intervals, on both sides of the

line, and these are staggered to give 20 metres between successive refuges.

3.  Where clearance is limited on one side of the line only, staff must take refuge on the opposite side.

4.  In rock cuttings refuges will be marked in white paint.

5.  At certain overbridges/viaducts where refuges are not provided, an audible warning system is installed to give adequate advice of the approach of trains to enable staff to proceed to a point of safety. The midway point of these locations is marked to assist staff in deciding the nearest exit point. The instructions for operating the warning system are detailed in page 214 of the Sectional Appendix.

6.  At station platforms, step irons are provided on the platform faces at the same spacing as for refuges.

7.  On platform surfaces a yellow line is painted with associated warning notices displayed, instructing people to stay behind the yellow line clear of the platform edge.

8.  Trackside location cases are fitted with handrails.'

In these days, when fast running trains can approach so silently, some warning is in any case necessary where track clearances are limited; but their importance is more than ever underlined with the introduction of the APT, and that in the rugged country traversed by the West Coast main line in the upland country north of Gretna there are locations where the lineside clearances are limited. The instructions to staff in this matter require quoting in full:

## 'Safety and Protection of Staff— Warning System

At the undernoted locations with limited clearance on the Carlisle/Glasgow Central via Beattock line, refuges are not provided and the warning system detailed below is provided to advise staff of the approach of trains to enable them to proceed to a place of safety.

| Location | Structure | m | ch |
|---|---|---|---|
| Kirtlebridge | OB60 | 16 | 71 |
| Kirtlebridge/Lockerbie | OB87 | 22 | 32 |
| Lockerbie/Beattock South | OB184 | 38 | 66 |
| Beattock North/Summit | UB249 | 47 | 03 |
| (Harthorpe Viaduct) | | | |
| Summit/Abington | OB263 | 50 | 61 |
| Summit/Abington | OB288 | 54 | 36 |
| Abington/Symington | UB332 | 62 | 66 |
| (Lamington Viaduct) | | | |
| Lanark Junc/Carluke | OB446 | 80 | 53 |

### Operation of warning system

1.  Before entering restricted area, wait 10 seconds to ensure system is not already switched on, then operate one of the four switches provided at each corner of the area.

2.  The indication given and action to be take are as follows:-

(a)  Bleep sounding at 7 second intervals—System Functioning—No train approaching—Safe to enter restricted area.

**Top** *The prototype APT, one power car and six trailers, on trial near Carstairs* (British Railways).

**Above** *A broadside view of the prototype APT during trials in August 1979 south of Beattock* (T.H. Noble).

(b) Continuous Warning Horn—Train approaching—Do not enter restricted area. If already within restricted area, proceed to place of safety immediately.

(c) No Sound—System Failed—Do not enter restricted area. If already within the restricted area, leave it immediately and be prepared to lie down in cess if a train approaches.

Test switch to ensure that it has not been switched off by someone else.

Report failure to Signalling Centre.

**3.** When leaving the restricted area switch off the system by operating any of the four switches unless it is known that someone else is in the restricted area.'

During the period of road testing the APT was based at Shields Electric Traction Depot, and on five days a week proceeded to Carlisle for a series of shuttle runs from there to Beattock, and back. The timetable path provided called for a departure from Shields at 05.55 and from Polmadie at 06.43. Thence, the path was arranged to fit in with other traffic on the line, and the only sharp timing laid down from Carstairs to Beattock summit, 23.8 miles (38 km) in 15 minutes with an average speed of 95 mph (152 km/h), did not call for faster running than that made by the electrically hauled West Coast expresses. The principal test length for the APT, however, was between Beattock and Gretna Junction, where it was stated that, for purpose of the tests, it might travel at speeds in excess of the line speed, but at all times under the jurisdiction of the train supervisor and of the traction and operating inspectors always travelling on the train.

From its first arrival at Kingmoor up passenger loop at 08.36 till its departure for Glasgow at 17.22, three paths in each direction were provided for test running between Kingmoor and Beattock, with northbound departures at 08.52,

---

*APT trials in Scotland, 1979—a working notice.*

MONDAY 18 JUNE

**SHIELDS ETD, POLMADIE CSD, BEATTOCK AND KINGMOOR UP PASSENGER LOOP**

| | | 1Z22 | 1Z22 | 1Z22 | 1Z22 | | | 1Z22 | 1Z22 | 1Z22 | 1Z22 |
|---|---|---|---|---|---|---|---|---|---|---|---|
| Shields ETD | dep | 05 55 | | | | Kingmoor Up | | | | | |
| Shields Jn. | | 06 03 | | | | Passenger Loop | dep | 08 52 | 11 22 | 14 08 | 17 22 |
| Terminus Jn. | | 06 05 | | | | | | (6) | (6) | (6) | (6) |
| Larkfield Jn. | | 06 07 | | | | Gretna Jn. | | 09 04 | 11 34 | 14 20 | 17 34 |
| **Polmadie CSD** | arr | 06 10 | | | | Quintins Hill | arr | | 11* 35½ | 14* 21½ | 17* 35½ |
| | dep | 06 43 | | | | | dep | 09 05 | 11* 46 | 14* 41 | 17* 50 |
| Rutherglen E Jn. | | 06 45½ | | | | | | (6) | (6) | (6) | (6) |
| Newton | | 06 48 | | | | Signal MC.863 | | 09 13 | 11 55 | 14 50 | 17 59 |
| Uddingston Jn. | | 06 51 | | | | Lockerbie | | 09 21 | 12 03 | 14 58 | 18 07 |
| Motherwell | | 06 57 | | | | | | (12) | (12) | (8) | (12) |
| Shieldmuir Jn. | | 06 59 | | | | Beattock | arr | 09 41 | 12 23 | 15 14 | |
| Law Jn. | arr | 07* 04 | | | | | dep | | | | 18 27 |
| | dep | 07* 14 | | | | | | | | | (3) |
| Lanark Jn. | | 07 24 | | | | Summit | | | | | 18 37 |
| Carstairs | | 07 25½ | | | | Abington | | | | | 18 43 |
| Abington | | 07 35 | | | | Carstairs | | | | | 19 00 |
| Summit | | 07 40½ | | | | Lanark Jn. | | | | | 19 02 |
| Beattock | arr | 07* 48 | | | | | | | | | [4] |
| | dep | 08* 05 | 10 09 | 12 30 | 15 20 | Law Jn. | | | | | 19 11 |
| | | | (12) | (6) | (12) | | | | | | (2) |
| Lockerbie | arr | | 10* 31 | 12* 46 | 15* 42 | Motherwell | | | | | 19 18½ |
| | dep | 08 16 | 10* 37 | 12* 55 | 15* 50 | Uddingston Jn. | | | | | 19 22 |
| Signal MC.862 | | 08 26 | 10 47 | 13 05 | 16 00 | Newton | | | | | 19 24 |
| | | | (6) | (6) | (6) | Rutherglen E. Jn. | | | | | 19 26 |
| Quintinshill | arr | | | 13* 13 | | Larkfield | | | | | 19 31 |
| | dep | 08 28 | 10 55 | 13* 30 | 16 08 | Terminus Jn. | | | | | 19 32 |
| | | | | (2) | | Shields Jn. | | | | | 19 35 |
| Gretna Jn. | | 08 30 | 10 56 | 13 34 | 16 09 | Shields ETD | arr | | | | 19 42 |
| | | | (6) | (6) | (6) | | | | | | |
| **Kingmoor Up** | | | | | | | | | | | |
| **Passenger Loop** | arr | 08 36 | 11 07 | 13 44 | 16 19 | | | | | | |

**A.P.T.** Brake Test Runs.
Trailer Rake No.1, 2 Power Cars, Trailer Rake No.2.
Traction and Operating Inspectors to accompany train throughout.
For the purpose of the above tests APT Test train may travel at speeds in excess of Line Speed between Beattock and Gretna Jn. in accordance with the authorised table of speeds issued when instructed by Train Supervisor.

**Consequential Alteration**
4S06 17 50 MX Pcls Carlisle to Perth, Beattock 18 31, Summit 18 40, Abington 18 47, Carstairs arr 19 03
thence as booked.

*The APT prototype going south near Nethercleugh, passing one of the lineside boards indicating the higher maximum speeds permitted for the Advanced Passenger Train (T.H. Noble).*

11.22, and 14.08 and return trips at 10.09, 12.30 and 15.20. From the times laid down, none of these paths appeared to require any fast running at all; but each had a generous amount of recovery time. Two out of the three northbound trips included stops, on the loop line, at Quintinshill, and all three southbound trips included stops at Lockerbie, to clear the through line for regular traffic. The working times in force during the month of June 1979 were contained in special notices, and a page relating to that of the week commencing June 18 is reproduced herewith. On the northbound runs the stops at Quintinshill were to give a clear road to the 07.45, 10.45 and 13.45 electric Scots from Euston, while on the southbound runs the stops at Lockerbie, on the 10.09 and 12.30 runs were to clear the line for the 08.57 Edinburgh to Kings Cross (via Newcastle)— an HST service, and 08.50 Aberdeen to Euston. Both of these latter, it will be appreciated, were extra to the normal West Coast timetable occasioned by the blockage of the East Coast main line at Penmanshiel Tunnel.

On December 20 1979 in the course of these tests the train attained a maximum speed of 160 mph (257 km/h) breaking the previous British Railways speed record of 152 mph (244.6 km/h) attained near Swindon in 1976.

# Chapter 18

# Threshold of a new age

Having described the technical and operational aspects of these two great British railway developments, and the prowess of the HST in first class revenue earning service on lines extending from London to Bristol, Swansea, Aberdeen and Penzance, I turn in conclusion to the happy contemplation of something quite different—what the organisers called 'A Railway Spectacular', with a sub-title 'The Once in a Lifetime Extravaganza'. It might, of course, be thought that a reference, however brief, to an event in which steam locomotives played a pre-dominant part would be quite out of place in a book devoted to such ultra-modern developments as the HST and the APT. This is not so, however. The pageant of 'Rocket 150' certainly was a feast of nostalgia for the lovers of steam; and for Heaven's sake aren't we all! But it carried a far deeper and more vital significance. The approach of the HST and, finally, of the APT at the end of the great roll-past provided the ultimate dénouement, the exemplification of what it was all about.

Railways represent the embodiment of speed on land. Indeed, for at least half of the 150 year span since the opening of the Liverpool and Manchester Railway they were the fastest means of travel available to man in any sphere; and it is astonishing how all down the ages there have been prophets of woe who have cried out against every development towards higher speed. It is amusing to recall some of these utterances, in view of present day complaints expressed in letters published in *The Railway Magazine* and referred to in Chapter 13 of this book. Then, read what the Bavarian College of Physicians had to say in 1832: 'The rapid movement must inevitably generate in the travellers a brain disease, a special variety of the *Delirium furiosum*. If travellers are nevertheless determined to brave this fearful danger, the State must at least protect the onlookers, for otherwise these will be affected with the same brain disease at the sight of the rapidly running steam wagon. It is therefore necessary to enclose the railway on both sides with a high, tight board fence'. The modern equivalent of *Delirium furiosum* prophesied seems to be asphyxiation!

Samuel Smiles, the famous biographer of the Stephensons, a staunch supporter of railways, and later Secretary of the South Eastern Railway Company, recalled early days thus: 'The Public were appealed to on the subject, pamphlets were written and newspapers were hired to revile the railway. It was declared that its formation would prevent cows grazing and hens laying. The poisoned air from the locomotives would kill birds as they flew over them, and render the preservation of pheasants and foxes no longer possible. Householders were told that their houses would be burnt up by the fire thrown from the engine chimneys; while the air around would be polluted by clouds of smoke. There would no longer be any use for horses; and if railways were extended the species would become extinguished, and oats and hay rendered unsaleable commodities. Travelling by rail would be highly dangerous and country inns would be ruined. Boilers would burst and blow passengers to atoms. But there was always this consolation to wind up with—that the weight of the locomotive would completely prevent its moving, and that railways, even if made, could never be worked by steam power'.

The actual development from the steady running at 20 mph (32 km/h) by which the *Rocket* carried off the prize at Rainhill, in 1829, was astonishing. In May 1844 on the opening of the Bristol and Exeter Railway, a special train was run from London conveying guests to a grand celebration lunch at Exeter, and Daniel Gooch drove one of his celebrated 2-2-2 engines, the *Actaeon*, there and back in the day, 387 miles (619 km). On the return run the $193\frac{1}{2}$ miles (309 km) were covered in a running time of 4 hours 40 minutes, $41\frac{1}{2}$ mph (66 km/h). Following the 'Battle of the Gauges' there was often some very fast running in the late 1840s between Paddington and Swindon, with maximum speeds of well over 60 mph. The tragedy is that there was not one of Gooch's famous 8 ft (2.4 m) single 4-2-2 locomotives shown in the pageant at Rainhill, in 1980. The most famous of them all, the *Lord of the Isles,* was preserved at Swindon; but in 1906 G.J. Churchward, revered for so many things, but who evidently had no appreciation of archaeology, scrapped that priceless relic because it was taking up valuable space in the works!

From a time roughly marked by the Great Exhibition of 1851 in Hyde Park, London, there was a pause in the development of railway speed. The locomotive

*Pageantry at Paddington on March 1 1979, as* King George V *runs alongside the 11.20 HST to Bristol, outside the terminus* (Patrick Kingston).

engineers had drawn somewhat ahead of their colleagues in other railway engineering disciplines. They were running too fast for the track, too fast for the comfort of the passengers, and far too fast for the rather primitive methods of braking, and controlling of traffic along the lines. The pause, which in Great Britain lasted for roughly 30 years, was nevertheless marked by the introduction of many beautiful and richly adorned locomotives—*objets d'art,* as much as pieces of machinery—some of which were on parade at Rainhill in May 1980; but it was the Regulation of Railways Act of 1879, a hundred years ago almost to the month from the time of writing these lines, that really paved the way for the next big speed-up. By that Act of Parliament the fitting of continuous automatic brakes on all passenger trains was made compulsory, as was also the equipping of all passenger lines with the closed-block system of traffic regulation. Assured of ample warning of any obstruction on the line ahead, and with adequate brake power to stop in emergency, the way was clear for much faster running.

It is at this stage, both in history and in the pageant that *Hardwicke* begins to steal the show. There were, of course, many other classes than F.W. Webb's 'Precedents' involved in the racing of 1888 and 1895; but 'Rocket 150' celebrating the sesquicentenary of the Liverpool and Manchester Railway was primarily a party for the London and North Western, the LMS, and the London Midland Region. It is thus all the more gratifying that *Hardwicke,* and the LNWR can claim the fastest start-to-stop run of any made in either of the two Anglo-Scottish races—67.2 mph (107.5 km/h) over the 141.1 miles (225.5 km) from Crewe to Carlisle, on August 22 1895. More than this, *Hardwicke* set up something of a record in utilisation because, prior to the final night, she had worked the racing train 18 times between Crewe and Carlisle, and three times between Euston and Crewe. In the 34 days between the inauguration of much accelerated running and the final night she covered 3,153 miles (5,045 km) on the racing trains alone, quite apart from return mileage on other trains, and on other duties.

In 1895 the East Coast were not dragging their feet either, and it is only fitting that some of their beautiful engines should have been on parade at Rainhill, in May 1980; but, apart from sentiment and nostalgia, the chronicle of the Aberdeen race, seen in cold print, makes fantastic reading, in the rapidity with which the time was cut.

## London-Aberdeen : July-August 1895

| Date | Route | Arr Time am | Total time from London min | Av Speed mph |
|------|-------|-------------|----------------------------|--------------|
| Until July 15 | East Coast | 7.35 | 695 | 45.2 |
| July 15 | West Coast | 6.47 | 647 | 50.1 |
| July 28 | West Coast | 6.14 | 614 | 52.7 |
| August 19 | West Coast | 5.15 | 555 | 58.4 |
| August 20 | East Coast | 5.11 | 551 | 57.0 |
| August 20 | West Coast | 4.58 | 538 | 60.2 |
| August 21 | East Coast | 4.40 | 520 | 60.6 |
| August 22 | West Coast | 4.32 | 512 | 63.2 |

The respective mileages were 523.5 (837.5 km) East Coast, and 539.8 (863.5 km) West Coast, so that the final effort of the West Coast, in which *Hardwicke's*

**Above left** *A Royal occasion: HST 253 025 arriving at Weston-super-Mare on August 8 1977 conveying HM the Queen and HRH the Duke of Edinburgh on their Silver Jubilee tour of the County of Avon.* **Above right** *The Queen and Duke of Edinburgh after the arrival of the train* (Patrick Kingston).

record run from Crewe to Carlisle formed a vital part, was secured despite the handicap of 16.3 miles (26 km) farther to go. In the period shown above there had been a reduction of $26\frac{1}{2}$ per cent in the journey time, and an increase in average speed of 39.8 per cent.

These, of course, were highly significant figures, although made by only two trains daily, one on each route, and trains for which the most elaborate measures were taken to keep the line absolutely clear throughout. Although demonstrating the performance that engineering technology and the skill of keen and fearless enginemen had made possible, the time had not yet arrived for the general advance of British train services to such levels of speed. There was a further, and even more brilliant 'flash in the pan' nine years later, when an Ocean Mail special of the Great Western not only produced the first instance in the world to be authenticated of a maximum speed of 100 mph but, after changing engines, made a start-to-stop run which for average speed remained a record for many years afterwards: Bristol (Pylle Hill) to Paddington 118.7 miles (190 km) in $99\frac{3}{4}$ minutes, an average of 71.3 mph (114 km/h). As in the earliest days of railways such feats did not pass without the prophets of woe rushing into print as precipitately as they had done in the 1830s. At the time of the second 'Race to the North', in 1895, *The Engineer* had an amusing leading article:

'The graphic articles from the pen of Mr. Rous-Marten which we have published render it unnecessary that we should here say anything concerning the events of the railway race which has just been terminated. But much remains to be written on certain aspects of the race concerning which the most extraordinary mistakes have been made by correspondents of the daily press. There is, too, some reason to believe that a section of the general public has regarded the race as a dangerous and almost criminal transaction. Mr. John Burns, MP, has excelled himself in wild denunciation of the railway companies, and has drawn a lurid picture of the perils and sufferings of drivers and firemen, which only needed a small substratum of truth to be a really pathetic piece of oratory. It seems that Mr. Burns has been riding on an engine in the United

*HST and APT alongside—a study in profiles—prior to depot open-day weekend at Glasgow, Shields* (T.H. Noble).

States and found it hard work, and a little alarming. We are not surprised. The experience of any man who rides on the footplate of an express locomotive for the first time is rather startling, but it is not necessary that as a result he should rush into print. But Mr. Burns is by no means alone. Many other worthy people seem to regard with dread an attempt to accelerate communications with Scotland. It is just possible that a few words from us tend to reassure and comfort these gentlemen. No lady correspondent of the daily press has yet expressed her fears. Possibly the racing spirit that induced the old lady to give her cargo of hams to the captain of a Mississippi boat to enable him to make more steam and beat a rival still beats in the female breast in this country. We have been repeatedly told that the race to Scotland is dangerous; that the men in charge of the train are overworked; that the speed is so tremendous that the passengers' health must suffer; that there is no time to avoid collisions, that the risks of running off the line, breaking the rails, bursting up the engine, breaking bridges, and so on are simply enormous. All this is an admirable and instructive example of the way in which history repeats itself. We can almost see some of the correspondents of the daily press copying their letters from old newspapers and reviews. In 1830, and one or two succeeding years, anything that has been written during the last couple of weeks was written and printed. The modern terrorist has nothing new to say on the subject. All the fine old crusted stock arguments have been trotted out. We admit there has been one omitted. We have not heard a syllable about the risk of suffocation, of which such capital was once made by the opponents of railways; but this is a small matter. Neither has anything been said about a cow . . . .'

The pause from these peak achievements of 1895 and 1904 was again one of about 30 years, until 'The Cheltenham Flyer', 'The Silver Jubilee', 'The

Coronation' and 'The Coronation Scot' began to hit the headlines; and while the Great Western 'Castles', Sir Nigel Gresley's streamlined 'A4s', and Sir William Stanier's 'Coronation' 4-6-2s were writing new pages of British railway speed history, it was gratifying that some of the heroes of past speeding were being preserved. The London and North Eastern Railway had made a brave start in the establishment of the first railway museum at York, and *Gladstone* from the Brighton Railway and the 100 mph *City of Truro* from the Great Western had been added to former LNER examples. Although it was a long time before an opportunity arose for putting them on permanent display, the preserving by the LMS of the Caledonian 4-2-2 No 123 and the LNWR *Hardwicke* was also of the utmost significance. The presence of the great Stanier 4-6-2 engine *Duchess of Hamilton* in the spectacular roll-past at Rainhill in May 1980, together with the record-shattering *Mallard,* symbolised in two different ways the ultimate in British Steam locomotive achievement—in maximum sustained power output, by the sister engine *Duchess of Atholl* on a dynamometer car test run in 1939, and in making the world's record maximum speed with steam, 126 mph (201.5 km/h) in 1938. All these, however, like those of the *Rocket, Hardwicke, City of Truro* and of the Dean 4-2-2 *Duke of Connaught* which made the Bristol-Paddington record run in May 1904, were one-off performances. This is not to suggest that they *could* not have been repeated, but rather that the times were not ready for them to be repeated as daily events, or duplicated, or parallelled by many other trains on the line.

It is extraordinary how the pause of a period of nigh on 30 years between major events repeats itself in the history of British passenger train services, for it was not until 1966, with the introduction of the full electric service from Euston, that the first break-through towards an entirely new era took place. Then it was not a case of one or two specially selected trains accelerated to spectacular schedules, but the *whole service* uniformly and dramatically speeded up. For the first time in Great Britain every express train was required to run at 90 to 100 mph for long stretches of its journey, to keep time; and, instead of having groups of trains running at fairly widely spread intervals, there were 'flights' of five or six minutes apart at hourly intervals throughout the day. It is a pity that the Liverpool and Manchester line, passing through Rainhill, is not electrified and that one of the most remarkable locomotives on show, the class '87' electric, had to be drawn by a diesel. This brings a rather poignant reminder of the centenary celebrations of the Stockton and Darlington Railway in 1925. Prior to the grouping of 1923 the Board of the North Eastern Railway had decided to electrify the East Coast main line between York and Newcastle, and Sir Vincent Raven had designed and built an electric locomotive for express passenger work. In the pageant at Darlington it was drawn past the stand by a steam locomotive, but unfortunately the hope that this type would be the future East Coast power was born to die. At Rainhill, in 1980, the '87' took its place, with many years and a huge tally of mileage run to its credit.

Its diesel counterparts from other Regions of British Railways have recently begun to come under scrutiny because of the so-called Energy Crisis, which is another name for the realisation that the world's oil supplies will not last for ever. In railway enthusiast circles I am sometimes asked if it would not be a good thing to bring back steam. The many and various reasons why this would not be practicable are beside the point in the present context, but a more serious suggestion as to how to save oil fuel was made by a friend who thought that uniformly high speed services throughout the day were an expensive luxury, and that off-peak expresses should be run to slower schedules and high speed should be confined to peak business hours, and made subject to supplementary charges. He was, I think, writing without full knowledge of the traffic pattern. The outstanding feature of the massive London Midland speed-up of 1966 and onwards was that the new timetables brought an almost sensational increase in business, and that the so-called off peak trains became almost as well loaded as those in the morning and evening business hours. And it was the supreme attraction of much shorter journey times, combined with lavish, but quite justifiable, frequency of service that has set the pattern for subsequent service planning in other areas. But I have discussed the philosophy of high speed train service elsewhere in this book, and must leave it at that.

For those who went to Rainhill, and watched the great pageant roll past the stands, there were inevitably some who would have liked to have seen the 'Duchess' class 4-6-2s come back on the West Coast main line. The might and majesty of locomotives such as these (the '87' and the most powerful of the diesels) sweep into comparative obscurity, spectacle wise. But it is a sobering thought that it would need two 'Duchesses' to do the uphill work normally put forth by one '87', and down in the West Country on a comparison of horse-power alone, quite apart from how it would be used, it would need three 'Castles' to match the power units of an HST. Even these, brilliantly successful as they are proving, can only be regarded as the stepping stones to the future. They are, after all, diesel-powered and thus ultimately suspect from the 'energy crisis' viewpoint. But shortage of oil is not likely to hit British Railways sufficiently hard to influence the life span of the HSTs.

As discussed in earlier chapters of this book, however, the number of main routes on which the HSTs can make an impact sufficiently strong to win traffic back to the railways, both from the roads and the air is limited, and it is the APT that is the real 'hope of the side'. Apart from the occasional complaint, the

*Paddington, the all-HST look* (Brian Morrison).

HSTs have won universal acclaim wherever they have so far run, and the APT will bring HST standards of speed to those routes on which the full potential of the HST cannot be realised because of track geometry. In contemplating what we hope will be the large scale introduction of APTs, in the years to come, and viewing it against a background of Rainhill, and all that has happened since, it is a time to dwell with the greatest pride on an outstanding national achievement in the most advanced form of mechanical engineering technology.

As a nation we are not given to blowing our own trumpets. Sometimes this is rather a pity, when others blow theirs with far less justification. At the time of the electrification of the London Midland line from Euston I was still in engineering practice, and closely connected with several aspects of the work involved. It would, therefore, have ill behoved me to do too much in the way of trumpet blowing. But now I have been retired from professional engineering work for a number of years, and feel free to commend the achievements of a younger generation with the utmost enthusiasm. In the view of one who has made virtually a lifetime's study of locomotives, and all aspects of railway traction, the Advanced Passenger Train is one of the greatest *successful* innovations in land transport history. Inevitably, in reviewing the 1980 roll-past at Rainhill one recalls the many daring conceptions that did not come off: monorails, turbo-locomotives, the Bennie rail-plane, turf burning locomotives and so on; but the APT has every look of a winner in the grand manner, and as it was propelled past the stands at Rainhill I hope that all who saw it recognised it as such—however different it looks from a steam locomotive!

One fact about both the HST and the APT is the apparent anonymity of the designers. As the steam locomotives rolled by, names like Robert Stephenson, Trevithick, Allan, Webb, Stirling, Ivatt, Churchward, Gresley and Stanier were on everyone's lips; but who designed the HST? Whose idea was the APT? In writing this book I have been privileged to go behind the scenes at Derby and Crewe, and to talk to many of the men who have played very important parts. The names of some of them appear on papers contributed to various scientific bodies, at home and overseas, and some of these are listed in the bibliography; but by and large it has been a magnificent team effort, under the skilled guidance of successive Directors of Research, at the Railway Technical Centre at Derby and of chief mechanical engineers of the British Railways Board.

To those of us who were privileged to know personally some of the famous men of the steam age, however, the situation is not really so very different. One may talk of the Stanier Pacifics, for example; yet the immensely successful 'Coronation' class which, on being stripped of their streamlining, became generally known as the 'Duchesses', were designed and put into production by members of his team while Sir William himself was in India on one of his major consultancy projects. On the other hand, some of those who relied less on team work and, by their egoism became historic personalities in the railway engineering world, cannot be counted among the most successful. So, one salutes the HST and the APT as corporate team achievements of British Railways; but it is equally appropriate (at the time of writing) in this year of 150th anniversary, of memories and looking forward, that the Chairman of the Railway Division of the Institution of Mechanical Engineers should be Mr Kenneth Taylor, the Chief Mechanical Engineer of the British Railways Board, who carries the ultimate technical responsibility for these two great British projects which are taking us over the threshold into a new railway age.

# Appendices

## 1 Bibliography

**Technical papers**
D. Boocock & M. Newman, *The Advanced Passenger Train,* Institute of Mechanical Engineers, 1976.
B.G. Sephton, *The High Speed Train, Railway Engineering Journal,* 1974.
A.H. Wickens, *APT Technology Results,* The American Society of Mechanical Engineers, 1974.
A.H. Wickens and A.O. Gilchrist, *Railway Vehicle Dynamics—The emergence of a practical theory,* Council of Engineering Institutions MacRobert Award Lecture, 1977.

**Books covering the historical approach, by O.S. Nock**
*Britain's New Railway (the LMR electrification),* Ian Allan 1966.
*British Railway Signalling,* George Allen & Unwin, 1969.
*Electric Euston to Glasgow,* Ian Allan, 1974.
*Speed Records on British Railways,* David & Charles, 1971.
*British Railways in Transition,* Thomas Nelson & Sons, 1963.

## 2 Production HST technical data

### Power car

Engine, Paxman 'Valenta' 12RP 200L.
Initial service rating 1,680 kW.
Engine driven alternator & rectifier supplying DC to traction motors.
Engine driven auxiliary alternator supplying 450 kW at 415 v 3 phase, to the train.
Net power at rail (2 power cars) 2,420 to 2,700 kW.
Luggage van (caged area) 4.5 m$^2$.
Maximum service speed 200 km/h (125 mph).
Weight with supplies 70 tonnes.
Performance: 2 power cars, 7 carriages and varying electric load of air-conditioning, etc: Balancing speed on level 200 km/h, on 5 per cent or about 180 km/h.
Nominal operating range 2,300 km (1,400 miles).
Nominal fuel capacity 4,500 litres.

## Mark III carriage

**Features**

Lightweight welded steel shell; Grouped equipment modules on underframe; Air sprung disc braked bogies; Air conditioned; Automatically operated interior doors; Public address; Ergonomically designed seats; Double glazing; Provision for chemical toilets; Modular constructed interior trim.

**Types**

First class saloon 48 seats.
Second class saloon 72 seats.
Kitchen/saloon 23 seats.
Buffet/saloon 34 seats.
Weight 33-39 tonnes.

# 3   Specification for APT-P

## Power car

The APT-P power cars are lightweight steel semi-monocoque structures with deep side skirts.

Each power car is carried on two four-wheel bogies and contains thyristor electrical control equipment feeding four 750 kW body mounted traction motors. The motors drive the axles via a body mounted gearbox, cardan shaft and lightweight final-drive reduction gearbox. Each powered axle is hydro-kinetically braked, the brake being fitted to the body mounted gearbox in the mechanical drive to the axle.

Power cars are equipped with anti-tilt mechanisms to ensure that the pantograph remains level as the body tilts.

Each power car weighs 69 tonnes.

## Trailer cars

Trailer cars are arranged in identical rakes each side of the power cars. Three basic types of vehicle are required not only for low total train mass, but also for acceptable axle loads, especially on articulated axles. To meet the mass targets, APT trailer car bodyshells are constructed in aluminium alloy, giving a 40 per cent weight saving over conventional steel coaches.

The vehicle structures are designed to meet the UIC loading specifications for main line coaches, including the 200 tonne proof buffing load. The dominant design criterion tends to be stiffness rather than strength, as high flexural natural frequencies are essential for good ride quality at high speed.

Passenger doors are of the power-operated sliding-plug type with a retractable step. By having only two wide doors per vehicle located in diagonally opposite corners, it has been possible to accommodate 72 second class seats or 47 first class seats at standard pitch within a 21 m vehicle length.

Internal fittings such as seats, luggage racks and trim panels are modular and easily replaceable. Similarly, air conditioning, tilt control and brake control units are installed in the vehicle underbelly as pre-commissioned, readily-removable packs.

Substantial weight savings have been achieved by developing a chemical toilet, lightweight seats, and a low-energy air-conditioning system. This system uses a low fresh air charge and a high (80 per cent) re-circulatory flow, deodorised by carbon filters. The small intake and exhaust areas are sealed on entry to tunnels to protect passengers from transient pressures.

The 25 kV electric pre-production train (APT-P) comprised two rakes of articulated trailer cars between which are positioned one or two power cars. Each trailer rake consists of a number of two-axle intermediate cars and two three-axle end cars. Each power car has four axles. Power cars and trailer rakes are easily uncoupled from each other in order to satisfy operating and maintenance requirements.

The train can be formed into alternative versions. The 125 mph (200 km/h) (1 + 11) low-powered version, with 11 trailer cars, represents the longest train that can be hauled by a single power car. The 155 mph (250 km/h) (2 + 12) high-powered version, with 14 vehicles total, is the longest train which can be accommodated within the existing platform lengths.

The train configuration, with power cars positioned in the middle, has been adopted so that current can be collected satisfactorily, using only one pantograph, and so that excessive suspension buckling forces can be avoided when pushing with two power cars.

Communication between the two trailer rakes is normally available to staff only, via a corridor through the power car. Passengers are permitted access only in emergencies and when escorted by a member of staff. To minimise this disadvantage, each rake of trailer cars is self-contained, incorporating both first and second class accommodation and catering facilities. First class accommodation is in the middle of the train and second class towards the ends, the division being marked by the intermediate catering car. The catering unit provides full meals for first class passengers in their seats and a buffet service for all passengers.

## Coach tilting

APT vehicles tilt by up to 9 degrees on curves. The requirement to stay within the BR loading gauge leads to their characteristic shape.

Each vehicle is tilted individually by hydraulic jacks mounted within the bogies. Power for the jacks is provided by a hydraulic power pack mounted below the vehicle floor. Tilting is controlled by an electronic box that measures the lateral acceleration of the bolster. This measurement is made by a 'spirit level' accelerometer in which the position of the bubble is sensed by electrical connections. The tilt system design permits the vehicle body to adopt an upright position in the event of hydraulic system failure.

# Index

*The prototype APT speeding north in upland Border country during the commissioning trials* (T.H. Noble).